# Past Minds

*Religion, Cognition and Culture*

**Series Editors**

**Jeppe Sinding Jensen and Armin W. Geertz**
**Aarhus University**

This series is based on a broadly conceived cognitive science of religion. It explores the role of religion and culture in cognitive formation and brings together methods, theories and approaches from the humanities, psychology, and the social, cognitive and neurosciences.

The series is associated with the Religion, Cognition and Culture Unit (RCC) at the Department of the Study of Religion, Aarhus University http://www.teo.au.dk/en/research/current/cognition.

Published:
*Religious Narrative, Cognition and Culture:*
*Image and Word in the Mind of Narrative*

Forthcoming:

*Origins of Religion, Cognition and Culture*
Edited by Armin W. Geertz

*The Burning Saints: Emotion and Motivation in the*
*Fire-walking Rituals of the Anastenaria*
Dimitris Xygalatas

*Mental Culture: Towards a Cognitive Science of Religion*
Edited by Dimitris Xygalatas and William W. McCorkle, Jr.

# Past Minds

## Studies in Cognitive Historiography

Edited by

Luther H. Martin and Jesper Sørensen

LONDON   OAKVILLE

Published by Equinox Publishing Ltd.

UK: 1 Chelsea Manor Studios, Flood Street, London SW3 5SR

USA: DBBC, 28 Main Street, Oakville, CT 06779

www.equinoxpub.com

First published 2011

British Library Cataloguing-in-Publication Data

A catalogue record for this book is available from the British Library.


ISBN 978 1 84553 740 1 (hardback)
ISBN 978 1 84553 741 8 (paperback)


Library of Congress Cataloging-in-Publication Data

Past minds : studies in cognitive historiography / edited by Luther H. Martin and Jesper Sørensen.
p. cm. — (Religion, cognition, and culture)
Includes bibliographical references and index.
ISBN 978-1-84553-740-1 (hb) — ISBN 978-1-84553-741-8 (pbk.)
1. Religion. 2. Cognition and culture. I. Martin, Luther H., 1937– II. Sørensen, Jesper, 1968–
BL51.P28 2010
200.1'9--dc22
                2009045390


Typeset by Queenston Publishing, Hamilton, Ontario, Canada

Index by Richard Bartholomew

Printed and bound in Great Britain

# Contents

Contents

# Contributors

**Ulrich Berner,** is Professor of Religious Studies (Religionswissenschaft) at the University of Bayreuth, Germany. His main interests are European Religious History, African Christianity, and Method and Theory in the Study of Religion. He served on the Editorial Board (2000–2005) and on the Advisory Board (2005–2010) of SAPERE (*Scripta Antiquitatis Posterioris ad Ethicam Religionemque pertinentia*), and he is now a Principal Investigator at BIGSAS (Bayreuth International Graduate School of African Studies).

**Aleš Chalupa** is Assistant Professor at the Department for the Study of Religions at Masaryk University, Brno, Czech Republic. His field of research is ancient religions, especially Roman religion, ancient mystery cults, Graeco-Roman magic and Mithraism. In recent years, he has also focused on the cognitive science of religion and its possible contribution to the methodology of the study of ancient religious traditions.

**István Czachesz** is Privatdozent of the University of Heidelberg. He is the author of *Commission Narratives: A Comparative Study of the Canonical and Apocryphal Acts* (Leuven, 2007), *The Grotesque Body in Early Christian Literature: Hell Scatology and Metamorphosis* (London, 2011), co-editor of *The Apocalypse of Peter* (Leuven, 2003), *The Visio Pauli* (Leuven, 2007), and *Changing Minds: Religion and Cognition through the Ages* (Leuven, 2010). In Hungarian, he is the author of *Gaia's Two Faces* (Budapest, 1996), co-author of *Codex D in the Book of Acts* (Budapest, 1995), editor of *Disciples, Wonderworkers, Martyrs* (Budapest, 1997), and translator of *Tyconius' Book of Rules* (Budapest, 1997).

**Douglas L. Gragg,** Ph.D., is Associate Dean, Library Director, and Professor of Bibliography and Research at Louisville Presbyterian Theological Seminary. He is the author of several book chapters relating cognitive theories to the study of Graeco-Roman religions and the compiler of a bibliography of publications in the cognitive science of religion. He is currently revising the bibliography and writing a book with the working title, Forms and Modes of Religion in the Ancient Roman World.

**Christophe Heintz** is an Assistant Professor of cognitive science at CEU, Budapest, Hungary. He is working on cultural evolution and cognition in the domains of the history of science and behavioural economics. He has written on the role, in cultural evolution, of institutions, trusting behaviour, conceptual change, and innate cognitive capacities. Christophe Heintz was trained in Mathematics and Philosophy and did his Ph.D. in cognitive science at the Institut Jean Nicod, Ecole des Hautes Etudes en Sciences Sociales.

**Dirk Johannsen** is a postdoctoral researcher at the Departement of Science of Religion at the University of Basel. His main research interests include cognitive and narratological approaches to the study of religion, discourse analysis and Scandinavian religious history.

**Gabriel Levy**, earned his Ph.D. at the University of California, Santa Barbara. He is a comparative historian of religion, specializing in early Judaism and the philosophy of language. His dissertation examined the emergence of Rabbinic theology in the context of the transition in religious authority from prophecy to Midrash, and the role that the technology of writing played in that transition. He has been Visiting Scholar in the Department of Biblical Studies, Faculty of Theology at the University of Copenhagen and is currently an ekstern lektor in the Department of the Study of Religion, Aarhus University, Denmark.

**Anders Lisdorf**, Ph.D., is an independent scholar who earned his PhD in the History of Religions from the University of Copenhagen. His publications focus on how the cognitive science of religion can aid in understanding the historical reality of and the practice of divination in ancient Roman times.

**Luther H. Martin**, Professor of Religion Emeritus, University of Vermont, is the author of *Hellenistic Religions. An Introduction* (1987), an editor (with Panayotis Pachis) of *Theoretical Frameworks for the Study of Graeco-Roman Religions* (2002), of *Hellenisation, Empire and Globalisation: Lessons from Antiquity* (2004, also with Pachis), and is author of numerous articles in this area of his historical specialization. In addition, he is the author of many articles on theory and method in the study of religion, especially the study of Graeco-Roman religions from the perspective of cognitive science of religion. He is editor of several volumes of essays in this area, including (with Harvey Whitehouse), *Theorizing Religions Past: Archaeology, History and Cognition* (2004), and with Roger Beck, *Data from Dead Minds? Challenges on the Interface of History of Religions (in Graeco-Roman Antiquity) and the Cognitive Science of Religion* (forthcoming). During 2005–2007, Martin was a Distinguished International Fellow in the Institute of Cognition and Culture at Queen's University Belfast.

**Christian M. Prager** is Associate Lecturer for Mayan studies and cultural anthropology at the Department of Anthropology of the Americas, University of Bonn, Germany. His key areas of research include Classic Maya epigraphy and religions of the Americas and he serves on the board of WAYEB, the European Association of Mayanists.

**Jesper Sørensen**, MINDLab Associate Professor at the Department for the Study of Religion, Aarhus University is the author of *A Cognitive Theory of Magic* and *Religion: I Psyke og Samfund* (in Danish) together with Olav Hammer. He has published numerous articles on magic, ritual, conceptual transmission, Western esotericism and theoretical issues pertaining to the scientific study of religion. Formerly an International Fellow at the Institute of Cognition and Culture, Queen's University Belfast, Sørensen is currently involved in a number of experimental research agendas investigating the effects of ritualized behavior on human cognition.

**Peter Westh** teaches at the Department of Cross-cultural and Regional Studies, University of Copenhagen, Denmark. He specializes in Mesopotamian religion. He is secretary of the Danish Association for the Study of Religions.

**Donald Wiebe**, Ph.D., is Professor of Theology at Trinity College, University of Toronto. His primary areas of research interest are philosophy of the social sciences, epistemology, philosophy of religion, the history of the academic and scientific study of religion, and method and theory in the study of religion. He is the author of *Religion and Truth: Towards an Alternative Paradigm for the Study of Religion* (1981), *The Irony of Theology and the Nature of Religious Thought* (1991), *Beyond Legitimation: Essays on the Problem of Religious Knowledge* (1994), and *The Politics of Religious Studies: The Continuing Conflict with Theology in the Academy* (1999). He has edited several books and sets of congress proceedings, and edits the series "Toronto Studies In Religion" for Peter Lang Press. In 1985, he was the co-founder (with Luther H. Martin and E. Thomas Lawson) of the North American Association for the Study of Religion which became affiliated to the IAHR in 1990; he twice served as President of that Association (1986–1987, 1991–1992).

# — Preface —

Luther H. Martin and Jesper Sørensen

In May 2007, the Institute of Cognition and Culture, Queen's University Belfast, sponsored an international symposium on the theme of this volume, "Past Minds: Evolution, Cognition, and History." The papers in this volume are selected from among those presented at this symposium, especially those focusing on historical examples of ancient religions and those addressing theoretical issues relevant to that study. We would like to thank all of those who participated in this symposium, especially those who revised their papers for this volume. And we would like to thank the Institute of Cognition and Culture, its students, and its director, Dr. Jesse Bering, and the European Office of Aerospace Research and Development, Air Force Office of Scientific Research, United States Air Force Research Laboratory, for their generous support and for their contributions to the success of this conference and this volume.

The book is divided into four parts. *Part One, Introduction*, contains two chapters. In the first, Luther H. Martin outlines the historical development of the relation between historiography on the one hand and evolutionary and cognitive theorizing on the other. He traces the shifting attitudes towards both mentalist and Darwinian approaches all the way from nineteenth and early twentieth century scholars such as Macallister and Harrison to current discussions between selectionist and attractor-based notions of human cultural transmission. In the second chapter, Christophe Heintz discusses how cultural epidemiology might inform historiography by modeling the influence of evolved cognitive systems on the spread of particular ideas and, subsequently, how this might be said to account for both cultural stability and historical change.

The four chapters that constitute *Part Two, Minds and Ancient Civilizations*, each address a particular empirical case. In Chapter 3 Gabriel Levy investigates the case of Judaism and argues that bottom-up approaches cannot account for particularities of Jewish culture as well as the impact of its particular mental abilities such as intelligence. Instead he opts for a top-down approach claiming that niche-construction and co-evolutionary processes have influenced genetic selection in the Jewish population and, as such, contingent historical factors can have a significant impact on evolutionary processes as well as vice versa. In Chapter 4 Peter Westh addresses how the cognitive optimum theory of religious representations argued by Pascal Boyer can be applied to ancient textual sources, in this case Assyro-Babylonian divine epithets, and to what extent this type of textual data should lead to a revision of the theory. Westh argues that textual sources might result in a more intuitively informed description of gods (i.e. being less counterintuitive than expected) as texts provide an alternative way to transmit cultural knowledge that does not depend on individual humans' memory. Turning to a comparative case, Christian Prager discusses the evolutionary and cognitive underpinnings of a particular symbolic phenomenon in Chapter 5. Based on cognitive understandings of symbolism as well as knowledge of aesthetically preferred landscapes stemming from evolutionary psychology, Prager investigates the often noted, but rarely explained, world-wide dispersal and stability of tree-symbolism and, in particular, its role in Mesoamerican cultures. In Chapter 6, Dirk Johannsen discusses how cognitive theories can help explain the co-existence and persistence of an oral tradition of the "Hidden People" together with standardized Lutheran Christianity in eighteenth and nineteenth century Norway. Making use of Pascal Boyer's repertoire of domain-violations and access to social strategic information, as well as of cognitive narratology, he analyzes how such violations dramatically enhance the explicability of life-events (e.g. sudden disease) and, at the same time, serve a narrative function as a central aspect of the plot.

*Part Three, Roman Minds*, consists of five chapters each of which addresses a historical case in the Roman period. In Chapter 7 Anders Lisdorf analyses the extensive use of omens and prodigies in the Roman Republic during a 200-year period. Lisdorf argues that understanding human cognitive systems can shed new light on the type of prodigies accepted, as well as how these were distributed through different strata of Roman society. In Chapter 8, Aleš Chalupa discusses how cognitive science might help answer the old riddle of the origins and rapid spread of Mithraism. Focusing on questions of ritual performance and transmission of religious ideas can supply new information to help the historian fill in the gaps in the historical record and thus reconstruct a likely historical scenario. Keeping with the theme of ritual, in Chapter 9 Douglas Gragg tests the ritual form hypothesis of Lawson and McCauley on the description of a ritual initiation found in a literary source, *The Golden Ass* by Apuleius. Gragg argues that an apparently potential problem for the theory, Lucius' second and third initiation into the mysteries of Isis, in fact supports the theory as these are regarded as extraordinary in the narrative itself. Turning to the topic of anthropomorphism, Ulrich Berner points in Chapter 10 to the important role of this concept in recent cognitive theories of religion as well as to its ancient roots in Greco-Roman scepticism in general and in the writings of Lucian of Samosata in particular. He warns that explaining religious conceptualization does not amount to an explanation of religion in general and that other methods must complement cognitive approaches in order to create a fuller picture. Finally, in Chapter 11 István Czachesz develops a cognitive explanation of magic and tests it from early Christianity. He argues that situations of operant conditioning with a variable reinforcement in themselves produce a ritualized magical response and, when combined with widespread miracle stories as well as explicit explanations, a positive feedback loop emerges whereby stories and explanations reinforce rituals and vise verse.

In the final part of the book, *Conclusion*, the perspective is once again widened in two chapters that discuss at the theoretical level the relation between historiography, cognitive science and evolutionary models. In Chapter 12, Don Wiebe critically accesses the potential role of social science and historiography for current evolutionary psychology. He criticizes evolutionary psychology for being overly reductionistic and, in fact, leaving no room for complementary approaches. Instead he calls for a pluralistic approach that acknowledges emergent levels of explanations of human phenomena and the need for a combination of evolutionary, cognitive and social scientific / historiographical approaches. In Chapter 13 Jesper Sørensen points to the inherent tension in historiography between contingent and particular facts, on the one hand, and the more or less explicit systems or structures understood as binding events together in narrative strings, on the other. He outlines three analytical models of the relation between psychology, socio-cultural systems and contingent historical events and discusses these in relation to the temporal scope as well as the explicit investigative concern of the historian.

But what is all the fuss really about? Why do historians need to concern themselves with cognitive science and evolutionary modeling? While this book has a lot to say in that regard, a short quote at the outset might point to a common denominator between the different views expressed. In his 1994 article, E. Thomas Lawson concluded that historians have a stake in the debate over the role of cognitive [and evolutionary] theorizing for historiographical method (Lawson 1994, 482). If historians *"are willing to make assumptions about the transmission of tradition, then it is their job,"* he challenges, *"to help in identifying the mechanisms which underwrite such a process"* (Lawson 1994, 483, emphasis original). From this perspective, historians—including historians of religion—are not only beginning to employ evolutionary and cognitive theorizing in their historiographical work but are becoming potential contributors of evidence for our understanding of such theorizing. We hope that the contributions to this volume might contribute to this project by offering some examples of such historiographical work while at the same time inquiring into the relevance and inferences of evolutionary and cognitive theorizing for that work.

## Reference

Lawson, E. Thomas. 1994. "Counterintuitive Notions and the Problem of Transmission: The Relevance of Cognitive Science of the Study of History." *Historical Reflections/Réflexions Historiques* 20: 481–495.

# — 1 —

# Evolution, Cognition, and History

## Luther H. Martin

> The true difference [between history and poetry] is that one relates what has happened, the other what may happen. Poetry, therefore, is the more philosophical...for poetry tends to express the universal; history the particular.
>
> Aristotle (*Poetics* 1415b)

Aristotle's view of history as the expression of unique events has characterized historiography from its establishment as an academic field in the mid-nineteenth century until the present. Nineteenth-century proposals for "scientific history," for example, were strictly concerned with an empirical description of facts—a position of particularism often unfairly associated with Leopold von Ranke's dictum that the historian should only show *wie es eigentlich gewesen* (Ranke 1824, vii).[1] Subsequently, historiographical methods were advanced that relied on the idiosyncratic *Gefühl* of the historian. Among others, R.G. Collingwood, for example, claimed that "the historian is doing something which the scientist...cannot do," namely, understanding the thought behind the particular events (Collingwood 1956, 214). This empathetic method of historiography, while still focused on particulars, assumed a humanistic view of understanding (*Verstehen*) that distanced the human sciences from the explanatory methods of the natural sciences as advanced for historiography by von Ranke. Similarly, Carl Hempel, in a classic 1942 essay, problematized Aristotle's distinction between a focus on the particular in historiography and a poetic (philosophical) concern with the general with his complaint that historians are "concerned with the *description* of particular events of the past rather than with the search for general laws which might govern [i.e., *explain*] these events" (Hempel 1965, 231). "In history as anywhere else in empirical science," he wrote:

---

1.  Ranke actually exhorted historians "to rise... from the investigation and contemplation of the particular to a general view of events and to the recognition of their objectively existing relatedness" (Ranke 1971: 23). Thus, the sense of "*eigentlich*" in Ranke's "dictum" should not be understood as a mere description of "actual" facticity but as a methodological exhortation for an "accurate" *reconstruction* of the past (Iggers 1983, 63–64, 76–80).

the explanation of a phenomenon consists in subsuming it under general empirical laws; and the criterion of its soundness is not whether it appeals to our imagination, whether it is presented in terms of suggestive analogies or is otherwise made to appear plausible—all this may occur in pseudo-explanations as well—but exclusively whether it rests on empirically well confirmed assumptions concerning initial conditions and general laws.

(Hempel 1965, 240).

Since the publication of Charles Darwin's *On the Origin of Species* (1859), one of the candidates most often proposed as providing a general law of history has been that of evolution. This is not surprising since biological evolution and human history both deal with past events reconstructed on the basis of surviving bodies of incomplete evidence and with an interpretation and chronological synthesis of these events (Nitecki and Nitecki 1992, vii). Both presume "that human beings are a part of nature in both the biological and the cultural sense" and both adhere "to materialist explanations" (Allen 1992, 216). And Darwin's theory has proven to be remarkably robust in accounting for biological change even as alternative theories of social and historical change have proven to be just as remarkably strained.

Already in 1882, the Dublin anatomist Alexander Macalister sought to apply to historical change "the operation of those great laws which [he considered also to] work in other departments of the material and moral world" (Macalister 1882, 4), that is, the "laws" of Darwinian evolution. In his scientific work, Macalister had provided a Darwinian account of anatomical variations (e.g., Macalister 1894) and had sought evolutionary connections between human and primate physiology (e.g., Macalister 1871b, 1873; Livingstone 2007, 77). He had reviewed Darwin's *Descent of Man* the year it was published (Macalister 1871a) and, subsequently, his work had been cited by Darwin (e.g., Darwin 1872, 10, n.13; 1879, 31, n. 30). Macalister's proposal for understanding the course of history in terms of Darwinian evolution anticipated basic assumptions for subsequent such programs:

When, in the history of any set of phenomena, we find that at certain successive stages the sequences vary, and that these variations are directly and recognizably related to the external surrounding conditions, we assume that there is a direct connexion between these external conditions and the modified sequences, and we say that the resulting state of things is due to evolution. The fundamental postulates are a capacity of variation in the train of sequences, and external modifying influences, and the latter may be either the direct action of the environments on the phenomena, or may be due to a power from without, overruling and directly ordering the modifications. In this sense evolution may be defined as the principle in accordance with which phenomena are modified to keep them in harmony with their surrounding conditions. (Macalister 1882, 10)

Macalister recognized that "no such [historical] process of moulding can take place" unless its theoretical object may be viewed as an "organism" that is "a central growing force of its own" (Macalister 1882, 36). His own case study for his proposal was the history of the Christian Church, the "vitality" of which he understood to be found in the "the sum" of its "component members" (Macalister 1882, 36). Macalister's presumption of social groups evolving through the effects of natural selection has been reintroduced by contemporary proponents of social evolution (e.g., Wilson 2002).

Seventeen years later, the Cambridge classicist Jane Harrison, in her contribution to the fiftieth anniversary commemoration of the publication of the *On the Origin of the Spe-*

*cies* (Seward 1909), also proposed a Darwinian approach to history, again with respect to religion. Unlike Macalister, however, who had exempted the human psyche (or soul) from "the operation of those great laws which work in other departments of the material and moral world" (Smith 1923, xxxv; Livingstone 2007, 78). Harrison, citing Darwin's own anticipations for the future of psychology, proposed a history of religion that would focus on "the necessary acquirement of each mental capacity [for specific religious practices and ideas] by gradation" (Darwin 2003, 458; Harrison 1909, 497). Her proposal for understanding religion as an ensemble of evolved behavioral features presciently articulated the recent agenda of contemporary evolutionary psychologists and cognitive scientists.

By the early twentieth century, in other words, both a (social) evolutionary and a (proto-) cognitive approach to the study of history had been proposed—both, interestingly, with respect to the history of religions. And both of these proposals focused on microevolutionary processes: the sum of the individual members of the Church, for Macalister; the evolved mental capacities of humans for specific religious ideas and practices, for Harrison. This initial focus on microevolutionary processes eluded many of Darwin's followers—especially among social scientists—and contributed to the rise of social Darwinism. These social Darwinists accepted uncontroverted descriptions of a continual historical relationship between more recent societies and their antecedents and they committed themselves as well to a lawful explanation for such historical and social change, which evolutionary theory seemed to provide. However, the growing body of ethnographic evidence increasingly contested their views of socio-cultural development as adaptive, i.e., as inevitably progressive, while the rediscovery of Mendel's laws of heredity challenged analogies of cultural transmission to heredity by showing that natural selection was neither the mechanism whereby variations were produced, as they had assumed, nor their source (Tax and Krucoff 1968, 404–405).

In 1989, a group of biologists, historians, and philosophers gathered in Chicago to address the implications of contemporary, i.e., post-Mendelian or neo-Darwinian, evolutionary theory for historical method and their conclusions, edited by Matthew and Doris Nitecki, were published in 1992 as *History and Evolution*. The primary issue debated by participants in this symposium—and, as we shall see, continue to be discussed today—was the relationship, if any, of the artificial and intentional selection of historical variation from the nonintentional and non-teleological processes of biological variation (Ruse 1992, 174).

Perhaps the most significant contribution to this 1992 volume—because the position advanced continues at the forefront of contemporary discussion—is Robert Boyd's and Peter Richerson's article "How Microevolutionary Processes Give Rise to History" (Boyd and Richerson 1992, 179–209). Boyd and Richerson correctly note that the "amount of data available from the past is usually very limited, and the number of possible reconstructions of the past is correspondingly large." Consequently, they conclude, "[s]ome sort of theory has to be applied to make some sense of the...isolated facts" (Boyd and Richerson 1992, 201).

What makes patterns of change over time "historical," they contend, is, first, that the "[t]rajectories are not stationary on the time scale of interest," i.e., they represent an occurrence of long-term change that does not repeat itself (Boyd and Richerson 1992, 185, 202) and, second, that "[s]imilar initial conditions give rise to qualitatively different trajectories" (Boyd and Richerson 1992, 186, 202). Building upon their earlier arguments in *Culture and the Evolutionary Process* (1985), Boyd and Richerson identify three processes that affect historical variation: "random forces," which, they argue "are the cultural analogs of mutation and drift in genetic transmission"; "biased transmission" or "decision-making forces," which "result when individuals evaluate alternative behavioral variants and preferentially adopt some variants relative to others"; and "natural selection," which "may operate directly on cultural variation" (Boyd and Richerson 1992, 182). While historians readily acknowledge the first two of these processes, it is natural selection that is at the center of theoretical analogies to evolutionary views of culture and history and the most problematic because of questions concerning the mechanisms for the heritable variation that is theoretically requisite. There have, however, been no analogues identified for genes whereby culture might self-replicate—apart, of course, from Richard Dawkin's suggestion of memes, or cultural "units of imitation" that might be transmitted from "brain to brain" (Dawkins 1989, 192). Although Dawkins' proposal has attracted some interest within cultural studies, it has not been widely accepted by the scientific community as it is, of course, but yet another biological analogy for historical transmission. Boyd and Richerson seek to escape this problem, however, by reverting to a pre-Mendelian Darwinian orthodoxy. "Darwin formulated a clear statement of natural selection," they write,

> without a correct understanding of *genetic* inheritance because it is a force that will operate on *any* system of inheritance with a few key properties. There must be heritable variation, the variants must affect phenotype, and the phenotypic differences must affect individual's chances of transmitting the variants they carry. (Boyd and Richerson 1992, 182; emphases theirs)

"That variants are transmitted by imitation rather than sexual or asexual reproduction," they continue, "does not affect the basic argument, nor does the possibility that the source of variation is not random" (Boyd and Richerson 1992, 182). Boyd and Richerson's view of historiography would seem, therefore, to meet the generalizing condition for scientific explanation advocated by Hempel. The question is whether Darwinian evolution provides an appropriate generalizing condition for a scientific explanation of history or simply represents the kind of suggestive analogy that Hempel judged to be a pseudo-explanation.

Like Hempel, Karl Popper had rejected evolutionary theory as an explanation for history, indeed, for anything, apart from "a host of biological and paleontological observations" (Popper 1957, 106). However one might argue against Popper's logical inference of a historical determinism in such lawful explanations (Popper 1957, vi–vii), and against his subsequent characterization of social processes in terms of a Darwinian evolutionary epistemology as a "metaphysical research programme" (Popper 1976, 167–189), Matthew Nitecki simply dismisses such criticisms (Nitecki 1992, 15). Rather, he asserts, somewhat salvifically, that since "[h]istory, like evolutionary biology, *must* explain human life, *must* help in understanding human life," "we *must* try to shape and control future events"—"[i]n spite of Popper" (Nitecki 1992, 15, emphasis added; but see, in the same volume, the brief comments by Robert Richards [1992, 20] and by Michael Ruse [1992, 156, 163–164])!

The journal *History and Theory* subsequently published a theme issue on "Evolutionary Ideas and History" (Shaw and Pomper 1999) which continued and extended the discussions of historical and cultural change as the products of evolutionary forces that had been initiated by the Niteckis a decade earlier—though with little notice taken of contributions to this earlier volume. What stands out in this later debate, however, is the contribution by the historian Joseph Fracchia and the biologist Richard Lewontin criticizing evolutionary views of history as a "problematic conflation of historical and evolutionary processes" (Fracchia and Lewontin 1999, 60). Even if history were in some sense law-like, they ask, "does that make a historical process evolutionary" (Fracchia and Lewontin 1999, 57?)

The methodological issue raised by evolutionary views of history, according to Fracchia and Lewontin, is whether they are to be understood as isomorphic with or analogous to

Darwinian theory. If isomorphic, the appropriateness of applying a theory developed to explain the data of one domain, organic speciation, to those of another, the behavioral and ideational productions of a single species, must be raised. If analogical, the conflation of historical and evolutionary processes is achieved, they argue, by substituting for features from various biological elements of Darwinian theory features from culture that are taken to be analogous (Fracchia and Lewontin 1999, 68)—transmission with heredity, for example. They consider such substitutions to be "slights of conceptual hand" (Fracchia and Lewontin 1999, 68, 69) by which analogies of cultural evolution to natural selection are more isomorphic with Darwinian vocabulary than with Darwinian theory (Fracchia and Lewontin 1999, 68). Whatever one might conclude about attempts to apply the Darwinian theory of organic evolution to cultural and historical change, whether directly or by analogy, the fundamental question posed by Fracchia and Lewontin is whether any "useful work is done by substituting the metaphor of evolution for history" (Fracchia and Lewontin, 1999, 52, 78?) And, it might be asked further whether selectionist models other than the biological might be more appropriate for explaining historical change—economic models of the marketplace, for example (e.g., the essays in Hogarth and Reder 1987; Young 1997).

Proposals for evolutionary views of history have primarily focused on generalized explanations for the production and transmission of culture—the "stuff" of history—but they have not specifically considered that impulse by which Aristotle had defined history and which continues to concern the work of most historians—an "interest in singular events" (Popper 1957, 144–145, n. 1). In the same issue of *History and Theory* in which Fracchia and Lewontin criticized evolutionary theories of culture, the anthropologist Donald Brown, perhaps best known for his earlier groundbreaking argument for human universals (Brown 1991), nevertheless concluded that an "attention to particulars" will be required if the influence of evolution for human affairs is not simply to become a "vacuous truism" (Brown 1999, 155). And in the same Darwinian commemorative volume to which Harrison had contributed her evolutionary proposal for a history of religions, the historian John Bury concluded that while general principles may embody the necessary conditions for any particular sequence, they do not provide sufficient conditions, whether in history or in biology (Bury 1909, 539).

The reconsideration of historical particulars which began to appear in the contributions to the special issue of *History and Theory* focused, however, on the expressions of evolved panhuman capacities of individual minds (as recognized by Harrison), which highlights the particulars of historical events if not their singularity. Whatever their position, most of the contributors to this volume now acknowledged the significance of evolutionary psychology, especially as articulated by John Tooby and Leda Cosmides in their contribution to *The Adapted Mind*, "The Psychological Foundations of Culture"—published the same year as the Niteckis' volume (Barkow *et al.* 1992) and subsequently developed by cognitive scientist such Scott Atran (1990, 2002), Pascal Boyer (1994, 2001) and Lawrence Hirschfeld (e.g., 1994), among others.

Dan Sperber, for example, has formulated a hypothesis of cognitive attractors as an alternative to that of the selectionist model favored by evolutionists such as Boyd, Richerson and their collaborators (Sperber 1996, 98–118). For Boyd and Richerson, culture is largely transmitted by imitation and learning, a view that no behaviorist would deny but which the cognitive revolution has challenged. However transmitted, Boyd and Richerson argue that culture can impact genes in a gene-culture

5

co-evolution. But, as Sperber observes, although "[h]uman culture has been around long enough for biological evolution to have been affected by it" and can help explain "the existence in humans of abilities that are specifically geared to cultural interaction, such as the language faculty"… "[g]ene-culture co-evolution," is just "too slow a process to explain cultural changes in historical time" (Sperber 1996, 114). Rather, Sperber identifies a probabilistic cognitive bias—evolved cognitive defaults—that stabilize the transmission of cultural information (Sperber 1996, 112).

In the view of Sperber and the cognitivists, these cognitive "adaptations to an ancestral environment, "tend to fix a lot of cultural content in and around [particular] cognitive domains" (Sperber 1996, 113; see Sperber and Hirschfeld 2004). Although Sperber and his colleagues accept that the conformity- and prestige-biased explanations for cultural transmission favored by the selectionists contribute to the macro-stability of culture, cognitive attractor biases function especially to stabilize the transformations of and modifications to information at the micro-level of transmission within populations and across generations (Claidière and Sperber 2007, 91). Sperber concludes that his model of cultural attraction is nevertheless Darwinian in that "it explains large-scale regularities" in culture and in history "as the cumulative effect of micro-processes" (Sperber 1996, 118). Such an "epidemiological" explanation for culture, based on an exploration of micro-processes, is not completely alien to historians. William McNeill, for example, has studied the effects of a series of micro-processes on world history—that of the spread of infectious diseases being perhaps the most well known (McNeill 1976; see also 1982 and 1995, and Gaddis 2002, 25–26).

Régis Debray, the self-styled *médiologiste*[2] and caustic critic of Sperber (Debray 1997; 2000, 88–98; see also Tanney 1998), has differentiated between information that occurs and is communicated in a cultural present from that which endures and is transmitted over time (Debray 2000, 3). Whereas communication bears no necessary mandate for transmission, transmission over time not only requires communication (Debray 2000, 7) but it gives relief and dimension to the fleeting things that are simply communicated (Debray 2000, 5). In contrast to the epidemiological model of communication proposed by Sperber, in which processes of communication are basically ones of transformation, however stabilized (Sperber 1996, 83; also Debray 2000, 27), processes of transmission, according to Debray, struggle to make inroads towards permanence, that is, towards history (Debray 2000, 4). Historical transmission unaided, Debray argues, is simply inadequate. Rather, historical permanence, he insists, requires an exteriorization of individual meaning and memory into material culture (Debray 2000, 10, 78, and *passim*). Anything significant enough to be encoded in neural networks, Debray argues, may also be considered significant enough to be inscribed and conserved in *material* culture as well (Debray 2000). Such inscribings—from the first flint tools to writing itself—can provide the historian with way stations for describing continuing mnemonic and reflexive traditions of transmission and exegesis. As Aviezer Tucker has recently emphasized, "[o]ur knowledge of history is "limited by the information-preserving evidence that survived the obliterating ravages of time in the historical process" (Tucker 2004, 261). "The common scientific theoretical background that allows historians to reach uncoerced consensus concerns the transmission of information in time, not the evolution of society." Whatever one concludes about the relationship of history and evolution, for "historiography and archaeology" Tucker concludes, "the *evolution of society* and the *transmission of*

---

2. Debray coins the term *médiologie* to designate study dedicated to the material transmission of cultural meanings (Debray 2000, viii).

*information* on past events are *independent of each other*" (Tucker 2004, 260).

Despite the discussions on the possible relationship of and potentials of evolutionary and cognitive theorizing for historiography, historians have been and continue to be reluctant to extend their explorations to the evolved panhuman capacities of and constraints upon human minds. In a recent article that surveys "what's happening in history now?," for example, the medieval historian Caroline Bynum notes that over the past three decades there have been a number of discussions concerning "the application of what is known generically as 'theory' to 'historical scholarship'" (Bynum 2009, 73). She notes that, in broad terms, these discussions have turned from an earlier concern with social theory to cultural (linguistic, textual) theory (Bynum 2009, 73) but this "linguistic turn," she concludes, has produced "no new theory or theory that has swept the field—or even commanded much attention from professional historians" (Bynum 2009, 74). Bynum does identify two new approaches to historiography that have emerged over the past decade, both of which we might characterize as a "return to science," to refer to the title of the theme issue of *History and Theory* cited above (Shaw and Pomper 1999).[3]

The first of the new approaches to historiography that Bynum identifies is a "renewed interest in material culture and physical objects" (Bynum 2009, 77). This renewed interest is, of course, the consequences of scientific advances in archaeological methods. Bynum mentions, for example, dendrochronology, zooarchaeology, and analyses of mineralogical emissions. The second of the new approaches that she acknowledges is the subject of this volume, the explicitly scientifically informed "enthusiasm for what one might call deep structures, represented both by an upsurge of so-call 'big' or 'deep' history and a renewed recourse to sociobiological and cognitive explanations for human behavior" (Bynum 2009, 77). However, she argues, as do some of the critics of those who seek to understand historical by biological change (referenced above), that "in the hands of most professional historians, even cognitive science and parallels from the old field of ethology…tend to be used analogously" (Bynum 2009, 78). In this way, Bynum is able wistfully to reaffirm cultural studies as usual rather than exploring recent scientific advances in historiographical methods. "The study of 'the material', she concludes, "is not…beyond the cultural turn" (Bynum 2009, 80). And "[e]ven 'deep history' at its best," she argues, "involves understanding that physical or physiological structures are always mediated through our ways of knowing them, and hence through culture" (Bynum 2009, 78).

Two recent exceptions to Bynum's nostalgic pronouncements are a study by the Canadian historian Gregory Hanlon of *Human Nature in Rural Tuscany* (2007) and that by the Harvard historian Daniel Lord Smail *On Deep History and the Brain* (2008; referenced by Bynum 2009, 77 n. 20). Similar to Sperber's proposal for evolved cognitive attractors that stabilize and constrain the transmission of cultural materials, Hanlon organizes and interprets detailed archival evidence within the theoretical constraints of evolutionary psychology and cognitive science, "the larger context" of which, he argues, "sets the limits of what can and cannot occur or endure beyond the short term" (Hanlon 2007: 8). In his prolegomenon to "deep history," which embraces that of *H. sapiens* since their emergence, Smail also focuses on the evolved capacities and constraints of human brains. By example, he considers the panhuman proclivity for mind-altering substances (e.g., alcohol, drugs) and practices (e.g., religious rituals), their institutionalization, and their commodification

---

3.   This is also referenced by Bynum (2009, 77 n. 19)—although Bynum prefers instead to characterize these new approaches as "a retreat from the textual" (Bynum 2009, 77).

over time. In this way, Smail suggests precise mechanisms whereby culture (or, more precisely, social institutions) might act upon evolved biological and cognitive proclivities to alter the human phenome (but not necessary the human genome).

Discussions about the relationship between social and cultural history and the more recent "scientific" history continue as do those among the "natural selectionists" and the "cognitive attractionists," as well a wide range of discussions among those seeking to understand the implications of Darwin's initial insights for an interpretation—even an explanation for—historical change, or, at least, aspects of that history. The studies in this volume, primarily by historians of religion, offer contributions—both theoretical and applied—to these continuing discussions.

# References

Allen, Garland E. 1992. "Evolution and History: History as Science and Science as History." In *History and Evolution*, edited by M. Nitecki and D.V. Nitecki, 211–239 Albany: SUNY Press.

Atran, Scott. 1990. *Cognitive Foundations of Natural History: Towards an Anthropology of Science*. Cambridge: Cambridge University Press.

———. 2002. *In Gods We Trust: The Evolutionary Landscape of Religion*. Oxford: Oxford University Press.

Barkow, Jerome H., Leda Comides and John Tooby, eds. 1992. *The Adapted Mind: Psychology and the Generation of Culture*. Oxford: Oxford University Press.

Boyd, Robert and Peter J. Richerson. 1985. *Culture and the Evolutionary Process*. Chicago, IL: University of Chicago Press.

———. 1992. "How Microevolutionary Processes Give Rise to History." In *History and Evolution*, edited by M. Nitecki and D.V. Nitecki, 179–209. Albany: State University of New York Press.

Boyer, Pascal. 1994. *The Naturalness of Religious Ideas: A Cognitive Theory of Religion*. Berkeley: University of California Press.

———. 2001. *Religion Explained: The Evolutionary Origins of Religious Thought*. New York: Basic Books.

Brown, Donald. 1991. *Human Universals*. New York: McGraw-Hill.

———. 1999. "Human Nature and History". *History and Theory* 38(4): 138–157.

Bury, John B. 1909. "Darwinism and History." In *Darwin and Modern Science: Essays in Commemoration of the Centenary of the Birth of Charles Darwin and of the Fiftieth Anniversary of the Publication of the Origin of the Species*, edited by A.C. Seward, 529–542. Cambridge: Cambridge University Press.

Bynum, Caroline W. 2009. "Perspectives, Connections and Objects: What's Happening in History Now?" *Daedalus* 138(1): 71–86.

Claidièr, Nicolas and Dan Sperber. 2007. "The Role of Attraction in Cultural Evolution." *Journal of Cognition and Culture* 7: 89–111.

Collingwood, R.G. 1956. *The Idea of History*. Oxford: Oxford University Press.

Dawkins, Richard. 1989. *The Selfish Gene*, new ed. Oxford: Oxford University Press.

Darwin, Charles. 2003 [1859]. *On the Origin of Species*. London: John Murray, New York: Penguin.

———. 1872. *Expression of the Emotions*. London: John Murray.

———. 1879. *The Descent of Man*, London: John Murray; New York: Penguin, 2004.

Debray, Régis. 1997. "A Plague Without Fleabites." Commentary in *Times Literary Supplement*, 4 July: 14–15.

———. 2000. *Transmitting Culture*, E. Rauth, trans. New York: Columbia University Press.

Fracchia, Joseph and Richard C. Lewontin. 1999. "Does Culture Evolve?" *History and Theory* 38(4): 52–78.

Gaddis, John Lewis. 2002. *The Landscape of History: How Historians Map the Past*. Oxford: Oxford University Press.

Hanlon, Gregory. 2007. *Human Nature in Rural Tuscany: An Early Modern History*. New York: Palgrave Macmillan.

Harrison, Jane E. 1909. "The Influence of Darwinism on the Study of Religions." In *Darwin and Modern Science: Essays in Commemoration of the Centenary of the Birth of Charles Darwin and of the Fiftieth Anniversary of the Publication of the Origin of the Species*, edited by A.C. Seward, 494–511. Cambridge: Cambridge University Press,

Hempel, Carl G. 1942. "The Function of General Laws in History." *The Journal of Philosophy* 39(2), (Jan. 15): 35–48 (reprinted in Hempel, *The Aspects of Scientific Explanation and Other Essays in the Philosophy of Science*, 231–242. New York: The Free Press).

Henrich, Joseph and Robert Boyd. 2002. "On Modeling Cognition and Culture: Why Cultural Evolution Does Not Require Replication of Representations." *Journal of Cognition and Culture* 2: 87–112

Hirschfeld, Lawrence A. and Susan A. Gelman, eds. 1994. *Mapping the Mind: Domain Specificity in Cognition and Culture*. Cambridge: Cambridge University Press.

Hogarth, Robin M. and Melvin W. Reder, eds. 1987. *Rational Choice: The Contrast between Economics and Psychology*. Chicago, IL: The University of Chicago Press.

Iggers, Georg G. 1983. *The German Conception of History: The National Tradition of Historical Thought from Herder to the Present*, rev. ed. Hanover, NH: University Press of New England.

Livingstone, David N. 2007. "Science, Site and Speech: Scientific Knowledge and the Spaces of Rhetoric." *Journal of the History of the Human Sciences* 20(2): 71–98.

Macalister, Alexander. 1871a. "Review of Charles Darwin, *The Descent of Man, and Selection in Relation to Sex*." *Dublin Quarterly Journal of Medical Science* 52: 133–152.

———. 1871b. "On Some Points in the Myology of the Chimpanzee and of Primates." *Annual Magazine of Natural History* 7: 341–351.

———. 1882. *Evolution in Church History*. Dublin: Hodges, Figgis.

———. 1873. "The Muscular Anatomy of the Gorilla." *Proceedings of the Royal Irish Academy* 11: 501–506.

———. 1894. *Some Morphological Lessons Taught by Human Variations and so on; the Robert Boyle Lecture No. 3 1892*. London: Henry Frowde.

McNeill, William H. 1976. *Plagues and Peoples*. Garden City, NY: Doubleday.

———. 1982. *The Pursuit of Power: Technology, Armed Force, and Society since A.D. 1000*. Chicago, IL: University of Chicago Press.

———. 1995. *Keeping Together in Time: Dance and Drill in Human History*. Cambridge, MA: Harvard University Press.

Nitecki, Matthew H. 1992. "History: La Grande Illusion." In *History and Evolution*, edited by M.H. Nitecki and D.V. Nitecki, 3–15. Albany: State University of New York Press.

Nitecki, Matthew H. and Doris V. Nitecki, eds. 1992. *History and Evolution*. Albany: State University of New York Press.

Popper, Karl. 1976. *Unended Quest: An Intellectural Autobiography*. La Salle, IL: Open Court.

Ranke, Leopold von. 1824. "Vorrede," *Geschichten der romanischen und germanischen Völker von 1494 bis 1514*, iii-viii. Berlin: Duncker and Humblot.

———. 1971. *The Theory and Practice of History*, Georg G. Iggers and Konrad von Moltke, eds. Indianapolis: Bobbs-Merrill.

Richards, Robert J. 1992. "The Structure of Narrative Explanation in History and Biology." In *History and Evolution*, edited by M.H. Nitecki and D.V. Nitecki, 19–53. Albany: State University of New York Press.

Ruse, Michael. 1992. "A Threefold Parallelism for our Time? Progressive Development in Society, Science, and the Organic World." In *History and Evolution*, edited by M.H. Nitecki and D.V. Nitecki: 149–178. Albany: State University of New York Press.

Seward, A.C., ed. 1909. *Darwin and Modern Science: Essays in Commemoration of the Centenary of the Birth of Charles Darwin and of the Fiftieth Anniversary of the Publication of the Origin of the Species*. Cambridge: Cambridge University Press.

Shaw, David Gary and Philip Pomper, eds. 1999. *The Return of Science: Evolutionary Ideas and History*. Theme Issue of *History and Theory* 38(4).

Smail, Daniel Lord. 2008. *On Deep History and the Brain*. Berkeley: University of California Press.

Smith, Grafton Eliot. 1923. "Obituary Notices of Fellows Deceased: Alexander Macalister, 1844-1919." *Proceedings of the Royal Society of London*, Series B 94(633): xxxii–xxxix.

Sperber, Dan. 1996. *Explaining Culture: A Naturalistic Approach*. Oxford: Blackwell.

Stern, Fritz, ed. 1956. *The Varieties of History: From Voltaire to the Present*. New York: Meridian Books.

Tanney, Julia. 1998. "Investigating Cultures: A Critique of Cognitive Anthropology." *Journal of the Royal Anthropology Institute* (N.S.) 4: 669–688.

Tax, Sol and Larry S. Krucoff. 1968. "Social Darwinism." In *International Encyclopedia of the Social Sciences*, edited by D.L. Sills, vol. 14: 402–406. New York: The Macmillan Company and The Free Press.

Tooby, John and Cosmides, Leda. 1992. "The Psychological Foundations of Culture." In *The Adapted Mind: Evolutionary Psychology and the Generation of Culture*, edited by J.H. Barkow, L. Cosmides and J. Tooby, 19–136. Oxford and New York: Oxford University Press.

Tucker, Aviezer. 2004. *Our Knowledge of the Past: A Philosophy of Historiography*. Cambridge: Cambridge University Press.

Wilson, David Sloan. 2002. *Darwin's Cathedral: Evolution, Religion, and the Nature of Society*. Chicago, IL: The University of Chicago Press.

Young, Lawrence A., ed. 1997. *Rational Choice Theory and Religion: Summary and Assessment*. New York: Routledge.

# — 2 —

# Cognitive History and Cultural Epidemiology

## Christophe Heintz

Cultural epidemiology is a theoretical framework that enables historical studies to be informed by cognitive science. It incorporates insights from evolutionary psychology and from Darwinian models of cultural evolution. Its research program includes the study of the multiple cognitive mechanisms that cause the distribution, on a cultural scale, of cultural representations and material cultural items. By a detailed analysis of the social cognitive causal chains that occurred in the past, one can find out—and specify—which are the factors of attraction that account for cultural stability as well as historical cultural change.

After reviewing recent research and developments in cognitive history, I present the concept of a cultural attractor and explain why cultural attractors are historically variable. In doing so, I emphasize the role of the historically constituted cognitive mechanisms, which account for much of historical cultural developments. I argue that the framework of cultural epidemiology can better account for these important historical phenomena than either evolutionary psychological accounts of culture or dual inheritance theory. I conclude that describing and explaining the history of cultural attractors is a good research goal for historians.

## Cognitive History and Cultural Change

### Rationale for cognitive history: the cognitive makeup of history

Historians are brought to hypothesize on the mental states of the agents who have lived and acted in the period they study. Describing the intentions, desires, motives, feelings, and thoughts of past agents is fully part of the historians' agenda. In particular, explaining past behaviors implies specifying the mental states that generated these behaviors. Thus, historians propose explanations that draw on psychological concepts and lead to psychological theorizing about agents' thoughts and intentions. Cognitive history is research done with the assumption that psychology and cognitive science provide useful tools and theories for historiography. There are several reasons for thinking that studies in cognitive history will foster better understanding of the past, which I will spell out in the rest of this chapter.

The relevance of psychology to the social sciences has been emphasized in the last two decades, most notably by Tooby and Cosmides (1992) and Sperber (1996). Although their main target was social and cultural anthropology, their arguments also apply to historiography. Cosmides and Tooby denounce the social scientists' assumption that humans are born with a mind like a blank slate, upon which culture can write. They argue, with evidence from psychology, that the inferential devices implemented in brains are content-loaded and constrain behavior and culture in significant ways. Sperber specifies the way in which psychological properties affect social and cultural phenomena. Cognitive processes, Sperber (2006) explains, are comprised of causal chains where the output of a process constitutes the input of another process; they form Cognitive Causal Chains (CCCs). Many events that are part of these causal chains happen within the brain (perception, memory, mental inferences, and motor control), but some other relevant events involve elements "outside of the skull." In particular, cognitive processes can involve social interactions: Chains of cognitive processes can extend across individuals and have a social character. In the simplest cases, the behavioral output of some individual's CCC may serve as a perceptual input for other individuals' CCCs and link them in a single Social CCC, or SCCC for short (Sperber 2006).

Sperber gives the simple example of someone ordering a pizza, where information is passed on from the client to the person taking the phone call, to the cook, and then to the deliverer. At each step information is transmitted and processed, and actions are taken. Historical events are also composed of such social cognitive causal chains. Take a chain of events leading to Saint Bartholomew's Day Massacre in 1572 in France: the Guise family forms the intention of assassinating the Huguenot Coligny, the action is planned, the instructions are given to the would-be assassin, but the attempt fails. The Huguenots want the culprits to be found and punished. In order to preempt possible retaliation from the Huguenots, Catherine de Medicis organizes, together with her son, the King of France, the assassination of the main Huguenot leaders staying in Paris. Orders are given to the municipal authorities and to the King's Swiss Guard; Catholic citizens are armed against possible uprising of the Huguenots. Following the first murders, the people of Paris, of strong Catholic conviction, murder some 2000 Huguenots. The violence then spread throughout France. This chain of events is causal by the production, transmission, and transformation of representations. The chain is cognitive because it is best explained by invoking semantic relations between what agents thought, perceived, and communicated. Thus, the *mental representations* of the members of the Guise family had an effect, through a causal chain unknown to historians, on the would-be assassin. The attempted assassination *informed* the Huguenots of others' *intentions* and power to harm them; they had *interests* in asserting their rights to justice. Catherine de Medicis *construed a mental representation* of the intentions she attributed to the Huguenots ("Huguenots want to retaliate"). She *anticipated* their possible actions. She *communicated* her solution for avoiding what she *thought* might be a danger (the Huguenots' retaliation). The emphasized terms are semantic descriptions of some events, and their relations are themselves expressed in terms of the production and flow of representations; mental representations are causes of the actions of people having them, and public representations cause the production of mental representations, as in communication for instance where sounds cause the listener to reconstruct what the speaker means.

Historians attempt to reconstruct Social Cognitive Causal Chains by using simple assumptions drawn from naïve psychology. In general, this reconstruction is done by using simple assumptions of the kind: people have beliefs, desires, and interests, and these account for their decisions and behavior. In fact, the above historical account is controversial:

we do not know for certain who first ordered the assassination of Coligny, and we do not know for certain the origin of the plan to murder Huguenot leaders. Was it Catherine de Medicis or rather her son, King Charles XI, who initiated the plan? Was it the result of pressures from the Guise family? Was it directly planned by the brother of the king and Henri de Guise, who were in search of authority and power? In order to tell apart the numerous possible chains on the basis of limited evidence, the historiographer needs to be generous in psychological assumptions. In the end, it is not only the historical data that determine historical theories, but also the psychological intuitions of the historians, who try to understand the characters they study, their beliefs, goals, and interests. Historians use their naïve psychological abilities to provide informative historiography. Couldn't historiography benefit from input from scientific psychology and cognitive science?

## Current Developments in Cognitive History

### Cognitive history of science and technology

The need for cognitive history has been felt in the history of science and technology, where the cognitive processes are non-obvious and historically highly significant. A simplified psychology relying only on beliefs and desires as explanatory concepts is largely insufficient for accounting for conceptual innovation.[1] Nersessian (1995) introduces the methodology and prospects of a cognitive history of science as a subfield of cognitive science that studies the thinking practices "through which scientists create, change, and communicate their representations of nature" (194). Cognitive history of science reconstructs historical events that are amenable to cognitive analysis. It already includes analyses of the works of Faraday (Tweney 1985, 1991; Gooding 1990), Maxwell (Nersessian 1984, 1992, 2002), Bell and Edison (Gorman 1992) as well as studies in the history of natural history (Atran 1990) and the history of mathematics (Netz 1999; Heintz 2007b, chapters 7 and 11). These works attempt to reconstruct scientists' thoughts and activities by using cognitive notions such as "schemata," "mental models," "heuristics," "naïve theories," "analogical thinking," "thought experiment," "deductive" and "inductive reasoning," and "procedural knowledge." They analyze through which cognitive processes innovation and conceptual change arise in history. In return, the study of these historical events can contribute to the understanding of cognition because it provides new data on cognition occurring in non-experimental settings. As opposed to research tasks performed in the psychologists' laboratory, the cognitive history of science analyzes how scientific cognition is at work in the scientists' own working environments.

The cognitive history of science uses cognitive psychology as a source of information for historians about the thought processes available to scientists while scientific cognition is analyzed as it occurred in historical contexts: scientists are socially situated, and this situation accounts in part for their thoughts and behavior. The cognitive historian also attempts to account for the behavior of scientists by generating hypotheses about the cognitive processes that are actually implemented. The historical case studies furnish empirical data for cognitive theories. There should be, as Nersessian (1995) puts it, a virtuous circle where some assumptions from cognitive science are accorded privileged status in order to get the historical analysis "off the ground" but could be subject to further critical scrutiny. Cor-

---

1.  The point is not that scientists' desires and interests do not play an important and pervasive role in scientific knowledge formation (see Barnes 1977), but that using only naïve psychology in social studies of science leads to a partial picture of the processes of scientific knowledge production.

rective insights should come from both directions: from experimental cognitive science to cognitive history and vice verse.

## Cognitive history of religion

The question of the usefulness of cognitive science to history has also been raised in the domain of the history of religion (Whitehouse 2005; Martin 2005). The cognitive science of religion has theorized on the psychological factors that make religious ideas likely to become widespread in time and space. Boyer (2001, chapter 2) and Atran (2002, section 4.7) show that minimally counterintuitive beliefs are more attention arresting, more easily remembered, and more willingly communicated. Religious beliefs are mostly made of such minimally counterintuitive beliefs, and this accounts for their large distribution and recurrence across time and societies. Performing this analysis requires knowledge of cognitive psychology, because whether a given belief is minimally counterintuitive depends on how intuitive beliefs are produced, and whether their content is constrained by universal features of the human cognitive apparatus. The resulting theory can bring some explanatory power to the history of religion. For instance, Vial (2005) explains why Luther's theology has been more successful than Zwingli's by pointing out features of Luther's theology that made his claims easier to cognize than Zwingli's.

Whitehouse's theory of *modes of religiosity* (2004) also draws on psychology and provides tools for historians. He specifies two distinct ways through which religious beliefs can be memorized: through memories of things seen and felt (episodic, autobiographic, memory), or through memories of specific content (semantic memory). Thus, religious beliefs can take the form of either episodic or semantic memories, which are distinct cognitive types of mental representations. The production and transmission of these two types of mental representations require different means: the production and transmission of episodic memories rely on rituals that ensure, through emotional arousal, that the course of events will be remembered as autobiographically salient memories. This is the imagistic mode of religiosity. The production and transmission of semantic memories rely on explicit and repetitive teaching; it implicates institutionalized learning and deferential behavior towards teachers. This is the doctrinal mode of religiosity. Whitehouse argues that the two modes coexist in any religion but that specific religions tend towards one or the other. Martin (2005) points out that this cognitive theory of cultural transmission predicts a "divergence of transmissive trajectories *over time*." The imagistic mode of religiosity implies transmission through emotionally loaded rituals, which create strong feelings of solidarity between those who went through it. The doctrinal mode of religiosity implies institutionalized teaching, and thus a social hierarchy.

## Cognitive economic history

It is likely that cognitive history will soon be applied to other domains, e.g. economic history. Several factors could lead to the development of cognitive economic history. First, economists have started to realize that psychology is most useful for understanding and predicting the actual behavior of economic agents. This led to the thriving field of behavioral economics (see for instance Gilovich *et al.* 2002). Second, another developing field of economics is information economics, which studies how information affects economic decisions and the consequent economic performances (the archetypical problem being "information asymmetries," see, e.g. Akerlof 1970; the relevance of the distribution of knowledge is explicated and analyzed by Martens 2004). Information economics emphasizes the economic importance of information, its transformation and distribution among economic agents. Third, the dissatisfaction with neoclassical economics and its unrealistic model of the economic agent is felt among economists who want to account for economic changes. Evolutionary economists, in particular, have been searching for alternative models to the neoclassical *homo œconomicus*, which are better suited for modeling operations on markets than for describing how economies evolve. Evolutionary economists are thus led to use more complex models of economic agents (e.g. Potts 2000, chapter 5) and integrate theories from psychology (mainly sociobiology and evolutionary psychology) and behavioral economics (e.g. Witt 2003, chapters 8 and 9).

Douglas North, a major figure in economic history and winner of the Nobel Memorial Prize in Economic Sciences in 1993, incited research in the direction of cognitive economic history. North (2005) argues as follows: in order to understand economic change, one has to account for changes in the institutional infrastructure that importantly determine economic decisions and overall performance. The institutional changes are brought about by economic agents acting on the institutional infrastructures on the basis of their beliefs about what is the case, what should be the case, and how to achieve the intended change. Thus, understanding the process of economic change requires investigating the psychological processes through which agents' intentions emerge. The history of the Soviet Union, briefly reviewed in a chapter of the book, provides a clear account of how (Marxist) beliefs about the world caused political actions that framed institutions. This led to undesired consequences (e.g. low agricultural production) and several attempts to adjust beliefs, policies, and perceived results. The history of the western world also illustrates the process: "belief structures" such as English people's perception of the rights of the individuals in the sixteenth century determined institutional structures such as the Petition of Right of 1628, which in turn changed the environment and later beliefs.

Understanding economic processes seems to call for an analysis of how beliefs evolve, are distributed, and processed in the population of economic agents. Historical changes provide one of the main sources of empirical data.

## Cultural Epidemiology and Cultural Change

### Cognitive cultural history

Cognitive history has been shown to be useful in the domains of religious and science studies, and it promises to give important insights for economics. Independently of the domain, the accounts are all about human thought processes in historical context and the factors that constrain the flow and transformation of information.

There are at least two reasons that make a social cognitive causal chain of interest for the historian. First, a social cognitive causal chain can be relevant to us because we know it led to some important, desirable or not, consequence. We then want to understand which change in which variables could have led to a different outcome. The chain of events leading to the Massacre of Saint Bartholomew, for instance, is highly relevant because we judge that the killings were disastrous. Moreover, the massacre led to a cultural change that has had further historical consequences, including the exodus of the Huguenots' intelligentsia after the revocation of the Edict of Nantes (1685). Cognitive chains that led to less adverse effects are also of interest: for instance, Faraday's reasoning in his laboratory has had important consequences for the future distribution of scientific representations and on our living conditions.

Second, social cognitive causal chains of the past are of interest to historians to the extent that they are representative causal chains—they often recurred in the past and are informative of the past culture. Here, the scope changes from an important single chain of events to recurrent chains of less important events. Recurring cognitive causal chains produce cultural phenomena. For instance, studying religious beliefs and practices implies reasoning on relatively large populations where not all actions and thoughts need be tracked down. It is not so important for the historian whether the blacksmith Jacques Martin living close to the Bastille went to Mass on the first Sunday of September 1571. What is important, however, is that the population of Paris is mainly composed of strong believers in Catholicism. Most inhabitants of Paris went to the Catholic mass in the years that preceded the massacre. It is the large *distribution* of strong Catholic beliefs as well as beliefs about one's own identity and that of other religious communities (the heretics) that constitute an important phenomenon. This phenomenon is cultural: it is not only constituted by the content of the beliefs (Catholicism, beliefs about Protestant beliefs) or their relations with singular actions and events, but also by the distribution of the beliefs in the French population of the sixteenth century.

In the first and second case, the cognitive historian questions which are the cognitive chains that produced the representations observed in the historical records (public representations such as letters or reports) or ascribed to historical agents by historians in order to make sense of their behavior. In the second case, the recurrence also needs to be explained. The question is: What are the principles that account for the change and stability of the distribution of representations in the population? The mechanisms that distribute representations can involve psychological properties, as when representations are attention-arresting, have inferential potential or are more emotionally provocative. They can also importantly rely on properties of the environment, which can itself be the result of social and historical processes, as when institutions determine who has the authority and means to distribute information (e.g. who can broadcast on radio). Doing cognitive cultural history[2] implies specifying the factors that led to the advent of cultural phenomena through the description of the recurrent social cognitive causal chains and the constructive cognitive mechanisms that are repeatedly triggered. In particular, the historians explain the evolution of distribution of representation in terms of probabilistic reasoning based on psychological notions (e.g. a representation being memorable or salient). The probabilistic reasoning has itself a causal cognitive underpinning: the cognitive historian specifies a cognitive causal chain that is likely to occur, given what is known of the properties of the human mind and the histori-

---

2. This is cultural history that draws on the explanatory power of cognitive science. By "cultural history" I refer to the historiography of cultural phenomena. However, "cultural history" also refers to a research program, especially in French historiography. It will appear that there are many similarities in the questions and goals of cultural history and cultural epidemiology: cultural history is characterized as "social history of representations" (Ory 2004), which departs from the previous history of mentalities because it refuses to use the concept of collective mentalities. Cultural history takes on the project to track down public representations as they were produced and distributed in the period studied, but also which mental representations these public representations generated at the time. For instance, Chartier (1990) insists on the "modes of reading" and the operations through which readers construct the signification of texts. Chartier argues that the reading practices of the eighteenth century encouraged critical discussion, which was a condition of possibility of the French Revolution, because it sapped the monarch of its mystical authority. The proponents of cultural history seem to rejoin cultural epidemiology's view of cultural phenomena as distributions of representations, and they likewise aim at identifying the social cognitive causal chains that distribute cultural representations.

cal context. Boyer notes that representations have more or less *"cultural fitness [...] under-stood as the likelihood* that a particular representation found at generation *n* will be found, in some roughly similar version at *n* +1" (1998). One much studied means for a cultural representation to have cultural fitness is to trigger and exploit evolved cognitive abilities. Evolved cognitive abilities constrain cognitive development and lead to universal psychological properties. For instance, the evolved capacity to speak a natural language constrains development so that nearly all adults having grown up in a common social environment speak the same natural language. Likewise, all "normal" adults ascribe beliefs and desires to others thanks to cognitive development of an evolved capacity for what is called naïve psychology.[3] These universal properties of the mind inform the cognitive social scientist about which mental cognitive causal chains are most likely to occur in specified conditions. Boyer talks about "inheritance tracks" when describing how cultural input is likely to be processed by situated agents, given their human evolved abilities.

### Cultural epidemiology as a theoretical framework for historians

Sperber (1996) argues that understanding the specifics of mental cognitive causal chains is as important for the study of culture as the study of pathologies is for medical epidemiology. Cultural phenomena are cultural because they involve *recurrence* of cognitive processes and *spread* of cultural items. Cultural epidemiology aims at studying the reasons for such recurrences and spread, taking into account theories from psychology. Cultural phenomena, Sperber says, can be characterized as distributions of mental representations and public productions in communities and their habitat. For instance, different versions of a tale may be instantiated as mental representations in children and adults' memory, and the versions can be instantiated as public productions in sound wavelength or written inscriptions. A story is cultural to the extent that its versions are well distributed in space and time. A tale, for example, is being told across several generations and is known by numerous member of a community of the same generation.

Cultural epidemiology provides a good theoretical framework for cognitive cultural history: it allows for a diachronic analysis of cultural phenomena, which are characterized as distributions of representations *in time* as well as in space. Cultural representations are made of token representations that remain recognizably similar to *past*, *antecedent*, token representations; these token representations must span relatively long periods of time in order to achieve a cultural status. The causes of the existence of cultural representations are also inscribed in time: Sperber points out that the social cognitive causal chains that stabilize representations are "long and lasting" (2001).

Studies in cultural epidemiology (i.e., the work of Atran, Boyer, Hirschfeld, and Sperber) have focused on the conditions—in particular the psychological conditions—for the resilience and continuity in content of some representations. Why and how do representations happen to spread successfully? Why are some taken on and spread, while others are rejected, radically transformed, or simply forgotten? These questions pertain to cultural history, but are phrased in terms of causal chains that go through people's brain. Which are these causal processes and mechanisms that distribute representations in a community and its habitat?

What has interested historians most is not only how some beliefs spread and last, but also how and why beliefs change. Cultural change, however, also falls into the epidemiologi-

---

3. People with autism have limited capacities to develop naïve psychology.

cal rationale: the stability of a cultural representation is always partial and depends on the environmental and culturally contingent conditions that sustain it. Studying how changes in the environmental conditions affect the stability of a representation is indeed a genuine epidemiological question, i.e. one that can fruitfully be answered within this theoretical framework. I will further argue for this claim by showing how historical contingency can be taken into account in the framework of cultural epidemiology. I will emphasize that historically and psychologically well-informed descriptions of social cognitive causal chains can enable the historian to discover the causes of the recurrent production of similar cultural items and thus the different factors of cultural change and stability. By contrast, the restricted focus of evolutionary psychology on evoked culture and dual inheritance theory on transmitted culture lead these two approaches to culture to neglect the rich interaction between the environment and the cognitive processes that distribute representations and thus produce cultural phenomena.

## The Historicity of Cultural Attractors

One central research goal of social and cultural anthropology is to account for cultural diversity across space, with people from one region having behaviors and beliefs that are relatively similar among themselves, but very different from people from another region. Likewise, cultural history has to provide explanations of cultural diversity across time. In this section, I present the notion of a cultural attractor as enabling accounts of cultural change and diversity while at the same time incorporating the universal aspects of human psychology.

### *Beyond the evoked/transmitted culture dichotomy*

It has often been assumed that cultural diversity is based on psychological diversity: evolutionary theories of the early nineteenth century presupposed differences in the mental abilities of peoples of different cultures (e.g. Lévy-Bruhl on pre-logical thinking); and contemporary anthropological relativist theories assume that the mind is so malleable that enculturation accounts for all those psychological properties that ground cultural thinking and behavior. Cultural diversity could be seen as providing an argument against ascribing a role to the universal psychological properties of the mind in framing cultures. If people were bound to think in the same ways, the argument goes, how come they have such different beliefs and types of behaviors across cultures? Cultural epidemiologists and evolutionary psychologists have argued that cultural diversity can be based on properties of the mind that are shared cross-culturally. Their answers, however, differ in ways that I will now try to explain.

Cosmides and Tooby (1992, 209) argue that even though there is a rich set of universal properties of the mind that strongly constrains cultural production, cultural diversity can arise because the universal mental mechanisms are put to work on different inputs from different environments: people living in the same location are likely to experience similar circumstances, which evoke similar responses, whereas people living in different locations experience different circumstances that evoke different responses. One obvious example is that people living in hot places tend to be lightly clothed, while people living in cold places wear clothes that keep them from the cold. Thus the variation of environmental conditions provides local similarities and general diversity of responses leading to diverse cultures. Cosmides and Tooby call "evoked cultures" the cultural responses to diverse environments, i.e., the local "similarities [in thoughts and behaviors] triggered by local circumstances"

(Cosmides and Tooby 1992, 210). Transmitted culture, by contrast, "is the process whereby the thought and behavior of some individuals (usually from the preceding generation) is passed on to other individuals, thereby causing the present pattern."

Social transmission and environmental evocation are two ways in which cultural diversity can be brought about. Although Cosmides and Tooby do think evocation and transmission operate together in the production of cultures, their work and that of evolutionary psychologists and sociobiologists in general, has largely focused on evoked culture. In order to emphasize the role of evolved cognitive abilities in shaping cultures they have attempted to explain many cultural phenomena as evoked culture rather than as the result of social transmission. The topics investigated in this way include kinship, mating behavior, and parental investment—where Hamilton and Trivers' work has provided much insight for evolutionary theorizing (see, e.g., Salmon and Shackelford 2007).

In order to re-establish the balance, Richerson and Boyd (2005) emphasize the role of transmitted culture. They provide several cases of cultural phenomena that cannot be accounted for by evocation alone. Technical knowledge, for instance, is cultural knowledge that it is not re-invented by each member of the culture or each generation. Rather, it is transmitted among the members of the culture. It "improves" through Darwinian processes and can become quite complex. Boyd and Richerson have advocated dual-inheritance theory, according to which both genes and cultural variants are transmitted across generations through two different channels. Yet, the evolved cognitive mechanisms they consider as psychological foundations of culture are mainly *enabling* cultural transmission (Richerson and Boyd 2005, chapter 4) and *selecting* cultural variants (transmission biases: Richerson and Boyd 2005, 69–77). Dual inheritance theorists have given little attention to the cognitive mechanisms that *construct* cultural representations on the basis of input from social interactions. In their models, imitation is mostly a black-boxed cognitive process. It is assumed that the process is such that the output (imitated behavior) will be sufficiently similar to the input (the model) in enough cases for the stabilization of cultural items to occur.

Evolutionary psychologists and dual-inheritance theorists form two schools of thought that emphasize the causal effect of either evolved faculties or social transmission on culture. But in fact, the evoked/transmitted dichotomy is more an artifact of debates between Darwinian theorists of culture than a fruitful way to categorize cultural phenomena.[4] It results indeed in some misleading oversimplification:

4.  Atran (2001) states that the divide may originate in "vulgar sociobiology" and the reactions it triggered:
    I suspect that Dawkins and colleagues tend to disregard or underplay the role of evolved cognitive architecture in constituting culture for many of the same reasons that motivate Stephen Gould (1980) and colleagues to take a similar stance: as an answer to vulgar sociobiology (i.e., identifiable classes of genes directly cause identifiable classes of cultural behavior). The central message of memetics is that human beings can still be purely Darwinian creatures and yet possess a significant measure of independence from their selfish genes and from the blind processes of natural selection that ruthlessly govern biological evolution. (242–243)
    He then proposes cultural epidemiology and modularity of mind as a third way:
    But sociobiology is not the only Darwinian alternative to memetics. The multimodular mind, too, allows for obvious human creativity and much free play in thought. Unlike memetic hand waving, it does so by attempting to actually specify the cognitive tools available and the recurrent rules of their use in building cultures. (243)
    My argument is similar with regard to dual inheritance theory and evolutionary psychology, which tends to perpetuate the aforementioned dichotomy, but I will draw attention to the theory of cultural attraction rather than to the modularity of mind hypothesis.

by trying to show the importance of the role of either evocation or transmission, one tends to ignore the constructive processes that involve both what is socially transmitted and the properties of the mind. On the one hand, studies of evoked culture emphasize that cultural items are the output of some mental cognitive processes; they tend to ignore that this output contributes to framing the environment in which neighboring agents, present and future, live. On the other hand, studies of transmitted culture tend to downplay the role of the constructive processes that produce the output.

An important fact that is concealed by the evoked/transmitted dichotomy is that the constructive processes themselves are not limited to evolved mental mechanisms. The constructive cognitive processes can evolve as a result of cultural transmission. First, mental processes evolve as a consequence of the feedback action of the distribution of cultural items. *Enculturation* is a particular feedback consequence of cultural phenomena since culture plays a role in mental development. People are not only learning new things, they are also learning to learn, as scientists in education like to say. Enculturation thus refers to more psychological phenomena than the incremental acquisition of transmitted cultural beliefs and values. Enculturation and learning in general have consequences on the *generative* mechanisms sustaining cultural evolution.

Second, the feedback actions of cultural phenomena change not only the mental processes but also the non-psychological environment that distributes cultural items. For instance, the availability of technical devices and other artifacts sometimes enables specific actions and thoughts. Mechanisms of distribution can involve mental and non-mental processes. This is the case with most institutions, which can include infrastructures and other material means (e.g., coercive means) as well as memorized procedures (Heintz 2007a).

Rather than assuming which processes produce cultural phenomena (imitation in dual inheritance theory or evocation in evolutionary psychology), cultural epidemiology prompts to describe these processes and thus enables going beyond the evoked/transmitted dichotomy. Social cognitive causal chains are, indeed, much more complex than simple reactions on some external and independent environment, and more complex than simple transmission chains. Historiographers are well aware of the numerous contingent and contextual causes that determine the course of history. I will now argue that such causes can be described within the framework of cultural epidemiology.

### Contextual causes in the production of cultural phenomena

By a careful analysis of the distribution of cultural items and other environmental input to cognitive mechanisms *and* a description of the cognitive mechanisms that occur at a time and place one can specify which are the cognitive processes that most probably occur, and thus which representations occur more often and eventually stabilize so as to constitute cultural phenomena. Careful analyses of environmental stimuli (including cultural items) are already included in the historiographers' agenda. The analysis of the cognitive mechanisms that occur at a time and place, however, may require the aid of cognitive psychology. Cultural epidemiologists have used and developed hypotheses about the structure of the mind that rely on methods from evolutionary psychology. On the basis of such psychological hypotheses, they have been able to specify the cognitive mechanisms that had a significant role in the formation of this or that cultural phenomenon (especially religious beliefs; Boyer 2001). Yet, constraints coming from universal properties of the mind are but one factor that can stabilize representations in a population. Ecological and psychological factors issued from learning and enculturation do play an important role. As these factors may change over time, their dynamics can also account for historical cultural changes.

Here are examples of contextual historical factors that induced or permitted the recurrence of types of events in social cognitive causal chains:

## Material means of communication

Social interactions and communication are key events out of which cultures evolve. Social interactions happen when the input of some agent's mental processes is made of the output of some other agent's mental processes; this output is a change in the external environment but this change is itself constrained by the environment. For instance, a book can be produced at low cost only when the environment provides affordances for printing. Means of communication have been shown to have an important impact on cultural production. They eventually have major consequences on which cognitive processes get implemented (see, e.g., Goody 1977; Donald 1991).

## Social constraints on the flow of information

Pre-existing distributions of representations can regulate who can talk to whom and about what. For instance, access to people with political power is often restricted to a small minority of the governed population. The use of the media for distributing one's idea is also regulated. Eventually, the flow of information across the population can be highly regulated by existing institutions. In particular, there can be local systems that assess the trustworthiness of sources of information and partly determine whether these sources can get the attention of some audience. Two examples are familiar: the differential prestige of scientific journals and search-engines mediated access to Web documents (Heintz 2006).

## Access to resources

More generally, access to resources, symbolic or other, is historically contingent, and determines which social cognitive causal chains there can be. This important Marxist point may be overlooked by studies of cultural evolution based on a definition of culture restricted to information acquired from others through social transmission (teaching, imitation, etc.).

## Enculturation

The historical context has some impact on psychological factors, since it governs enculturation. Max Weber's study on the Protestant ethic is a case in point: it shows how religious complex and abstract ideas about an afterlife can have effects on personality formation and then on behavior. From a distribution of theological ideas, a distribution of ideas about oneself evolves (e.g. as being "chosen"), which partly determines economic decisions.

The first reason why cultural evolution is contingent upon historical factors is its cumulative aspect. For instance, it is only if I already know how to make a good kayak that I can improve it by using, e.g., some new sewing techniques. Yet, the examples above show that historical contingency is involved in several ways other than the ones due to the accumulation of cultural knowledge: significant factors in cultural evolution can include the existing artifacts, social organization, and inter-relations of apparently independent beliefs. Rather than "cumulation," Wimsatt and Griesemer (2007) talk about "scaffolding." They give several examples where complex cultural features arise from several pre-existing cultural phenomena. Their analysis of the history of Sears' Kit Houses, for instance, shows the rich set of factors that lead to the spread of those houses in the US from the 1890s to the 1930s. The Sears company advertised houses through catalogues and sold houses were sent in pieces by train. The factors of the success of the company, and thus of its cultural impact, include the railway infrastructure and low postal rates, the availability of cheap paper, and the fact that most Americans in the countryside did not have ready means to travel to retail stores in urban centers.

> Thus, mail order emerged as means of extending the reach of department stores beyond the "neighborhood" defined by the travel distances of consumers, but it also leveraged a national expansion of successful retail stores. Both extensions took place through the catalog, scaffolded by the various institutional, technological and organizational innovations of society and government mentioned above. The Sears catalog became an icon of American popular culture. (Wimsatt and Griesemer 2007, 239)

How can we deal with this multiplicity of factors and their historicity? The best way is to come back to the events as they historically took place, and, I sustain, describe the social cognitive causal chains as they occurred. Of most interest to cultural historians, are the social cognitive causal chains that are representatives of recurrent types. These constitute mechanisms of distribution of cultural representations.

### Contextual factors of attraction

Sperber (1996) talks about *cultural attractors* as positions in the space of possible "cultural items." In this space, two items are close to each other when they resemble each other, so a cultural phenomenon is constituted by the existence of many items close to each other in this space of possible items, and that are distributed in the population and its habitat, and through time. An attractor is "an abstract statistical construct" (112). The notion of attractor is not intended to be explanatory, but to enable the description of cultural phenomena that are constituted by the regular production of resembling cultural items. The regularities that are described with cultural attractors are such that the produced cultural items are statistically gathered around one ideal-type variant, which is then called the attractor. In the case of social transmission, social cognitive causal chains are made of repeated transmissions, where a first item leads to the production of a second one that resembles the first (e.g., a causal chain where a mental representation is reproduced in someone else's head). Such chains of repeated transmissions lead to the stable distribution of resembling representations and constitute cultural phenomena. Sperber argues that in most cases the social cognitive causal chains of cultural transmissions are such that there is a high probability that the produced cultural items resemble the cultural attractor more than does its antecedent variant in the cognitive causal chain. The result is that, in the space of possible items, cultural items gather around cultural attractors: new items tend to resemble the cultural attractor as much as they tend to resemble the antecedent variant in the transmission chain.

Sperber (1996, chapter 5) argues that the notion of cultural attractor is a useful notion to describe cultural phenomena because there is no high fidelity in transmission and reproduction of cultural items. But, even though there is a lack of fidelity at the level of cultural transmission (see also Sperber 2000), there is nonetheless stability at the population level. "Resemblance among cultural items is to be explained to some important extent by the fact that transformation tend to be biased in the direction of attractor position in the space of possibilities" (Sperber 1996, 108). The social cognitive causal chains constitutive of social transmission often take the form of cognitive mechanisms that reliably produce an output that resemble the cultural attractor in spite of some variations in the input. For instance, a tale can be memorized and recounted in the same way independently of the pitch of the initial narrator, but also, and more importantly, independently of the specific words she used, and even with a relative independence of some of the events initially recounted. The causes of stability are therefore to be found in the constructive processes at work in social cognitive causal chains, such as the specifics of human memory and the reliance on evolved cognitive abilities. Cultural stability results from causal factors of attraction, which have for consequence a gathering of cultural items around cultural attractors.

There are multiple factors of attraction, and these can be local and historical as well as universal (more precisely, derived from universal properties of the cognitive apparatus). Epidemiological studies of religious beliefs (Boyer 2001; Atran 2002) have focused on universal human psychological properties as factors of attraction. However, the position of attractors always depends on both properties of universal aspects of human psychology and of the shared context, local beliefs, development of local psychological properties, etc. As Sperber says, "the factors that make for a good form [i.e. a form seen as being without either missing or superfluous parts, easier to remember, and more attractive] may be rooted in part in universal human psychology and in part in a local cultural context" (Sperber 1996, 108). Cultural phenomena can indeed act as ecological or psychological factors of attraction.

First, properties of local material culture such as the already mentioned material means of communication can *foster* and *constrain* further cultural production. For instance, a type of musical instrument makes some tune easier to play and more pleasant to listen to because of its shape and specific sounds. There exist two types of bassoon, the Buffet bassoon and the Heckel bassoon, which require different fingerings for many notes and have distinctive sounds. Each type of bassoon seems to have a repertoire for which it is more adequate: the Heckel bassoon is more widely used, but the Buffet bassoon, which originated in France, is favored for playing music composed by Frenchmen. So it seems that the specificities of instruments have consequences on the music that is being composed and vice versa.

Second, psychological factors are not always anchored directly in universal psychology. The local cultural context can determine psychological development in such a way that the ensuing psychological properties act as factors of attraction. For instance, the ability to play chess or to use an abacus influence human behavior on a cultural scale. These abilities also create a demand for material objects—a chess game or abacus in our case—and can have consequences for social organization—chess club or the organization of the market place and the form of economic exchange. More controversially, the specificity of the language spoken has some consequences on thinking (cf. the literature on the Sapir-Whorf hypothesis).

Here is a further illustration of the context dependency of the position of cultural attractors. Sperber's example of a form of a tale as a cultural attractor is as follows:

> suppose that an incompetent teller has the hunters extract Little Red Riding Hood from the Big Bad Wolf's belly, but forgets the grandmother [...] hearers whose knowledge of the story derives from this defective version are likely to consciously or unconsciously correct the story when they retell it, and, in their narrative, to bring the grandmother back to life too. In the logical space of possible version of a tale, some versions have a better form: that is, a form seen as being without either missing or superfluous parts, easier to remember and more attractive (Sperber 1996, 108).

Why does the defective version have a bad form? Sperber does not tell at this point, leaving it to the intuition of the reader that the normal form is more attractive than the defective. A hypothesis, however, is that it is understood that the hunters are benevolent, since they are acting against the bad wolf. But benevolent people cannot so easily forget about the well-being of a grandmother—this is, at least, what our naïve psychology leads us to expect. Of course, cultural information also plays a role in the fact that we want to satisfy this expectation: the tale is intended for children for whom maximal relevance (Sperber and Wilson 1986) may be attained when explaining how difficult situations can be sorted out (one just needs some benevolent hunters). Imagine however that the tale was to be told to teenagers among whom poking fun of grandmothers is highly appreciated. Telling a tale that goes against the expected behavior would increase the relevance of the story: it would raise the question "why did the hunters leave the grandmother in the wolf's belly?," opening up inferences such as "leaving grandmothers in wolves' bellies is more benevolent than taking them out," "we are better off when grandmothers remain in wolves' bellies" and so on. In both cases, both evolved cognitive abilities (I mentioned the working of naïve psychology in producing expectations about the hunters' behavior) and cultural background information play a role as factors of attraction towards a specific form of the tale. In this example, the existence of a cultural attractor results from psychological factors of attraction. But these psychological factors are themselves changing, depending on age-related expectations and interests: benevolence and problem solving in the case of young children and the undermining of moral norms of respect due to elderly people in the case of contemporary European teenagers. Of course, one can also note the dependence of the cultural attractor on kinship system or other factors, which can always be situated on a continuous scale from universal to local and contextual.

Cultural historical research mainly consists in specifying which factors gave rise to cultural phenomena. These factors may be multiple and historically contingent in a way that is not always recognized by current evolutionary theorists of culture. For instance, Richerson and Boyd (2005, 31–35) illustrate the power of cultural transmission in the face of variations in institutional and social environment by pointing out that post-Soviet countries have kept or recovered their own regional culture in spite of Soviet actions against these local cultural traits. Indeed, transmissions of national values and ideas have played a great role in the formation of post-Soviet countries, but other factors also come into play. In particular, the structure of the incentives should not to be ignored: what is to gain by adopting traditional values? In the repertoire of traditions, why choose this one rather than that one? In the Republic of Moldova, one of the post-Soviet countries, many people regret the fall of the Soviet era. The Communist party has known a large success in recent years. Also, in a referendum in 1994, the people massively voted against the unification with Romania, with which they share most of their past and traditions. These events occurred in spite of the fact that around 72% of the population is Romanian. Discussions of what should be the national language (Romanian or Romanian renamed "Moldovan," or whether Russian should have a special status) show that past traditions are differentially promoted in the Republic of Moldova and that political and local interests have important effects. In the village where I stayed (10/04–01/05), on the bank of the Dniester, it clearly appeared that job prospects, opportunities to gain a little more money, were thought to be in Russia—Western Europe was still thought of as too inaccessible. There is a parallel between the selection of traditions that are maintained and the selection of features of the tale in the above example: what constitutes a good form, with a potential to stabilize, is contingent on current interests.

Does recognizing the multiplicity of factors directing cultural change make the attempt to develop and use cultural evolutionary theory in history hopeless? No: But understanding the multiplicity of factors and mechanisms of evolution requires relying on historiography as an important source of data. In spite of the multiple contingent factors that intervene in fixing the position of cultural attractors, there is nonetheless regularity in the cognitive causal chains producing items on a cultural scale. In order to account for this regularity, Boyer (1998) talks about "cognitive tracks." Cognitive tracks are cognitive causal chains that are more probable to occur than others, given a range of input. Their higher probability of occurrence is due to the fact that there are cognitive mechanisms already in place that are triggered by cultural inputs with the result that sets of inputs generate similar sets of output. Boyer emphasizes the role of intuitive ontologies as forming the cognitive mechanisms that shape cognitive tracks and constitute factors of attraction. I have, on my part, emphasized that such cognitive mechanisms can also be the product of history: they can result from enculturation or be implemented through a preexisting distribution of representations and its effect on the social organization of cognition (social management of the flow of information, social distribution of cognitive tasks). My claim, therefore, is that explanations in cultural historiography can take the form of specifying which cognitive mechanisms are in place; this in turn can explain which are the cognitive tracks likely to be taken given the input (e.g., the structure of incentives as causally implied in beliefs about expected utilities) and also which input is more likely to be produced in social interactions. Boyer (1998) notices that when intuitive ontologies are not more or less directly relied upon, material and institutional support must be implicated in the production and distribution of items on a cultural scale. To this analysis I add that the material and institutional support can also take the form of cognitive mechanisms upon which the production and distribution of cultural items rely. In other words, cognitive explanation spans larger than cognitive psychology, as has been shown by students of distributed cognition (Hutchins 1995). Cognitive mechanisms can be realized outside of the boundaries of the skull and so cognitive tracks can often cross-cut brains and environment.

## Conclusion

Factors of attraction come from the properties of the cognitive mechanisms in place (i.e. present in a given population and its habitat at a given time). Recognizing that cognitive mechanisms can change over time (especially because of enculturation and distributed cognition) is to give to cognitive studies of cultural evolution a new historical dimension: factors of attraction themselves can change over time. The historicity of these factors tends to be ignored in accounts of cultural evolution of both evolutionary psychology and dual inheritance theory. Cultural epidemiologists also have not yet given full attention to the processes through which factors of attraction change. They have mostly focused on unchanging psychological factors. Yet, one aspect with which cultural epidemiology makes a difference with respect to competing evolutionary theories of culture is its ability to integrate and develop theories about multiple and changing cognitive mechanisms at work in the distribution of cultural items.

I hope that the arguments I have developed in this chapter will appear to be more than hand waving towards historians: when advocating the use of cultural epidemiology in cultural history, I have spelled out the advantages of the approach. Cultural epidemiology aims at describing the social cognitive causal chains out of which cultural items are being produced and distributed, it aims at specifying the behavioral and cognitive bases of cultural phenomena, and it provides the conceptual tools (Sperber, 2001) for such inquiries. Explanatory power is gained by providing the opportunity for historiographers to use theories in cognitive science. Theories about intuitive ontologies have been the main focus of studies in cultural epidemiology, although a cognitive theory of communication (relevance theory of communication, see Sperber and Wilson 1986) has always been in the background (especially as an alternative to theories of cultural transmission that completely rely on "imitation" as an ability for culture). In this chapter, I have argued that studies of enculturation and of situated and distributed cognition can also integrate into and benefit from studies in cultural epidemiology. Integrating such studies in cultural epidemiology should enable the cognitive study of what Wimsatt and Griesemer (2007) have called "scaffolding" and "generative entrenchment"—the fact that the historical context constrain and makes possible the generation of new cultural items—in cultural evolution. It would provide some important bases for the development of a *cognitive cultural history*, enriching our understanding of the cognitive mechanisms that distribute cultural items.

# References

Akerlof, G.A. 1970. "The market for 'lemons': Quality uncertainty and the market mechanism." *Quarterly Journal of Economics* 84(3): 488–500.

Atran, S. 1990. *Cognitive foundations of natural history: Towards an anthropology of science.* Cambridge: Cambridge University Press.

———. 2001. "The trouble with memes." *Human Nature* 12(4): 351–381.

———. 2002. *In gods we trust: The evolutionary landscape of religion.* New York: Oxford University Press.

Barnes, B. 1977. *Interests and the growth of knowledge.* London: Routledge and Kegan Paul.

Boyer, P. 1998. "Cognitive tracks of cultural inheritance: How evolved intuitive ontology governs cultural transmission." *American Anthropologist* 100(4): 876–889.

———. 2001. *Religion explained: the evolutionary origins of religious thought.* USA: Basic Books.

Chartier, R. 1990. *Les origines culturelles de la Révolution francaise.* Paris: Seuil.

Clark, A. 1997. *Being there: Putting mind, body and brain together again.* Cambridge, MA: MIT Press.

Cosmides, L. and J. Tooby. 1992. "Cognitive adaptations for social exchange." In *The adapted mind: Evolutionary psychology and the generation of culture,* edited by J.H. Barkow, L. Cosmides and J. Tooby, 163–228. New York: Oxford University Press.

Donald, M. 1991. *Origins of the modern mind: Three stages in the evolution of culture and cognition.* Cambridge, MA: Harvard University Press.

Gilovich, T., D. Griffin and D. Kahneman eds. 2002. *Heuristics and biases: The psychology of intuitive judgment.* Cambridge: Cambridge University Press.

Gooding, D. 1990. *Experiment and the making of meaning: Human agency in scientific observation and experiment.* Dordrecht: Kluwer.

Goody, J. 1977. *The domestication of the savage mind.* Cambridge: Cambridge University Press.

Gorman, M. 1992. *Simulating science: Heuristics, mental models and technoscientific thinking.* Bloomington, IN: Indiana University Press.

Heintz, C. 2006. "Web search engines and distributed assessment systems." *Pragmatics and Cognition* 14(2): 387–409.

———. 2007a. "Institutions as mechanisms of cultural evolution: Prospects of the epidemiological approach." *Biological Theory* 2(3): 244–249.

———. 2007b. Scientific cognition and cultural evolution: Theoretical tools for integrating social and cognitive studies of science. Unpublished doctoral dissertation, Ecole des Hautes

Etudes en Sciences Sociales, Paris. Available at http://christophe.heintz.free.fr/thesis.

Hutchins, E. 1995. *Cognition in the wild*. Cambridge, MA: The MIT Press (Bradford Books).

Martens, B. 2004. *The cognitive mechanics of economic development and institutional change*. New York: Routledge.

Martin, L. 2005. "Introduction: Imagistic traditions in the Graeco-Roman world." *Historical Reflections/Réflexions Historiques*, 31(2): 297–307.

Nersessian, N.J. 1984. *Faraday to Einstein: Constructing meaning in scientific theories*. Dordrecht: Kluwer.

———. 1992. "How do scientists think? capturing the dynamics of conceptual change in science." In *Cognitive models of science*, edited by R.N. Giere, 3–45. Minneapolis: University of Minnesota Press.

———. 1995. "Opening the black box: Cognitive science and history of science." *Osiris* (2nd Series) 10: 194–211.

———. 2002. "Maxwell and 'the method of physical analogy': Model-based reasoning, generic abstraction, and conceptual change." In *Essays in the history and philosophy of science and mathematics*, edited by D. Malament, 129–166. Lasalle, IL: Open Court.

Netz, R. 1999. *The shaping of deduction in greek mathematics: A study in cognitive history*. Cambridge: Cambridge University Press.

North, D.C. 2005. *Understanding the process of economic change*. Princeton, NJ: Princeton University Press.

Ory, P. 2004. *L'histoire culturelle*. Paris: Presses Universitaires de France.

Potts, J.D. 2000. *The new evolutionary microeconomics: Complexity, competence and adaptive behaviour*. Cheltenham: Edward Elgar.

Richerson, P. J. and R. Boyd. 2005. *Not by genes alone: How culture transformed human evolution*. Chicago, IL: The University of Chicago Press.

Salmon, C.A. and T.K. Shackelford eds. 2007. *Family relationships: An evolutionary perspective*. New York: Oxford University Press.

Sperber, D. 1996. *Explaining culture: A naturalistic approach*. Oxford: Blackwell.

———. 2000. "An objection to the memetic approach to culture." In *Darwinizing culture: The status of memetics as a science*, edited by R. Aunger, 163–173. Oxford: Oxford University Press.

———. 2001. "Conceptual tools for a natural science of society and culture." *Proceedings of the British Academy* 111: 297–317.

———. 2006. "Why a deep understanding of cultural evolution is incompatible with shallow psychology." In *Roots of human sociality: Culture, cognition and interaction*, edited by N. Enfield and S. Levinson, 431–449. Oxford: Berg.

Sperber, D. and D. Wilson. 1986. *Relevance: Communication and cognition*. Cambridge, MA: Harvard University Press.

Tooby, J. and L. Cosmides. 1992. "The psychological foundations of culture." In *The adapted mind: Evolutionary psychology and the generation of culture*, edited by J.H. Barkow, L. Cosmides and J. Tooby, 19–136. New York: Oxford University Press.

Tweney, R. 1985. "Faraday's discovery of induction: A cognitive approach." In *Faraday rediscovered: Essays on the live and work of Michael Faraday*, edited by D. Gooding and F.A.J.L. James, 189–210. New York: Stockton Press.

———. 1991. "Faraday's notebooks: The active organization of creative science." *Physics Education* 26: 301–306.

Vial, T. 2005. "Can memory fill in gapes of memory? Applications of the cognitive science of religion to the history of religion." *Historical Reflections/ Réflexions Historique* 31(2), 283–295.

Whitehouse, H. 2004. *Modes of religiosity: A cognitive theory of religious transmission.* Walnut Creek, CA: AltaMira Press.

———. 2005. "Cognitive historiography: when science meets art." *Historical Reflections/ Réflexions Historiques* 31(2): 307–318.

Whitehouse, H. W.C. Wimsatt and J.R. Griesemer.

———. 2007. "Reproducing entrenchments to scaffold culture: The central role of development in cultural evolution." In *Integrating evolution and development: From theory to practice,* edited by R. Sansom and R. Brandon, 227–323. Cambridge, MA: MIT Press.

Witt, U. 2003. *The evolving economy: Essays on the evolutionary approach to economics.* Cheltenham: Edward Elgar.

## — 3 —

# Technology and Past Minds:
# The Case of Jewish Niche Construction

## Gabriel Levy

## Introduction

Though it is an extremely controversial line of argument for obvious (though nonetheless important) reasons, there is pretty good evidence to indicate that human mental function, and perhaps corresponding brain structures have changed in the past 40,000 years, even the past two thousand years (Smith 2007; see also Hawks *et al.* 2007).[1] If one approaches this history within traditional evolutionary psychology, this argument may present somewhat of a problem.[2] Scholars in this field usually want to insist that we basically have a Pleistocene mind, and what has changed is not biology, but culture. But if we really espouse a consilience approach to biology and culture, this idea must be challenged. Culture is not the outer, inauthentic manifestation of biology, but a materiality that feeds back into evolutionary processes. The human brain may be "relatively" the same as it was in the Pleistocene, but of course the big question is just how relative and what difference it makes? In this essay I present an evolutionary argument that attempts to explain Jewish "intelligence," not so much because I endorse the explanation, but because I think this is the type of problem that cognitive science presents useful tools to answer. Furthermore I think the case complicates the naïve viewpoint that sees modern day humans simply as Pleistocene hominids with the accoutrements of modern life attached to us willy-nilly. The basic point is that technological forms such as writing and cities that

---

1. Merlin Donald notes in a personal communication that he thinks "humans have continued to evolve, well into the period of modern occupation of the continents, and well into the period of increased population density... Many quite recently differentiated subgroups—Jewish people are probably one such subgroup, in a cultural sense, although not really genetically homogenous at this point—were subjected to unique environmental pressures for centuries, and it is unlikely that they were not subjected to some serious selection pressures. I would be very surprised if there were no major differences between such groups, especially when they can be identified as sharing certain genetic traits" (email message, September 14, 2007). More will be said about this below.

2. For some other related problems of traditional evolutionary psychology, see Buller 2005.

persist long enough over time can in principle have stable biological significance (Clark 2004).

On the one hand, since we do not have a Pleistocene brain around to study, we are left with very indirect evidence to make our case. On the other hand, we have an abundance of material artifacts and evidence of change over the past 100,000 years. It is quite obvious that the cognitive niches that humans have constructed over time have changed dramatically, for example, with the emergence of urban centers. Perhaps some of these significant changes are instantiated in the biological brain; for example, a great deal of research has come out in the past few years concerning the biological effect of technologies like television (Miller and Borzekowski 2007; Anderson and Pempek 2005; Escobar-Chaves *et al.* 2005; Van Evra 2004; Vandewater *et al.* 2005). It is not obvious that these technologies are persistent enough to have an *evolutionary* biological effect, but at least we now understand some very clear mechanisms to talk about the continual feedback between biology and culture.

## A Word of Warning

There is a great deal of controversy around the subject of Jewish "intelligence." A psychologist at California State University named Kevin MacDonald was probably first to reapply principles of natural selection to Judaism. As early as 1994, he used group selection theory in a simplistic fashion to try to account for Jewish intelligence, arguing that Jews have consciously used eugenics and selective breeding throughout their history to achieve it. Though this article is in sympathy with an attempt to reconcile evolutionary biology with the study of culture and history, there have been significant doubts raised about MacDonald's motivations—specifically his association with the far right—that urge me to distance myself from his body of work.

There are immense implications for the emerging field of the cognitive science of religion concerning these questions. To complicate matters, any argument made on this subject will be taken up by political operatives to justify their own particular agenda. The so-called "Jewish Question" has been at the core of much political theorizing in the modern West. Indeed, *any* materialist theory that takes up Judaism as a subject-matter will be forced to deal with the "Jewish Question."[3] With regard to Judaism then, the notion of consilience is dangerous. But I insist it will do us no good to approach this subject with our backs turned from difficult and controversial problems. I do claim that Jews on average excel at certain types of intelligence, namely verbal and reasoning ability. I explain this by way of the theory of niche-construction and downward causation. All of these terms are open to further interrogation.

If my arguments entail a political point it is that an overly deterministic narrative that seeks to integrate biology and culture is the wrong way to go. Culture is radically underdetermined by biology, and just as biology affects culture, so too culture affects biology. Biology cannot mix itself into detailed historical narratives, except perhaps as a rhetorical trope, because the folkish, intention-oriented type of causation that forms the basis of historical narrative is not the same as the causation in scientific inquiry and explanation.

3. For the first polemic, see Marx's *On The Jewish Question* (1843). We are not now outside of "The Jewish Question." The scholar cannot step outside of it and understand its origins and causes. MacDonald's morally myopic work yet again points to the dangers of applying evolutionary theory to history. Since historiography is primarily driven by narrative and rhetoric, while science is driven by falsification in the pursuit of knowledge, it is extremely tricky to base political policy on either one. However, I still insist that evolutionary biologists and cognitive scientists of religion (especially) should not turn their backs on the relation between biology and history.

## Ashkenazi "Intelligence"

In a story about Jacob in Genesis 30: 35 we find an excellent parable for the case to follow. This is a story about sexual selection. To make a long story short: Jacob goes far and wide to try to get the proper wife, and he winds up with two after a series of negotiations. Somewhere along the line Jacob's father-in-law Laban tries to trick him. Laban says he will give Jacob goats of a certain color, but Laban removes the goats from the flock before Jacob will get them. Jacob in turn devises a way to breed the goats he needs. Jacob peels poplar and other sticks to make white streaks on them, and then uses these sticks to organize the breeding of the flock (33: 41). Later in the story, Jacob will be renamed Israel and become the father of the Twelve Tribes. Jacob's miraculous fortune is owed to his use of symbolic forms (the white streaks), but also involves the skilled manipulation of economic, social, and biological domains. On the surface this is simply an example of domestication or "artificial breeding," but as scholars since Darwin have known, artificial selection is merely *natural* selection with environmental constraints imposed consciously by human masters.

Opening this line of argument in relation to the question of Jewish intelligence I reiterate is a particularly controversial place to start, but it is so crucial to the points I want to make in this essay that I cannot avoid it. By pointing to Jewish history as an example for the process I want to highlight, I am not making the claim that it is only in the Jewish case that processes like it are in place, nor that this is the only explanation. Furthermore, in making the case for a biological account, I am not claiming that historical factors, such as the emancipation of Jews in Europe during the nineteenth century play no role in the story about Jewish intelligence. Quite to the contrary I am looking for a suitable way to integrate the insights from cognitive science and evolutionary theory into the study of Judaism that does justice to both biological nature and the irreducible contingency of history.

To be clear, the concept of race has been thoroughly debunked as a biological category. So, there is no such thing as the Jewish race. However, we cannot deny the existence of discrete genetic forms or inheritances in different human populations. This fact is attested in the growing phenomenon of genetic ancestry tracing. For the most part, these tests (often imprecisely) determine where a person's ancestors came from, and often little else. Geography is a dominant factor in human history because it can isolate certain populations, allowing for adaptation to particular environmental circumstances and thus producing characteristic genetic forms. In the case of Judaism, to put it bluntly, the question is whether a cultural technique of isolation could serve the same purposes as geographic isolation. Indeed, the ghetto wall and the *shtetl* were forms of geographic isolation. It is still an open question the extent to which Jewish populations were isolated in Europe over the past 2000 years, though in the case of the Ashkenazim most researchers now come down on the side of genetic isolation (Nebel 2001 and 2005, 388).

Susan Kahn has recently noted that Ashkenazi Jews in particular have been a boon for genetic researchers because, apart from their willingness to be tested, the population also exhibits some classic mechanisms in the theory of evolution, namely 1) the founder effect, "in which a population that is descended from a small handful of ancestors historically shuns intermarriage or is forcibly ghettoized, thereby maintaining genetic lineages (including disease-causing mutations)," and 2) "the theory of genetic drift or bottleneck, which occurs when a genetic mutation becomes common because the population in which it is found dwindles due to famine, war, epidemic, or other event, as has happened frequently

among Eastern European Jews" (Kahn 2005, 180).[4] Indeed, there is an immense literature on this subject, exploring such questions as the prevalence of Tay Sachs disease in
Ashkenazi populations. Tay Sachs is a genetic disease where a fatty acid derivative called a
ganglioside accumulates in the nerve cells of the brain. Cochran *et al.* (2006) argue that the
disease is tied to Jewish "intelligence," but there are also other theories that explain it, such
as genetic drift, or adaptation to TB (Slatkin 2004).[5]

That having been said, there may be an evolutionary explanation for "Jewish Genius,"
the fact that, according to Charles Murray (of *Bell Curve* fame/infamy), an extraordinarily
disproportionate number of Noble Prize winners are Jewish and that Jews appear to score
better on I.Q. tests than other groups on average. Though these tests are extremely controversial if we take them as a measure of intelligence writ large, it is clear they do accurately
measure certain intelligence abilities.

Murray (2007, 3) notes in his study *Human Accomplishment* that there were only seven
Jewish "significant figures" from 1200–1800 c.e. (see Murray 2003). After Jewish emancipation in Europe however, when they were no longer excluded and no longer excluded
themselves from broader European society, there were 170 (by 1950). Murray notes that
"in the first half of the twentieth century, despite pervasive and continuing social discrimination against Jews throughout the Western world, despite the retraction of legal rights,
and despite the Holocaust, Jews won fourteen percent of the Nobel Prizes in literature,
chemistry, physics, and medicine/physiology" (Murray 2007, 3). In the second half that
figure more than doubled. Since Jews constitute two-tenths of one percent of world population, these numbers seem staggering. In terms of IQ, Jews are about average on tests of
visual-spatial skills, "but extremely high on subtests that measure verbal and reasoning
skills," so their overall average is about "one standard deviation higher than the north-
western European average" (Murray 2007, 3; Cochran 2005, 659).

Murray (2007) notes two popular genetic explanations for these facts: "winnowing by
persecution," and "marrying for brains". He dismisses the former as cutting both ways
because "the kind of intelligence that leads to business success or rabbinical acumen" is not
of much help when the "Cossacks are sweeping through town" (4). The latter explanation
also does not help very much, as the data is simply not there to address how much the
"attractiveness of brains" played in selecting marriage partners. Instead Murray offers the

---

4. For more on the genetic picture, see the interesting literature on the so-called Levite Haplotype in
Ashkenazi populations. The data points to a common (or relatively few) male ancestor for Ashkenazi
Levites within the last 2000 years (Nebel *et al.* 2004). The mitochondrial evidence in Jewish women is
more variable, thus "the striking dissimilarities in the genetic signatures of these women suggest that
diasporic Jewish communities were established when Jewish male traders from the ancient Near East
intermarried with local non-Jewish women along their trade routes" (Kahn 182, citing Thomas *et al.*
2002; for the debate on the Cohen Modal Haplotype, see Zoossmann-Diskin 2001).

5. The point of this paper is not to make moral or ethical claims, but simply to propose that *some* Jews
have ancestors who adapted to a particular cognitive niche, which in turn enhanced a certain type of
intelligence. Obviously intelligence is far too complex a concept so that it could be fully captured by a
test. Rather than making a Hobbesian point here I mean to be emphasize that human intelligence itself
is plastic. If we understand the brain more like an elephants' trunk, only far more plastic and adaptive,
it is not hard to conceptualize the type of change I am envisioning. In the same way that skin color or
eye color vary, so do intelligences. Indeed, the well-known rebuttal to a biological argument for IQ has
been evidence of the "Flynn Effect" which shows that IQ scores rise with every generation since the
testing began. Thus some have argued that IQ tests do not test how intelligent one is, but how modern
(Gladwell 2007).

32

research of Cochran and his colleagues (2006), who propose that

> the high intelligence test scores observed in the Ashkenazi Jewish population are a consequence of their occupation of a social niche over the last millennium that selected strongly for IQ . . . that there was an increase in the frequency of genes that elevated IQ as a by-product of this selective regime, which led to an increased incidence of hereditary disorders. (659).

The "social niche" Cochran *et al.* and Murray, point to, is the "managerial" (sales, trade, finance) occupations of urban life that Jews were confined to (or confined themselves) for approximately 900 years (Cochran *et al.*, 670). These scholars argue that the Malthusian collusion between economic, intellectual, and biological success meant that wealthier families tended to have more offspring. In turn more children tended to survive into adulthood in the "successful" entrepreneurial families. In the case of Judaism, since its inception there has been a tendency to equate biological and intellectual fecundity—an especially stark distinction from Christianity whose scholars remained celibate until Luther let the dogs out.

I recognize just how controversial the equation of economic and biological success is, and I will not go too much into the argument here,[6] for my purpose is simply to cite an example of a relatively isolated cultural group adapting to a socio-economic niche, for which there was presumably corresponding *cognitive* changes in the brain. In terms of the physiology, these changes may statistically apply to brain volume, volumes of specific regions, density, reaction times, and brain glucose utilization rate (662). This would be a paradigmatic example of evolutionary processes active in human history and in the development of past minds. In this case culture is not simply the explanandum to be explained away, but must be understood as part of evolution itself. Indeed, the integration and interaction of cultural technologies (such as those of different occupations) and cognitive biology goes back the very origin of *Homo sapiens*. These findings clearly point to the more plastic dimensions of the human mind/brain—its ability to adapt to different cognitive and ecological niches relatively quickly. In this case, I am less concerned with the controversial points about Jewish intelligence than I am in giving an exemplar of downward causation (Bøgh Andersen 2000).

Written language and Biblical culture, I would argue, have been the primary mechanism for the creation of the cognitive niche in which Jews have been so "successful"—namely late twentieth century liberal societies. These societies are the ultimate form of what Merlin Donald calls "theoretical culture."[7] In another world we might expect that those specific forms of intelligence noted in the articles above would not be very beneficial. It just so happens that present day Western society finds things like Nobel Prizes extremely valuable.

In all of these arguments about Jewish intelligence literacy is a crucially important factor, for Cochran *et al.* note that "the key cultural precondition among the Jews was a pattern of social organization that required literacy, strongly discouraged intermarriage, and that could propagate itself over long periods of time with little change. Literacy (which does not itself require high intelligence) was probably important in the shift from a nation to an urban occupational caste ... " (667; see also Botticini and Eckstein 2005). Murray even goes so far as to argue that the difficulty of interpreting the Biblical text would increase the number of "low intelligence" deserters (2007, 8). But what is it about literacy that makes it a characteristically Jewish form of intelligence, and how does it relate to verbal and math-

---

6. For more on this Malthusian logic, see Clark and Hamilton 2006.

7. Though I cannot develop it here, I think the last chapter of *A Mind So Rare* (Donald 2001) has profound implications for the argument I make.

ematical reasoning? What is the connection between these managerial trades and cognitive changes in intelligence? What is the process under which a cultural niche can have such effects? In what follows I will present the rudiments of an answer by going back to cognitive origins of written language.

## The Evolution of Writing Systems in Children and History

Writing systems and the corresponding inventions of science and higher mathematics are forms of intelligence that the world had never seen before their emergence some 10,000 years ago. That is, these technologies mark a particularly distinct form of cognition one step removed from the cognitive processes that predominated in human cultures before them. The fact that so much of modern post-industrial life revolves around these forms of technology should give us pause, and we should be working hard to think of ways to understand post-industrial brains with the new tools of cognitive science. That having been said, the origins of written culture in the Western world goes back to the ancient near East, to southwestern Iran, where we find an intrinsic connection between writing and accounting.

We find evidence for a ratcheting effect[8] in the early story of writing from about 8000 to 3000 BCE as told by Denise Schmandt-Basseret (1992).[9] In the proto-stage, human beings sculpted figurines representing various gods and animals for ritual purpose. In the next stage tokens of basic geometric shapes representing simple food staples were made out of baked clay. Next, more complex tokens emerged that represented complex staples. These tokens would be sealed in clay envelopes for accounting purposes in the context of the rise of agricultural surpluses and cities. Since there is no way to tell what was in the envelope, in the next stage someone came up with the idea to embed tokens on the outside of the clay to tell what was inside, and thus a system of marks was developed for the same purpose. This facilitated a transition from three-dimensional objects to two-dimensional scratches.

Up to this point there was a one to one correspondence between an object and token, so for example, three jars of grain were represented by three tokens in or on the envelope. A sign represented the token inside the envelope, which in turn represented a commodity/staple. In the next stage clay tablets replaced clay envelopes and a sign mark on the tablet was used to represent a token, marked either with a stylus or the corresponding token. The first recordings of numerals occur with these tablets. In other words, there is no longer a one to one correspondence. Here the sign represents a concept, not the particular object in question, and we move to greater degrees of abstraction. In the next stage, which Schmandt-Besserat does not discuss, signs go from representing objects or concepts (pictures) to representing the sound of first syllable of the word for the concept (acrophonic principle) and eventually signs represent sounds.

In line with the current revival of Evo-Devo, a field of biology that examines ontogenetic development to find insight into evolution, I find it extremely interesting that this "evolutionary" trajectory is similar to the developmental progression of literacy in young

---

8. For the term "ratcheting" as applied here, see Tomasello 1999, 37–40 and Levinson *et al.* 2005, 10.

9. It is interesting to note that this is the time period for the emergence of *ASPM* (abnormal spindle-like microcophaly), a gene thought to regulate human brain growth. Martin (forthcoming, 16–17) points out that the evolutionary argument that ties brain size with cultural abilities is extremely speculative. In other words it has not been shown that the emergence of *ASPM* corresponds to any real phenotypic changes. However, this is an open question; these genes may indeed express themselves as variation in certain types of cognitive abilities (see Nitzan and Lahn 2007).

children. Homer and Olson studied pre-literate children's developing conception of writing (Homer and Olson 1999). There are striking parallels between this form of the development and the one noted in the case of writing. The basic gist of their finding was that as children age most move from a "token" based representational schema to a "type" based one. When preliterate children were asked to write "one dog, two dogs, no dog, red dog, blue dog" many used the individual word dog as a token one-to-one representation. Thus "two dogs" was written as "DOG DOG" and "no dog" many claimed could not be written. This points to the fact that many preliterate children believe there is some intrinsic non-arbitrary relation between the written word and the concept/thing to which it refers. As children progressed they learned that the sign "dog" could be annotated and modified with other signs, namely numerical ones.

The fact that both cognitive systems develop from an iconic stage to an indexical one has precedents in many other fields. More complex informational systems must, by definition, be built up out of simpler systems, for it would be impossible for the symbolic relation to emerge without a more basic layer of one to one relations. The iconic perspective would seem to be the default cognitive position that must be modified with training. Furthermore, we know that the relation between token and type is a key property of any informational or programming system, from MS-DOS to DNA (see Deacon 2004 and Clark 2006). In contrast to much of what has been written about the predominant effect of writing on the mind, perhaps the most revolutionary innovation for human development was the robust recognition of the type-token distinction, which simply put is an "ontological one between a general sort of thing and its particular concrete instances." For example, the sentence "a rose is a rose is a rose is a rose" has three word types and ten word tokens (Wetzel 2006). Training in literacy is training in higher-order characterization and organization, especially with regard to words and numerosity; for this reason the earliest forms of writing rarely distinguished between letters and numbers.

## Jewish Niche Construction: The Emergence of Writing and Cities

So types are higher order labels that apply to a configuration of tokens. Similarly, in discussing the emergence of what he calls the "Age four transition," the theoretical philosopher Mark Bickhard points out that

> knowing is an interactive, functional, relational property between systems and their environments, and ... such interactive systems ... themselves instantiate properties that could not be known (interacted with) by the systems themselves, but could be interactively known by systems at the next higher level.... The hierarchy of potential knowing levels is generated by iteration of the basic relationship of representational "aboutness"—each level's interactive representations are about properties of the lower level. (Bickhard, 2)

Bickhard points out that the hierarchy of interacting systems can be climbed only in a particular sequence because, to paraphrase, lower order arrangements provide the content for higher order systems. Though this example is meant to make sense of the important step in human development around the age of four when full-blown intersubjectivity becomes apparent in most human beings, we can equally well apply it to the "emergence" of writing. It is not unrelated to this transition at all: recent research in the psychology of literacy has shown that literacy tends to enhance or change precisely theory-of-mind/cognitive-embedding abilities that make their robust appearance in children around the age of four (Olson 2001).

35

David Olson, the foremost researcher in the psychology of literacy, is the first to point out that claims about the enormous effects of literacy during the 70s and 80s were somewhat exaggerated. Since then, literacy has been shown to "play less a causal role than an ancillary or instrumental one in psychological and social change." Thus "literacy played more of a role in the elaboration and adjustment of pre-existing structures and practices than in the actual creation of novel ones" (Olson 2001, 240). However, Olson does leave room for one extremely important locus of change that literate composition brings to this equation, and this concerns precisely the theory-of-mind mechanisms that are so central to culture and religion.[10] Literacy is in principle meta-linguistic because complex forms of written correspondence are forms of quoting oneself—one must disembed her own utterances from their normative environment of present speech in order to communicate in writing (Olson 2001, 243–244). So to put it more concretely, the idea is that literacy not only helps organize lower order representations like words and numbers, but robust literacy also helps to organize "higher-order" cognitive activities and propositions (see Levy 2010, 175ff.).

Writing did not begin this way. As Jared Diamond has pointed out: "anyone hoping to discover how Sumerians of 3000 BC thought and felt is in for a disappointment" (1999, 234). The first forms, as noted, were extremely cumbersome; they were what Diamond calls "telegraphic" in an analogy to another somewhat cumbersome communicative technology that has since been modified. Diamond reiterates Lévi-Strauss's point that the main function of ancient writing was "to facilitate the enslavement of other human beings" (235). The shift to expressive forms of resistance and poetry would come much later.

The points made above concerning perceptions about writing in young children must also be understood in light of a developmental progression. It is not that children who use the token method for accounting for writing are wrong, it is rather that at a certain stage when robust literacy emerges children are able to take higher order inputs, such as Theory of Mind concepts, into processes of communication and thought. The emergence of writing as a historical phenomenon must have gone though a similar developmental process.

But the development of various "knowing levels," in Bickhard's terminology, are not one-dimensional, linear events. Knowing levels are processes where higher levels are made up of a variety of lower order processes, which themselves do not reduce to one another. This is so because the organization itself of each micro-system is a key property for higher order processing (Bickhard and Campbell 2000, 342–343). Bickhard's model gives an extremely compelling framework for making sense of the Age 4 transition in neurological and cognitive terms. There appears to be a consensus from a variety of angles, including Baron-Cohen, that mentalizing takes as its input simulations of interactions between social agents—thus the organization of lower level interactions, similarly, will be a central focus when moving between "knowing levels" (see Baron-Cohen 1995, 38–40).

---

10. Dunbar (2006, 176–177) also makes the connection between "cultural evolution" and Theory of Mind. The evidence indicates that the neo-cortex grew in correlation (perhaps causally) to the size of human groups. The inference to take here is that the neocortical, non-modular, brain grew to keep track of *social relations*. A social relation is not a physical object; it is invisible. From keeping track of invisible social relations, it is a quantum step to keeping track of relations in general. Cognitive disembedding is simply a higher order form of this ability. It takes the outputs of lower order relation tracking as the inputs to higher orders of relation tracking. Thus the marked outcome of this cognitive process in most adult humans is the ability to retain comprehension while imbedding up to 5 or 6 propositions within a sentence. "I believe that you think that I want you to suppose that I believe that the world is flat" (173). Dunbar finds this embedding essential to teaching and learning, and thus to cultural transmission in general.

In the limited uses of early forms of writing, Diamond finds a clue for the reason why writing appears so late in the human narrative: it was for management and control of complex institutions. He notes that all forms of writing seem to have evolved in the context of "socially stratified societies with complex and centralized political institutions" (Diamond 1997, 236). Similarly Whitehouse, Goody, and Boyer also connect writing to complex polities, though they disagree concerning causes and consequences. While Whitehouse tends to favor the idea of writing emerging in the context of other technological and demographic changes, Goody and Boyer seem to indicate writing was the cause of the changes (see Boyer 2001, 313–315 and Goody 2004). I think a more fruitful line of approach to this subject is to see in literate societies the emergence of a novel ecological niche.

For our purposes it is sufficient simply to point out that higher-order phenomena, such as literacy (which is only of high-order from a certain perspective) is composed of a causal lattice among various interacting levels (Lemke 2000). A crucial element in this causal lattice is the social environment in which literacy develops. Indeed, in his 1997 book Diamond goes further to say that the change in food production technology was a necessary condition for the emergence of writing. This is not a trivial condition, for we saw that Schment-Besserat has shown the empirical connection between surplus storage, accounting techniques, and the emergence of writing. The store of surplus, in turn, allowed for the emergence of cities: "early writing served the needs of [complex and centralized] political institutions (such as record keeping and royal propaganda), and the users were full time bureaucrats nourished by stored food surpluses grown by food-producing peasants" (Diamond 1997, 236). Thus we find the movement and development of a "naturally" occurring ecological-social niche. Literate guilds slowly molded the social environment to be conducive to their own particular skills. Goody pointed to these connections long ago, between domesticating the savage mind and writing (Goody 1977).

But can we be more precise about the mechanisms by which biological and cultural ecology interact? Indeed we can. Levinson notes a number of relevant mechanisms of "twin track evolution with feedback" from culture (Levinson 2005, 4). The first is natural selection in an environment that "can be partly constructed by the organism itself." For example, the invention of fire "lies behind the progressive reduction of dentition" in hominids, due to the fact that fire softens food. The second is the Baldwin effect where "behavioral changes can feed back into the genome by exposing the organism to new environmental pressures." The example he gives is clothing, which encouraged humans to move into colder climates, which in turn lead to physiological adaptations. These first two probably fit under the rubric of niche construction illustrated by Odling-Smee *et al.* (2003). The third is group selection, which occurs when a group acts to affect its own fitness and the fitness of other groups; this process is a likely scenario for the extinction of the Neanderthals in northern Europe (Levinson 2005, 6). Related to group selection, the fourth is "kin selection in culture-bearing kindreds," where the well-known mechanism of altruistic behavior toward others of sufficient biological relatedness is regulated and modified by the perception of common culture. The fifth is sexual selection, or the "choice by females of their mates." Indeed much of culture and language has recently been theorized from this perspective (see Martin 2011, forthcoming and Deacon 1997, 379–381, 384–389). For example, Levinson notes that if a culture erects boundary conditions for reproduction, like the payment of a bride price, "it translates the biological foundation for those skills into reproductive success, thus ultimately fixing those skills in the genome." The last form of feedback Levinson terms "auto-domestication," by which Levinson means selective breeding in human populations, though there are "distinct limits to the extent to which humans have applied breeding techniques to their own kind" (2005, 7).[11]

Thus literate religions like Judaism do not evolve in a technical sense, but they do make lasting changes to human ecology, which in turn have their own selection pressures. Indeed there is a case to be made in terms of sexual selection that much of the human decoupling ability noted above, which would be so important to religion, evolved so that men could convince women (and their fathers) to give themselves over into a sexual relationship (marriage). In women, a pronounced cheater-detector *and* false-belief detector would be crucially important for sifting the respectable men out from sexual cheaters and smooth-talkers, respectively. These cognitive systems develop faster in girls and are more closely associated with estrogen; indeed "in the brain centers for language…women have 11% more neurons than men" (in contrast, men have "two and a half times the brain space devoted to sexual drive," see Brizendine 2007: 5).

However, knowing the mental states of potential suitors is crucial for all parties involved, not just the women. Wildgen makes a similar point concerning the origin of language. Citing Dunbar and Deacon, he adds that it is not just women who need to detect sexual cheaters, for while "females needed more and richer information on the males to select in order to be able to predict their future behavior in the caring for females and children," males had to be able to trust women sexually "when they were on long hunting excursions" because they "do not want to invest in the children of other males" (Wildgen 2004, 19). With these points we are reminded again of the story of Laban and Jacob, where language is again tied back to food and sex. To put it simply, with literacy—especially literacy of both sexes—a new biological phenomenon emerges: the love letter (*Shir ha-Shirim*) and its more modern incarnation in email and online matchmaking.

Apart from sexual selection, the classic example of cultural feedback and niche construction concerns diet: the phenomenon of lactose tolerance in human dairy farming populations (Levinson and Jaisson 2005, 7). In human groups where dairying has been practiced consistently, the enzyme lactase does not shut down after weaning, thus allowing people to continue drinking milk. Thus Durham has shown that "distinct food-preparation techniques have resulted in microevolutionary adaptations in human groups" (Durham 1991). Levinson finds that a thousand years, or about 40 generations, is sufficient for the kind of feedback discussed above to take place. Other interesting examples of "cultural adaptation on the genotype" are the cases of type II diabetes and hypertension, which are found predominantly in agricultural populations; Diamond explains this fact as due to the "unconscious domestication of humans by agriculture" (Diamond 2001, 707; Levinson, 8).

With these mechanisms in mind, let us return to the case of Judaism for a moment. The question as to whether Judaism is a sufficiently unitary category to warrant examination will be left for the reader to decide. From my perspective Judaism would seem to fit quite well into Levinson's notion of "culture-bearing kindreds." In other words, we are dealing here with a cultural unit with borders policed by individuals and groups, from both the inside and outside. The individual may identify as a Jew, but the institutions of the group may reject that identity. Outside institutions, like states (the Third Reich or the State of Israel), may also police Judaism's borders, defining who and who is not a member. The idea that Judaism could be a distinct biological category is an illusion that emerges out of this

---

11.  For a fuller picture of these mechanisms they should perhaps be juxtaposed with Tomasello's points about the way in which uniquely human forms of culture modifies previous (animal) forms of social cognition; see Tomasello (1999, 210).

dynamic model of border crossing and policing. These practices are not unique to Judaism, though it is perhaps the paradigmatic case, for Judaism must be understood as a cultural constellation that arose in relation and reaction to Christianity. Early Christianity largely colonized the pathways and networks already set in place by early "Judaism."

All of Levinson's mechanisms of cultural feedback into evolutionary processes thus appear to be present quite acutely in the case of Judaism. The niche that Judaism helps to set up is the urban environment and its accompanying technologies. This new environment of course leads to different environmental pressures on its inhabitants.[12] Perhaps one Talmudic passage will suffice as evidence: "A man should sell all he possesses in order to marry the daughter of a scholar, as well as to marry his daughter to a scholar" (Talmud Bavli, Tractate *Pesahim* 49a). A more operative question here must be to what extent the cultural imperative to educate sons—notably to teach them to read a second language, which was in most cases a foreign alphabet, starting at a very young age (before puberty)—has a persistent biological effect.

Botticini and Eckstein have recently proposed an intriguing model which argues that Judaism as an identity selected itself (i.e. Jews selected themselves) to urban skilled occupations that most often required literacy or the manipulation of symbol systems (mathematical, monetary, or legal). They argue that the implementation after the second century of the common era of the

> religious norm requiring Jewish fathers to educate their sons determined three major patterns in Jewish history: (i) a slow process of conversions from Judaism among illiterate Jewish farmers who lived in subsistence economies; (ii) a comparative advantage in urban skilled occupations in which the literate Jews selected themselves when urbanization and the development of a commercial economy provided them with the returns to their investment in education; and (iii) the voluntary diaspora of the Jews in search of worldwide opportunities in crafts, trade, and moneylending. (Botticini and Eckstein 2007, 886)

Similarly, Murray also ties selection to urbanization in his attempt to explain the facts that American Jews perform significantly better at verbal and reasoning skill portions of IQ tests and that Jews have won about 32% of the Nobel Prizes awarded in the twenty-first century. He summarizes Cochran *et. al* (2005, 659–693) to say that economic success in these occupations

> is far more highly selected for intelligence than success in the chief occupation of non-Jews: namely, farming. Economic success is in turn related to reproductive success, because higher income means lower infant mortality, better nutrition, and, more generally, reproductive "fitness." Over time, increased fitness among the successful leads to a strong selection for the cognitive and psychological traits that produce that fitness, intensified when there is low inward gene flow from other populations. (Murray 2007, 5)[13]

In this sense, Judaism throughout history was probably the first highly distributed net-

---

12. It is important to be clear on the point that religion in general is not an evolutionary adaptation, and is neutral or detrimental often with respect to fitness. Harris (2006) gives the example of Catholic priests discouraging the use of condoms in Africa, despite the HIV and AIDS epidemic. For more on the strange logic of adaptation see Maolem 2007. For the most recent critique of the use of functionalism in the study of religion, see Penner (2003, 390–392).

13. An important qualification is that where Murray says "intelligence," he means "verbal and reasoning skills" and significantly *not* "visuo-spatial skills" (nor other kinds of intelligences such as emotional and social intelligence).

work of people bonded in core beliefs of biological descent and common language. The technology of writing allowed for the network to expand intact. Interestingly, Greif (1994) has presented a game-theoretical model that tries to explain the success of Jewish (Maghribi) traders in the Middle ages. The Maghribi traders had a "collectivist" mentality as opposed to the "individualist" one of their Christian neighbors. As such they "invested in the sharing of information and the Genoese [Christians] did not. Each Maghribi corresponded with many other Maghribi traders by sending informative letters to them with the latest available commercial information and 'gossip,' including whatever transpired in agency relations among other Maghribis." In contrast, the Genoese Christian merchants "seem to have held an opposite attitude regarding information sharing" (Greif 1994, 923–924).

Botticini and Eckstein (2007) contend that "the network externality among Jewish traders highlighted by Greif could not exist without a common written language (Hebrew), high literacy levels, and a common law (Talmud)" (890). It is sufficient to note in conclusion that this particular case suggests an important amendment to the recent trend, exemplified in the excellent work of Bulbulia (2004/2005), that would take into consideration the role of technology in general and religious technology in particular as offering a new class of constraints or resources in the game-theoretical machinery and evolutionary modeling.

Judaism provides and important test case to understand the relation between cognition and past minds. I think bottom-up psychological processes tend to be overemphasized in cognitive accounts of culture and religion. Thus, the main purpose of this essay has been to give the rudiments of a plausible account of downward forms of causation that also does justice to biology and cognition. It is for this reason that I have focused on mechanisms of niche construction and gene-culture co-evolution. These concepts are powerful tools for explaining institutions like writing and religion, some of the primary cases of downward causation. I think these concepts also encourage us to leave behind a static picture of human cognition in which modern day humans are simply Pleistocene creatures wearing Versace.

# References

Anderson, Daniel R. and Tiffany Pempek. 2005. "Television and Very Young Children." *American Behavioral Scientist* 48: 505–522.

Baron-Cohen, Simon (1995). *Mindblindness: An Essay on Autism and Theory of Mind.* Cambridge MA: The MIT Press.

Bickhard, Mark H. "Commentary on the Age 4 Transition." Unpublished Manuscript. http://www.lehigh.edu/~mhb0/Age4Commentary.pdf

Bickhard, Mark H. and Donald Campbell. 2000. "Emergence." In *Downward Causation: Minds, Bodies and Matter*, edited by Bøgh Andersen, Peter, Claus Emmeche, Niels Ole Finnemann and Peder Voetmann Christiansen, 322–348. Aarhus: Aarhus University Press.

Borzekowski, Dina L. and Thomas N. Robinson. 2005. "The Remote, the Mouse, and the No. 2 Pencil: The Household Media Environment and Academic Achievement Among Third Grade Students." *Archives of Pediatrics and Adolescent Medicine* 159: 607–613.

Botticini, Maristella and Zvi Eckstein. 2007. "From Farmers to Merchants, Conversions, and Diaspora: Human Capital and Jewish History." *Journal of the European Economic Association* 5(5): 885–926.

———. 2005. "Jewish Occupational Selection: Education, Restrictions, or Minorities?" *The Jour-*

*nal of Economic History* 65: 922–948.

Brizendine, Louann. 2007. *The Female Brain*. New York: Broadway.

Bulbulia, Joseph. 2005. "Are There Any Religions? An Evolutionary Explanation." *Method and Theory in the Study of Religion* 17: 71–100.

———. 2004. "Religious Costs as Adaptations that Signal Altruistic Intention." *Evolution and Cognition* 10(1): 19–38.

Buller, David. 2005. "Get Over: Massive Modularity". *Biology and Philosophy* 20: 881–891.

Bøgh Andersen, Peter, Claus Emmeche, Niels Ole Finnemann and Peder Voetmann Christiansen, eds. 2000. *Downward Causation Minds, Bodies and Matter*. Aarhus: Aarhus University Press.

Clark, Andy. 2006. "Material Symbols." *Philosophical Psychology* 19(3): 291–307.

———. 2004. "Towards a Science of the Bio-technological Mind." In *Cognition and Technology: Co-existence, Convergence and Co-evolution*, edited by Barbara Gorayska and Jacob L. Mey, 25-36. Amsterdam: John Benjamins.

Clark, Gregory and Gillian Hamilton. 2006. "Survival of the Richest: The Malthusian Mechanism in Pre-Industrial England." *The Journal of Economic History* 66(3): 707–736.

Cochran, Gregory *et al.* 2005. "Natural History of Ashkenazi Intelligence." *Journal of Biosocial Science* 38: 659–693.

Davidson, Donald. 2001. *Subjective, Intersubjective, Objective*. Oxford: Clarendon Press.

Deacon, Terrence. 2004. "Memes as signs in the dynamic logic of semiosis: Beyond molecular science and computation theory." In *Conceptual Structures at Work: 12th International Conference on Conceptual Structures,* edited by Karl Wolff, Heather Pfeiffer and Harry Delugach, 17–30. Lecture Notes in Computer Science, vol. 3127. New York: Springer.

———. 1997. *The Symbolic Species: The Co-evolution of Language and the Brain*. New York: Norton.

Diamond, Jared. 2002. "Evolution, Consequences and Future of Plant and Animal Domestication. *Nature* 418: 700–707.

———. 1997. *Guns, Germs, and Steel*. London: Vintage.

Donald, Merlin. 2006. "Art and Cognitive Evolution." In *Artful Mind: Cognitive Science and the Riddle of Human Creativity*, edited by Mark Turner, 3–20. Oxford: Oxford University Press.

———. 2001. *A Mind So Rare: The Evolution of Human Consciousness*. New York: W.W. Norton and Co. Press.

Dunbar, Robin. 2006. "Brains, Cognition, and the Evolution of Culture. In *Evolution and Culture*, edited by S. Levinson and P. Jaisson, 169–179. Cambridge, MA: The MIT Press.

Durham, William H. 1991. *Coevolution: Genes, Culture and Human Diversity*. Stanford, CA: Stanford University Press.

Escobar-Chaves, S.L., S.R. Tortolero, C.M. Markham, B.J. Low, P. Eitel and P. Thickstun. 2005. "Impact of the Media on Adolescent Sexual Attitudes and Behaviors." *Pediatrics* 116: 303–326.

Gladwell, Malcolm. 2007. "None of the Above: What I.Q. Doesn't Tell You about Race." *The New Yorker*, December 17.

Goody, Jack. 2004. "Is Image to Doctrine as Speech to Writing? Modes of Communication and the Origins of Religion." In *Ritual and Memory: Toward a Comparative Anthropology of Religion*, edited by Harvey Whitehouse and James Laidlaw, 49–64. Walnut Creek, CA: AltaMira.

———. 1977. *The Domestication of the Savage Mind*. Cambridge: Cambridge University Press.

Greif, Avner. 1994. "Cultural Beliefs and the Organization of Society: A Historical and Theoretical Reflection on Collectivist and Individualist Societies." *The Journal of Political Economy* 102(5): 912–950.

Harris, Sam. 2006. *Letter to a Christian Nation*. New York: Knopf.

Hawks, John *et al.* 2007. "Recent Acceleration of Human Adaptive Evolution." *Proceedings of the National Academy of Sciences* 104(52): 20753–20758.

Homer, Bruce D. and David R. Olson. 1999. "Literacy and Children's Conception of Words." *Written Language and Literacy* 2(1): 113–140.

Kahn, Susan M. 2005. "The Multiple Meanings of Jewish Genes." *Culture, Medicine, and Psychiatry* 29(2): 179–192.

Kotik-Friedgut, Bella. 2006. "Development of the Lurian Approach: A Cultural Neurolinguistic Perspective." *Neuropsychology Review* 16(1): 43–52.

Lemke, Jay L. 2000. "Material Sign Processes and Emergent Ecosocial Organization." In *Downward Causation: Minds, Bodies and Matter*, edited by Bøgh Andersen, Peter, Claus Emmeche, Niels Ole Finnemann and Peder Voetmann Christiansen, 181–213. Aarhus: Aarhus University Press.

Levinson, Stephen C. and Pierre Jaisson. 2005. *Evolution and Culture: A Fyssen Foundation Symposium*. Cambridge, MA: MIT Press.

Levy, Gabriel. 2010. "Rabbinic Philosophy of Language: Not in Heaven." *Journal of Jewish Thought and Philosophy* 18(2): 167–202.

Majid, Asifa *et al.* 2004. "Can Language Restructure Cognition? The Case for Space." *Trends in Cognitive Science* 8(3): 108–114.

Martin, Luther H. Forthcoming 2011. "Origins of Religion, Cognition and Culture: The Bowerbird Syndrome." In *Origins of Religion, Cognition and Culture*, edited by Armin Geertz. London: Equinox.

Miller, Carlin J. and Dina L. Borzekowski. 2007. "Brief Report: Television Viewing and Risk for Attention Problems in Preschool Children." *Journal of Pediatric Psychology* 32: 448–452.

Moalem, Sharon (with Jonathan Prince). 2007. *Survival of the Sickest*. New York: Harper Collins.

Murray, Charles. 2007. "Jewish Genius." *Commentary Magazine*, April.

———. 2003. *Human Accomplishment: The Pursuit of Excellence in the Arts and Sciences, 800 B.C. to 1950*. New York: Harper Collins.

Nebel, Almut *et al.* 2005. "Y Chromosome Evidence for a Founder Effect in Ashkenazi Jews." *European Journal of Human Genetics* 13: 388–391.

———. 2001. "The Y Chromosome Pool of Jews as Part of the Genetic Landscape of the Middle East." *American Journal of Human Genetics* 69(5): 1095–1112.

Nitzan Mekel-Bobrov and Bruce T. Lahn. 2007. "Response to Comments by Timpson *et al.* and Yu *et al.*" *Science* 317(24): 1036b.

Odling-Smee, John F., K. Laland and M. Feldman. 2003. *Niche Construction: The Neglected Process in Evolution*. Princeton, NJ: Princeton University Press.

Olson, David. 2001. "What Writing Is." *Pragmatics and Cognition* 9(2): 239–258.

Penner, Hans. 2003. "On Self-Regulating Systems, Cannibals, and Cogs That Turn No Wheels: A Response to Joel Sweek." *Method and Theory in the Study of Religion* 15(4): 390–408.

Schmandt-Besserat, Denise. 1992. *Before Writing: From Counting to Cuneiform*, vols. 1–2. Austin: University of Texas Press.

Slatkin, Montgomery. 2004. "A Population-Genetic Test of Founder Effects and Implications for Ashkenazi Jewish Diseases." *American Journal of Human Genetics* 75(2): 282–293.

Smith, Allison. 2007. "Century-scale Holocene Processes as a Source of Natural Selection Pressure in Human Evolution: Holocene Climate and the Human Genome Project." *The Holocene* 17(5): 689–695.

Thomas, Mark *et al.* 2002. "Founding Mothers of Jewish Communities: Geographically Separated Jewish Groups Were Independently Founded by Very Few Female Ancestors." *American*

*Journal of Human Genetics* 70: 1411–1420.

Tomasello, Michael. 1999. *The Cultural Origins of Human Cognition*. Cambridge, MA: Harvard University Press.

Van Evra, Judith. 2004. *Television and Child Development*. Mahwah, NJ: Lawrence Erlbaum.

Vandewater, Elizabeth A., David S. Bickham, June H. Lee, Hope M. Cummings, Ellen A. Wartella, and Victoria J. Rideout. 2005. "When the Television Is Always On: Heavy Television Exposure and Young Children's Development." *American Behavioral Scientist* 48: 562–577.

Wade, Nicholas. 2005. "Researchers Say Intelligence and Diseases May Be Linked in Ashkenazic." *The New York Times*, June 3.

Wetzel, Linda. 2006. "Types and Tokens". *The Stanford Encyclopedia of Philosophy*, Edward N. Zalta, ed., http: //plato.stanford.edu/archives/sum2006/entries/types-

Whitehouse, Harvey and James Laidlaw, eds. 2004. *Ritual and Memory*. Walnut Creek, CA: AltaMira.

Whitehouse, Harvey and Luther Martin, eds. 2004. *Theorizing Religions Past*. Walnut Creek, CA: AltaMira Press.

Wildgen, Wolfgang. 2004. *The Evolution of Human Language: Scenarios, Principles, and Cultural Dynamics*. Amsterdam: John Benjamins Publishing Company.

Zoossmann-Diskin, Avshalom. 2001. "Are Today's Jewish Priests Descended from the Old Ones?" *Journal of Comparative Human Biology* 51(2–3): 156–162.

# — 4 —

## Illuminator of the Wide Earth; Unbribable Judge; Strong Weapon of the Gods: Intuitive Ontology and Divine Epithets in Assyro-Babylonian Religious Texts

Peter Westh

### Introduction

The basic contention of Pascal Boyer's "Cognitive Optimum Theory" (as indeed of most current, cognitive theories of religion) is that at some fundamental level—the level of what might be called "everyday, empirical knowledge" (Sperber 1985, 83)—humans everywhere and at all times understand the world in much the same way. Despite the cultural variability of conceptual systems and worldviews, the basic categories of what kinds of things there are in the world, their structure and the causal principles governing their behaviour in fact vary very little. In this sense, the human mind is endowed with what Boyer, following Keil (1979), calls an "intuitive ontology."

In principle, a workable theory anchored in insights into such a fundamental, panhuman level of cognitive representation carries great promise for the historical study of cultural material. By stipulating limits to cultural relativity, it may serve to constrain and inform our hermeneutical endeavours. The methodological and theoretical problems facing a cognitive study of ancient cultural material are numerous, however, and many of them boil down to the fact that Boyer's theory, and the Cognitive Science of Religion more generally, does not offer a principled way of working with textual, or even linguistic material. While it attaches great importance to the representation of superhuman agents and their actions, very little attention is paid to actual, linguistically encoded concepts of the divine as people speak them and write them down. This is something of a paradox, which needs to be overcome if a cognitive history of religions is to be a fruitful enterprise.

The following essay is a proposal for how that might be done. It uses the Assyro-Babylonian "sun god" Šamaš as a test case, and presents a way of subjecting a body of religious texts from antiquity to a quantitative analysis based on Cognitive Optimum Theory.[1]

---

1.  The present analysis is partly inspired by Laura Feldt (2007). I would like to thank her and Gabriel Levy for useful criticism in the process of preparing this manuscript.

## Intuitive ontologies and cognitive optimum theory

Boyer's theory has been explained and summarized numerous times elsewhere, so there is little need to recount other than the bare essentials here (Barrett 2000; Boyer 1994, 1996, 2000a, 2000, 2001, Chapter 2, 2002; Boyer and Ramble 2001; Lisdorf 2004). Boyer posits three broadly characterized cognitive systems or "domains of inference" that constrain and produce human, ontological assumptions: naïve physics, naïve biology and naïve psychology or "Theory of Mind". From these three he deduces five ontological domains: NATURAL OBJECT, ARTEFACT, PLANT, ANIMAL and PERSON (Boyer 2000b). NATURAL OBJECTS and ARTEFACTS both fall within the domain of naïve physics; PLANTS and ANIMALS both fall within the domain of naïve biology; and what distinguishes PERSONS from things in the other domains is that their behaviour can be understood in psychological terms. The relation between the three inference domains is hierarchical and transitive, so that naïve physics generates expectations regarding PLANTS, ANIMALS and PERSONS also, while naïve biology applies to PERSONS as well as ANIMALS and PLANTS.

Now, Boyer's claim is that religious concepts, even though they obviously do not fall within the purview of "everyday, empirical knowledge," nevertheless draw on these same, ontological, assumptions, but "tweak" them in particular ways (Boyer 2003, 119–120). On the one hand, religious concepts explicitly violate intuitive expectations, as when ghosts (a kind of PERSON) pass invisibly through walls. This makes them extraordinary and attention demanding. On the other hand, apart from these explicit violations, religious concepts are formed largely in accord with intuitive assumptions for their ontological domain, as when we tell stories about *who* the ghost is, and the past events that gave *him* or *her* their *motive* for returning to haunt the living. Concepts that strike the right balance between counterintuitive and intuitive properties—what Justin Barrett (2000) has dubbed "Minimally Counterintuitive" (MCI) concepts—constitute a "cognitive optimum"; they are easily remembered and transmitted, and thus more likely to become widespread in any given population. This, according to Boyer, explains the ubiquity, and some of the universal features of religious representations in all human cultures.

It follows from the logic of Boyer's scheme that violations of intuitive ontological assumptions come in two forms: As *breaches* of the assumptions associated with an ontological domain or its superordinate domains, or as *transfers* from a subordinate domain. By squaring his five ontological domains with his three inference domains, Boyer arrives at a catalogue of 15 different templates of religious concepts (Boyer 2000a, 2002; Barrett 2000; Atran and Norenzayan 2004, 721):

| OBJECT + violation of physical expectation | ARTIFACT + violation of physical expectation | PLANT + violation of physical expectation | ANIMAL + violation of physical expectation | PERSON + violation of physical expectation |
|---|---|---|---|---|
| OBJECT + transfer of biological expectations | ARTIFACT + transfer of biological expectations | PLANT + violation of biological expectations | ANIMAL + violation of biological expectations | PERSON + violation of biological expectations |
| OBJECT + transfer of psychological expectations | ARTIFACT + transfer of psychological expectations | PLANT + transfer of psychological expectations | ANIMAL + transfer of psychological expectations | PERSON + violation of psychological expectations |

46

A deductive scheme such as this should obviously not be taken too seriously, and it will not be necessary to go into its details here. For reasons that should become obvious below, only the two ontological categories of NATURAL OBJECT and PERSON, and the six templates for MCI-concepts based on them, are relevant to the present analysis. [2]

### Assyro-Babylonian religion

The history of ancient Iraq is a turbulent one, with periods of peace alternating with periods of war and general chaos, and small city-states expanding into major empires, only to wither as others rose to power. From 1792 BCE, the year of King Hammurabi's accession to the throne, until 539 BCE, when the entire area came under Persian rule, the main epicentres of these political fluctuations were the city of Babylon, around 85 kilometers south of present day Baghdad, and the city of Assur, about 250 kilometers to the north of Baghdad. Important differences and developments notwithstanding, this period can be treated as a continuous whole, both linguistically and culturally (Oppenheim 1964; Roaf 1990).

Broadly speaking, two institutions dominated Assyro-Babylonian society: the royal palace and the temple. The separation of secular and religious power at the institutional level was accomplished in prehistoric times, but the king continued to have numerous religious duties. The authority of the king was delegated through an extended network of officials; one branch of this network was the legal system, in which the king was the last instance of appeal (Postgate 1992).

Assyro-Babylonian religion was polytheistic; the number of divine names attested running into the thousands, but in most periods there were only about 10 prominent gods with a fairly stable hierarchy among them. In general terms, each god was attributed with particular identifying traits and a particular domain of relevance, although the picture is far from coherent. For example, the god Ea was described as cunning and wise, and was often called on in rituals of magic, while Šamaš usually was associated with justice and divination. Many gods were linked with natural phenomena, such as Nisaba, who was the god of grain and reed (and of writing, since reeds were used for writing cuneiform), Sin, the moon god, and Šamaš, whose name etymologically means "sun" (Lambert 1975; Black and Green 1992; Bottéro 2001).

The temple cult centered on the daily offerings to the gods who inhabited the city temples in the form of anthropomorphic statues. The, often massive, amounts of food served were later redistributed among the temple staff, and thus formed an important part of the temple economy.

The extant sources fall within a wide variety of types and genres. There are inscriptions recounting the exploits of kings, and myths and literary works recounting those of gods and heroes. There are prayers and hymns addressed to gods, and elaborate ritual instructions used in the temples or in and around the royal court. There are incantations concerned

---

2. The fundamental question is, how are Boyer's five ontological domains actually defined? They correspond roughly to the various headings under which cognitive psychologists subscribing to the theory of domain specificity have conducted their research (Hirschfeld and Gelman 1994a), but as Boyer has himself noted (Boyer and Barrett 2006): *The problem [...] is that the domains themselves are not construed in a principled way. In most studies of domain-specificity, the precise understanding of what are 'artifacts' (often oddly called 'objects') or 'animals' or 'living things' is left to the experimenter's commonsense, as if that was a privileged road to cognitive structure.* See also (Boyer and Barrett 2005). This weakness of the theory remains even if the empirical tests of its predictions are generally supportive (Boyer and Ramble 2001; Barrett and Nyhof 2001; Atran and Norenzayan 2004; Gonce *et al.* 2006; Lisdorf 2007).

with healing, exorcism and with averting future misfortune; many of these seem to have had the king as their patient, and may have served political purposes. The quantitatively largest group of texts deals with divination.

The texts come from all periods and places, though the bulk of them derive from excavations of the large royal library collection of the sixth and the seventh centuries BC. This does not necessarily mean that they were composed at that time, but rather that for the majority of texts we do not know the exact context in which they originated. There was no Assyro-Babylonian "canon," although certain texts were of course more popular and widely circulated than others.

## Divine epithets

"Divine epithets" can be defined as formulaic and conventionalized, linguistic expressions concerning superhuman agents. The following excerpt from a prayer put in the mouth of the Assyrian king Assurbanipal (668–627 BC) is a typical example of how epithets were used in Assyro-Babylonian religious texts (Foster 2005, 734; Ebeling 1953).

> O great lord who occupies an awe-inspiring dais in the pure heavens,
> Golden tiara of the heavens, symbol of royalty,
> O Šamaš, shepherd of the people, noble god,
> Seer of the land, leader of the people,
> Who guides the fugitive on his path,
> O Šamaš, judge of heaven and earth,
> Who directs the heavenly gods,
> who grants incense offerings to the great gods,
> I, Assurbanipal, son of my god,
> Call upon you in the pure heavens.

The first eight lines are made up entirely of epithets. The main argument for focusing on divine epithets in order to study conceptions of the divine is that they may give some indication of how the gods were conceptualized in everyday discourse. An epithet is the kind of thing you could say to or about a deity without anyone raising an eyebrow. If deities are indeed "culturally postulated superhuman agents," divine epithets are the actual cultural postulates being made regarding them.

The textual corpus used in the present analysis is delimited by the entries related to Šamaš in Knut Tallqvist's book *Akkadische Götterepitheta* (1938). In spite of being relatively old, Tallqvist's work is still cited as a reliable reference. The main problem with using it is of course that the number of relevant texts and textual fragments that have been excavated and published has at the very least doubled since 1938. In order to be conclusive, the following analysis should of course include this newer material, although it is unlikely that it would alter the overall pattern significantly. The following, then, should be seen as a pilot study.

Tallqvist cites 224 different texts from a wide variety of genres, containing 321 different epithets applied to the god Šamaš, distributed on 503 textual occurrences altogether. On the face of it, these figures seem to contradict the claim that divine epithets were conventionalized and oft-repeated. In fact, 59.8% of all epithets occur only once, and as little as 1.5% of all epithets occur more than ten times, the top scorer being "king of heaven and earth," which occurs 21 times in the corpus (thus accounting for 4.2% of all textual occurrences). This is hardly what would be expected, if epithets reflected widely held cultural concepts.

The figures are, however, somewhat misleading. Numerous epithets are synonyms or only slight grammatical variations on the same expression. There are, for example, five different epithets that literally mean "Illuminator of Darkness." More importantly, most epithets are simple permutations on a fairly limited repertoire of expressions, as the following examples illustrate:

> *Light of heaven and earth, Lord of heaven and earth, Judge of heaven and earth, Supreme judge of heaven and earth, King of heaven and earth, Creator of heaven and earth, King of Heaven, King of Justice, King of Mankind, King of the Land, Light of Above and Below, Light of Heaven, Light of the Earth, Light of Heaven and Earth, Light of the great Gods*

And so on ad infinitum. Clearly, the linguistic variation is far greater than the variation at the conceptual level. This is exactly why an ontological and semantic analysis is needed.

### *The problem of representativity*

A note needs to be made regarding the problem of representativity. It is in the nature of archaeological evidence that what has or has not been excavated is largely a matter of chance. In the present analysis, the term "text" refers to individual textual compositions, rather than individual extant fragments or manuscripts. This means that texts that were copied particularly often do not weigh relatively more in the analysis than esoteric or rare material. By analogy, this amounts to giving the same weight to the Lord's Prayer and John 1: 1–5 in a study of Christianity, even though the former is quite obviously massively more salient than the latter. There is no safe way out of this predicament. The only thing that can be done is to test for systematic differences within the material, whether for instance certain textual genres or texts from certain periods differ significantly from others. I have not been able to find such differences.[3] Epithets seem, in other words, to be coherently and evenly distributed across the corpus, which is a good argument that there are no strong biases in the material.

There are other, related problems in singling out divine epithets as our object of study. First of all, epithets are not the only way that deities are conceptualized in texts. Divine epithets are defined by certain grammatical and formal features, thus leaving out other expressions with the same or similar conceptual content. For example, the expression "the one who brings the day" is an epithet proper, while an expression such as "all humankind kneels at your rising" is not—although both expressions quite clearly conceptualize Šamaš in the same way: as the rising sun. Using divine epithets as an inroad to the study of god concepts is feasible only on the assumption that epithets are in fact a reliable index of how a deity is conceived in any given text. For present purposes, I will have to simply assert that this is the case. I am not aware of any texts where the conceptual content of the epithets used differs markedly from other elements in the text in which they appear. But clearly, this assertion could be criticized for being hermeneutically circular.

An even more difficult problem is that not all concepts are linguistically encoded. The context of an expression may implicitly suggest that a superhuman agent is to be conceived in a certain way, even though it is not expressed in language. I will return to this problem below. With these caveats and reservations in place, it is now time to turn to the actual analysis.

---

3.   My initial hypothesis in this study was that different textual genres would display massive and systematic differences in the epithets used.

### *Distribution of epithets across ontological domains*

The distribution of epithets across ontological domains is shown in Figure 4.1. The PER-SON category contains epithets that are clearly anthropomorphic such as "great lord," "unbribable counsellor," "warrior of the gods," "pre-eminent son" and so on, while the OBJECT category contains epithets that target the physical appearance and properties of the sun, such as "displayer of light," "who brings down feverish heat upon the earth at midday," "dressed in sparkles," "singular brilliance" and "radiant god."

The category that I have chosen to call "generic" expressions covers two kinds of epithets: 1) expressions that do not imply any ontological constraints on the object to which they are applied, and 2) expressions that might very well have done so, but which are opaque or ambiguous to modern scrutiny. Examples of the former are epithets such as "great," "exalted" and "all-powerful"; examples of the latter are "the one who reveals the evil-doer" and "lifegiver."

Unsurprisingly, the main ontological distinction that can be made is that between OB-JECT and PERSON. There is in fact a small group of epithets that formally conceptual-ize Šamaš as an ARTEFACT—namely "Shield of the white temple," "mirror of the wide earth," "strong weapon of the Gods" and the one quoted above, "Golden tiara of heaven." I will argue, however, that these should be understood as metaphorical expressions (Cf Heimpel 1968). "Weapon" and "Shield" are metaphors of strength and protective power

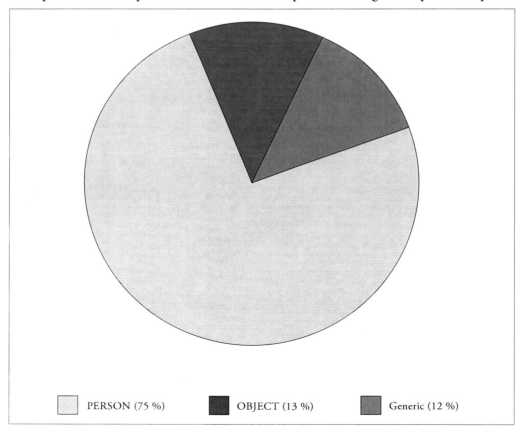

PERSON (75 %)     OBJECT (13 %)     Generic (12 %)

Figure 4.1 The distribution of divine epithets across basic ontological domains

("The white temple" being the names of two temples devoted to Šamaš, one in the city of Sippar and one in Larsa), "tiara" is a lyrical description of the luminance of the sun, while the word translated as "mirror" literally means something that is looked at or stared at—in other words, an object of prayer or devotion. Consequently, these expressions are counted as "generic" in Figure 4.1.[4]

Metaphorical language poses particular problems for a theory that focuses on ontological category violations, such as Cognitive Optimum Theory. The theory of domain specificity would seem to be incompatible with the "everything is metaphor"-view so influential in certain corners of cognitive linguistics (Johnson and Lakoff 1980). The fact that tables have "legs" or that clocks have "faces" lures no-one, save perhaps the occasional preschooler, into thinking that they have intestines as well, or produce offspring that inherit their properties (Keil 1994, 236). Clearly, metaphorical projections are constrained by the ontological status of the target domain.[5] Not all "concept combinations" have ontological implications (Franks 2003).

We need, in other words, to maintain the distinction between metaphorical and literal language. This is not always easy in the case of religious concepts, as it is exactly the ontological status of the entities to which these concepts are applied that we are trying to figure out. So how can we know? In many instances the ontological implications of an expression are made obvious by its immediate context, but often all we can do is make an educated guess. For all that we know that might have been what the ancients themselves did as well; we cannot assume that the meaning of all of these expressions was transparent to the people using them.

*Conceptual components of the person ontology*

The fact that the PERSON ontology accounts for three quarters of all epithets is hardly surprising. According to Boyer's theory, PERSON concepts will generally be more likely to be culturally successful, because they activate Theory of Mind, and thus have a very high "inference potential" (Boyer 1996). Šamaš is, by all counts, a classic example of what is generally termed anthropomorphism, the projection of human attributes onto the nonhuman (Guthrie 1993; Boyer 1996). But as Boyer has rightly argued, such an account is too imprecise to be of any explanatory use (Boyer 1996). We need to take a more detailed look at exactly *which* human features are projected onto the gods. This can be done by distinguishing the various semantic fields that comprise the PERSON ontology. I have identified eight such fields, as shown in Figure 4.2.

The field "Royal authority" covers such epithets as "King of heaven and earth," "Lord of truth and justice," "Leader of the people," "He whose command is not changed" and so on, while "Judicial authority" covers epithets like "Exalted judge of heaven and earth," "Unbribable judge," "Passer of verdicts," and "The one whose justice and decisions are quickly carried out." There is a considerable overlap between these two semantic fields, as well as between the royal field and the field of "Martial power"—indeed, epithets such as "great warrior," "conqueror of enemy lands" and "hero" are often applied to human kings.

---

4. To Assyriologists the most remarkable thing is perhaps that there is not a single epithet that conceptualizes Šamaš as an ANIMAL, animal imagery, such as "calf," "wild bull" and so on being otherwise extremely common in Mesopotamian religious language. (See Feldt 2007).

5. The failure to account for these types of constraints on metaphorical projections is arguably one of the major shortcomings of Conceptual Metaphor Theory (Murphy 1996; See also Hirschfeld and Gelman 1994b, 23; Keil 1979, 154).

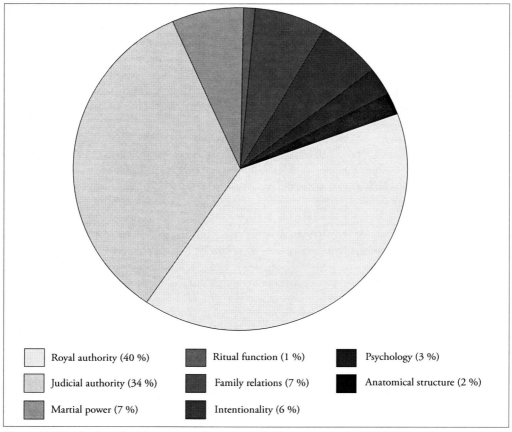

Royal authority (40 %)     Ritual function (1 %)     Psychology (3 %)

Judicial authority (34 %)     Family relations (7 %)     Anatomical structure (2 %)

Martial power (7 %)     Intentionality (6 %)

Figure 4.2 Distribution of epithets among the semantic fields comprising the PERSON ontology

The minute field "Ritual function" contains only a couple of epithets that describe Šamaš as a "seer," that is, a divination priest. Šamaš played an important role in rituals of divination, although these epithets are not particularly prevalent in that textual genre (Starr 1983).

Epithets in the category "Family relations," such as "Brother of Marduk" "Beloved of Aya" and "God who calms his father's heart" mainly address the relative status of various deities, while the target of an expression like "Father of the black-headed" is the relation between deities and men ("the black-headed" being a conventional expression for "humans."

The category "Intentionality" plays a role somewhat similar to that of the "generic" category in Figure 4.1. It covers concepts that clearly imply intentional action, but do not otherwise seem to constrain their object more specifically. Examples are "decider of destinies" (accounting for 2 out of 6%), "releaser of curses" and "the one who guides the fugitive on his path." Quite clearly Šamaš *does* something here, but exactly how and in what capacity seems underdetermined by the expression itself.

By contrast, the epithets in the "Psychology" field entail more definite conceptions of mental states and perceptual processes, such as "wise," "who hears prayers," "who sees through peoples hearts" and "who loves the living."

Lastly, the domain "Anatomical structure" covers epithets such as "Great god with long arms," "Who has a lapis-coloured beard" and so on. Two things should be noted here: First, the fact that there are very few of these epithets does not necessarily mean that Šamaš was not generally conceived of as having anatomical structure, as anthropomorphic pictorial representations of deities were very common—indeed, the lapis-coloured beard ascribed to Šamaš probably is a description of the divine statue of him that inhabited his temple. Second, the verb "treading" or "walking" should perhaps be interpreted as a metaphorical description of the movements of the sun across the sky, rather than as implying that Šamaš has anatomical structure (legs).

The most striking fact in this survey of the semantic fields falling under the PERSON ontology is of course that Royal, Juridical and Martial epithets together account for 81% of all epithets. What characterizes these epithets is that they are inherently social: they posit a clear, social hierarchy, and attribute specific social roles and modes of operation to the deity. Their source domain is Assyro-Babylonian society, and they are not explicitly concerned with belief-desire psychology or other aspects of "the mind." Incidentally, royal and martial epithets are widely applied to most Assyro-Babylonian deities, while the judicial epithets are, if not exclusive to Šamaš, at least mostly applied to him (Tallqvist 1938; Jacobsen 1976, chap. 4).

It could be argued that the scarcity of explicitly psychological concepts poses a problem for Boyer's claim that "anthropologists know that the *only* feature of humans that is *always* projected onto supernatural beings is the mind" (Boyer 2001, 163), but it seems reasonable to assume that the naïve psychology is there, even if it is left tacit. While the projection of mind or agency does not necessarily entail the ascription of more specific human features such as anatomical structure, family relations or social roles, the projection of these features will "almost invariably" entail the projection of agency and psychological properties (Boyer 2001, 163). A judge, a king or someone who has a beard is, by definition and by default, an intentional agent, a person.

### Anthropomorphism and the distinctness of ontologies

Part of the idea of anthropomorphism as a transfer of features from the human domain is that it is transferred *onto* some other, non-human domain. Šamaš, being a "sun god," would seem to be a classic example of this: A natural phenomenon, onto which human features are projected.

Boyer's explanation of the universality of this kind of transfer is twofold. First, as already explained, he claims that concepts that derive some of their structure from naïve psychology have a greater inference potential than other types of concepts; this goes both for concepts belonging to the PERSON ontology, and for transfers onto other types of concepts. Second, the transfer of features from the PERSON ontology onto the OBJECT ontology constitutes a breach with intuitive expectations, which makes such projections salient, in the sense of attention-grabbing; they become, in other words, MCI-concepts. These two features converge to make anthropomorphic projections particularly likely candidates for successful cultural transmission.

If this account is at all adequate in the case of Šamaš, we should be able to describe at least a significant portion of the Assyro-Babylonian concepts of Šamaš along the following lines, utilizing a scheme developed by Boyer (Boyer 2000a, 2000b; Boyer and Ramble 2001; Barrett 2000):

1. a pointer to the OBJECT domain
2. an explicit representation of a *transfer* of properties from the PERSON domain

3. a link to (nonviolated) default expectations for the OBJECT domain
4. additional encyclopaedic information
5. a lexical label: Šamaš

We have already seen in Figure 4.1 above that the number of "pointers" to the object domain is in fact rather small—13% of all epithets—the vast majority of epithets being explicit representations of the PERSON domain (and thus, in this scheme, belonging to point 2 and possibly 4). But of course, epithets do not occur in isolation; 65% of the texts in the corpus contain two or more epithets. If intuitive expectations deriving from the OBJECT domain are indeed fundamental to how Šamaš is conceptualized, and if the many epithets from the PERSON domain represent transfers onto the OBJECT domain, then we should expect epithets from the OBJECT domain 1) to occur, in most instances, alongside epithets from the PERSON domain and 2) to be fairly widely and evenly distributed across the corpus.

Figure 4.3 shows that while the first of these predictions is true, the second is clearly false. In this analysis, the texts are divided into four categories. The PERSON and OBJECT categories cover texts that contain one or more epithets that either belong to one of these ontologies exclusively, or a combination of these and generic epithets. The Blended category covers texts that contain two or more epithets from different ontological domains, while the generic category obviously covers texts with only generic epithets.

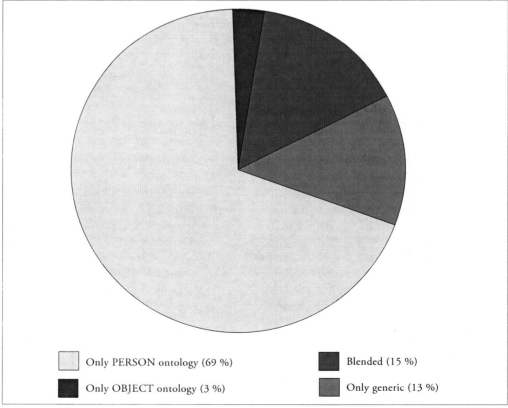

Only PERSON ontology (69 %)   Blended (15 %)

Only OBJECT ontology (3 %)   Only generic (13 %)

Figure 4.3  The relative number of texts with epithets pointing to the PERSON ontology, to the OBJECT ontology, to both, or with only generic epithets.

Of the 18% of the corpus that contain epithets from the OBJECT domain, only 3% contain epithets from that domain only. In so far as Šamaš is represented as an OBJECT, the ontological assumptions associated with this are usually followed by the explicit representation of features from the PERSON domain. Regarding the 3% of text where there are no evident transfers from the PERSON domain, it could be argued that this group of texts is an artefact of a too narrow definition of anthropomorphism. Even if Šamaš is addressed in terms that highlight only the experiential features of the sun, the fact that Šamaš is addressed at all—named, praised, prayed to, posited as a participant in rituals, in short: deified—entails the ascription of intentional agency, even if it is not fleshed out in explicitly anthropomorphic or psychological language. Either way there is some, albeit limited, support for the thesis that concepts of Šamaš were based on Boyer's template of religious anthropomorphism, that is as an OBJECTS with transfers of properties from the PERSON domain.

The fact remains, however, that 82% of the texts in the corpus contain no explicit pointers to the OBJECT domain whatsoever, nor any links to nonviolated assumptions from that domain. In these texts, Šamaš is conceptualized singularly and exclusively as a PERSON. This must mean that Boyer's template of divine anthropomorphism does not apply to these texts. Unless, that is, there are some tacit pointers or links to the OBJECT domain. This may not be as hopelessly *ad hoc* as it sounds; it is in fact an interpretative principle that has dominated the study of Ancient Near Eastern religion since Max Müller (Westh 2001). For one thing, the deity's lexical label, "Šamaš," could be construed as a pointer to the OBJECT domain. After all, the name does mean "sun," at least etymologically. Further, the individual occurrence of a deity cannot of course be understood in complete isolation from how the deity is described elsewhere, and pointers to the OBJECT domain may be recurrent enough to constitute a salient feature of a culturally stable conception of this deity.

This is a somewhat speculative line of argument, however. If indeed intuitive, non-violated default expectations deriving from the OBJECT domain play a significant part in the great number of explicitly anthropomorphic texts, we are in need of an explanation why it does not show at all at the surface level—indeed, why there is apparently no "link to (non-violated) default expectations for the OBJECT domain" in these texts (Boyer and Ramble 2001, 537). It is more reasonable then to simply accept that Šamaš was, in the vast majority of cases, construed as fundamentally humanlike. In other words, the data seem to fit very well with that part of Boyer's argument which explains the prevalence of anthropomorphic projections by their superior inference potential, but not with the claim that these projections are counterintuitive. Unless, that is, Šamaš, when construed as a PERSON, has some other counterintuitive properties.

### Counterintuitive concepts

Figure 4.4 shows the relative frequency of intuitive and counterintuitive epithets in the corpus. The category "default activation" covers epithets with no evident counterintuitive properties, whether they point to the OBJECT or the PERSON ontology. Examples of epithets based on the template PERSON + breach of physical or biological expectations are "who makes the dead alive," "who destroys lands at the blink of an eye" and "Great lord who occupies a terrifying dais in the pure heaven". Examples of epithets based on the template PERSON + breach of psychological expectations are "who sees through the evil of the enemy," "who watches over everything" and "who hears prayers".

As already noted, there are some interpretative difficulties here. Is an epithet such as "whose face is radiant" an OBJECT onto which a property from the PERSON domain (a

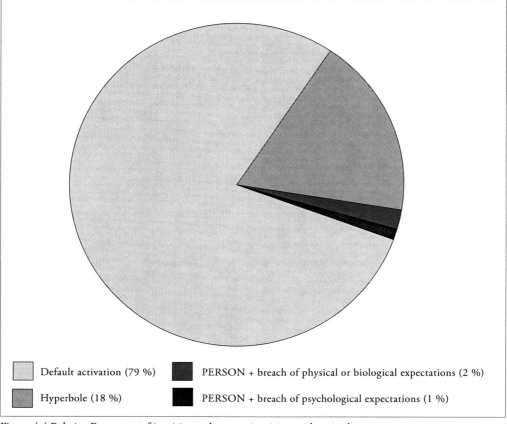

Figure 4.4 Relative Frequency of intuitive and counterintuitive epithets in the corpus.

face) has been projected, a PERSON that violates intuitive, physical expectations (people aren't radiant, literally speaking) or is it a metaphorical expression? Similar questions are posed by epithets such as "who wanders the roads of heaven and earth" and so on.

A comment is needed on the distinction made between counterintuitiveness and what I have called hyperbole. A fairly large group of divine epithets pointing to the PERSON ontology are hyperbolic in the sense of extending the scale of concepts beyond the realistic or humanly possible: "Leader of *everything*," "the exalted judge *who leads the upper and the lower lands*," "ruler of *the living*," "just shepherd *of humanity*" and so on. As extraordinary as these concepts are, they are hardly counterintuitive in the technical sense presupposed by Cognitive Optimum Theory. If anything, they are bizarre in the sense proposed by Barrett and Nyhof (2001). One could argue, however, that they *imply* counterintuitiveness; for example, "Leader of everything" might imply violations of psychological or physical assumptions such as sensory limitation or location in space. Again, there are interpretative difficulties—is "all-powerful" hyperbolic or counterintuitive? In any case, even if we grant hyperbolic expressions status as counterintuitive, the general picture is clear: MCI concepts are not all that prevalent in the corpus.

What does this entail for Cognitive Optimum Theory? One problem with the theory is that the scope of its predictions is not very specific. Does the theory entail that all religious concepts are minimally counterintuitive by definition, as some of Boyer's readers seem to think (e.g. Pyysiäinen 2003)? Does it predict that the distribution of intuitive and counterintuitive concepts in any tradition will converge toward the distribution in the recall experiments that have been made (Lisdorf 2004)? Does it entail, more modestly, that minimally counterintuitive concepts are generally a salient part of any religious system, although they need not be the only or even the dominant type (Atran and Norenzayan 2004, 722)? Or does it merely set out to explain the evolutionary paradox of why and how people entertain counterintuitive concepts at all, given a theoretical framework—modularity theory and evolutionary psychology—that otherwise has as its fundamental axiom that human cognition is governed by fairly tight intuitive constraints?[6] The first two readings would seem to be contradicted by the data presented here, while the last two are of course entirely compatible with them.

A possible counter-argument to the claim that most concepts of Šamaš were not MCI-concepts could be that the counterintuitive properties of Šamaš were somehow tacit. The very idea of a "god" is counterintuitive enough as it is; adding further intuitive violations in the form of epithets would only clutter the cognitive system unnecessarily, and would reduce the inference potential and memorability of concepts (Barrett 1999, 2004, 24f). There are at least two problems with this argument. First, it is vulnerable to severe methodological criticism as it, in effect, turns the absence of evident counterintuitive properties in a god concept into proof that the god concept is counterintuitive. Second, part of the very logic of Cognitive Optimum Theory is that, in order for MCI concepts to be entertained and transmitted, the violations of intuitive expectations that make them salient must be *explicit* (Boyer 1994, 407, 1998, 881, 2000b, 197; Boyer and Ramble 2001, 537; Sørensen 2007, 38). The whole point of the theory is that it is only the counterintuitive properties that need to be culturally transmitted; the intuitive properties are "filled-in" automatically and unconsciously. A tacitly counterintuitive concept is, simply, a contradiction in terms.

A more reasonable argument would be that the counterintuitive properties of these religious concepts are not tacit per se—only they are not encoded in the texts, but suggested by their ritual, pragmatic or social context. Addressing a prayer to a god who is not manifestly present, or who is present in the form of a statue made of wood, metal and precious stones, is about as counterintuitive as can be. This is an argument with some strength but, again, it reduces the notions of counterintuitiveness and cognitive optimum to *a priori* assumptions, and commits us to some very specific *ad hoc* assumptions regarding how these concepts were transmitted.

A more promising line of argument would be, I think, to simply accept what the data suggest and try to find an explanation for it. The obvious place to look is the medium through which these concepts have become available to us: writing. Although the sources analyzed here to some extent reflect an oral tradition, they are written texts, meticulously reproduced by a class of educated specialists. This means that the filtering effects of memory and communication were largely bypassed, and thus there was no need for god concepts to balance around the cognitive optimum (Sperber 1985) In most discussions of Cognitive Optimum Theory, MCI concepts are contrasted with explicitly and maximally counterintuitive, "theologically correct" concepts. The metarepresentational potential offered by writing and material culture is assumed to allow concepts to part ways with the intuitive, taking off into the spheres of theology, philosophy and science (Sperber 1985; Barrett 1999; McCauley 2000). In the case of Assyro-Babylonian religion, these same mechanisms

---

6.  I take it for granted that we can rule out the absurdly strong reading of Boyer's theory, that MCI-concepts will always and invariably have a transmission advantage over intuitive concepts (Alles 2006; Barrett 2004, 24).

may have permitted god concepts to move in the other direction, away from the cognitive optimum toward the predominantly intuitive. There's nothing in the theory that precludes that possibility. The question is, why would this happen?

A likely candidate for an answer comes from Figure 4.2 above. 81% of all epithets in the PERSON domain, or about 61% of all epithets in the corpus, have the political power structures of Assyro-Babylonian society as their source domain. The gods were, by and large, modelled on the king and his various officials. The prevalence of anthropomorphism in Assyro-Babylonian religion was, in other words, ideological (Benavides 1995; Binsbergen and Wiggerman 1999).

## Conclusion

When discussing the results of the present analysis with a close friend and colleague, one of his objections to the conclusion that Šamaš had in fact only very few counterintuitive properties, was: "As epithets—right? I mean, looking at the broader myths and rituals Šamaš is minimally counterintuitive—right?" It is an interesting question that reveals a lot about the methodological problems faced by a cognitive historiography. It is no problem, of course, to find instances of minimally, and perhaps "not so minimally counterintuitive" concepts in Assyro-Babylonian, as in probably any religious tradition (Barrett 2004, 29f). The problem is, why single out exactly those properties as salient and characteristic of religious concepts? Without some principled way of delimiting what is and what is not relevant data, and at what level of generality "concepts" are to be identified, any historical analysis along the lines of Cognitive Optimum Theory will be subject to a massive confirmation bias.

The route chosen here to avoid this trap was to keep the conceptual analysis very close to the level of actual, linguistic encoding, and to subject the data to a quantitative analysis. This strategy has numerous problems of its own, as it clearly risks throwing the baby out with the bath water by bracketing out the cultural and pragmatic contexts which ultimately give concepts their meaning. Even under these constraints, however, the results of the analysis gave a clear indication of the ways cognitive structures, material culture and social factors interact in the formation and transmission of religious concepts. Assyro-Babylonian concepts of the deity Šamaš do seem to fall rather neatly into the basic ontological domains proposed by Cognitive Optimum Theory; but the theory cannot account for the actual distribution of concepts across the different ontological domains, nor can it explain the semantic content of the concepts used. Violations of intuitive ontological assumptions do not seem to play the prominent role that the theory predicts.

Regarding the deity Šamaš, an Assyriologist could argue—and rightly so—that what has been uncovered here by means of cognitive theorizing is little more than the glaringly obvious. The prevalence of anthropomorphic god concepts in the Assyro-Babylonian period has been recognized by everyone within the field (Jastrow 1898; Dhorme 1910; Landsberger 1974; Kramer 1948; Lambert 1975, 1990; Jacobsen 1976; Selz 1997), and the notion that the source of these concepts was royal ideology is just plain common sense; what else would it be (Jastrow 1898; Jacobsen 1976; Binsbergen and Wiggerman 1999)? What may be new and controversial in the present analysis is not that Šamaš was anthropomorphic but that, despite being a "sun god," his association with the sun in fact played a rather marginal role in how he was conceived. (Cf Edzard 1965; Lambert 1971; Black and Green 1992; Bottéro 2001).

# References

Alles, Gregory D. 2006. "The so-called cognitive optimum and the cost of religious concepts." *Method and theory in the study of religion* 18(4): 25.

Atran, Scott, and Ara Norenzayan. 2004. "Religion's evolutionary landscape: Counterintuition, commitment, compassion, communion." *Behavioral and brain sciences* 27(6): 713–730.

Barrett, Justin L. 1999. "Theological correctness." *Method and theory in the study of religion.* 11 (4): 325–339.

———. 2000. "Exploring the natural foundations of religion." *Trends in Cognitive Sciences* 4 (1): 29–34.

———. 2004. *Why would anyone believe in God?*, Cognitive Science of Religion Series. Walnut Creek, CA: Altamira Press.

Barrett, Justin L. and Melanie A. Nyhof. 2001. "Spreading Non-natural Concepts: The Role of Intuitive Conceptual Structures in Memory and Transmission of Cultural Materials." *Journal of Cognition and Culture* 1(1): 69–100.

Benavides, Gustavo. 1995. "Cognitive and Ideological Aspects of Divine Anthropomorphism." *Religion* 25(1): 9–22.

Binsbergen, Wim van and Frans Wiggerman. 1999. "Magic in history. A theoretical perspective, and its application to ancient Mesopotamia." In *Mesopotamian Magic. Textual, historical, and interpretative prespectives*, edited by W. v. Binsberg, F. Wiggermann and T. Abusch, 3–34. Groningen: Styx publications.

Black, J. A., and A. Green. 1992. *Gods, Demons, and Symbols of Ancient Mesopotamia: An Illustrated Dictionary.* Austin: University of Texas Press.

Bottéro, J. 2001. *Religion in Ancient Mesopotamia.* Chicago, IL: University of Chicago Press.

Boyer, Pascal. 1994. "Cognitive constraints on cultural representations: Natural ontologies and religious ideas." In *Mapping the Mind*, edited by L.A. Hirschfeld and S.A. Gelman, 391–411. Cambridge: Cambridge University Press.

———. 1996. "What makes anthropomorphism natural: intuitive ontoloogy and cultural representations." *Journal of the Royal Anthropological Institute* 2 (1): 83–97.

———. 1998. "Cognitive tracks of cultural inheritance: How evolved intuitive ontology governs cultural transmission." *American Anthropologist* 100(4): 876–889.

———. 2000a. "Evolution of the modern mind and the origins of culture: religious concepts as a limiting-case." In *Evolution and the Human Mind: Modularity, Language and Meta-Cognition*, edited by P. Carruthers and A. Chamberlain, 93–112. Cambridge: Cambridge University Press.

———. 2000b. "Functional Origins of Religious Concepts: Ontological and Strategic Selection in Evolved Minds." *The Journal of the Royal Anthropological Institute* 6(2): 195–214.

———. 2001. *Religion Explained.* London: Vintage.

———. 2002. "Religious Ontologies and the Bounds of Sense: A Cognitive Catalogue of the Supernatural." http://ontology.buffalo.edu/smith//courses01/rrtw/Boyer.htm Access date: 18/08/2006.

———. 2003. "Religious thought and behaviour as by-products of brain function." *Trends in Cognitive Sciences* 7(3): 119–124.

Boyer, Pascal, and H. Clark Barrett. 2005. "Domain specificity and intuitive ontology." In *The handbook of evolutionary psychology*, edited by D. M. Buss, 96–118. Hoboken, NJ: John Wiley and Sons.

———. 2006. *Causal Inferences. Evolutionary Domains and Neural Systems.* Invited contribution to an Interdisciplines.org web-conference on Causation (edited by Anne Reboul), www.interdisciplines.org/causality Access date: 18/05/2007.

Boyer, Pascal and Charles Ramble. 2001. "Cognitive templates for religious concepts: Crosscultural evidence for recall of counter-intuitive representations." *Cognitive Science* 25(4): 535–564.

Dhorme, P. Paul. 1910. *La Religion Assyro-Babylonienne*. Paris: Librairie Victor Lecoffre

Ebeling, Erich. 1953. *Dia akkadische Gebetsserie "Handerhebung," Deutsche Akademie der Wissenscaften zu Berlin Institut für Orientforschung Veröfflichung*. Berlin: Akademie-Verlag.

Edzard, Dietz Otto. 1965. "Mesopotamien. Die Mythologie der Sumerer und Akkader." In *Götter und Mythen im vorderen Orient*, edited by W. Haussig, 18–139. Stuttgart: Ernst Klett Verlag.

Feldt, Laura. 2007. "On Divine-Referent Bull Metaphors in the ETCSL Corpus." In *Analysing Literary Sumerian—Corpus-based Approaches*, edited by J. C. Ebeling Graham, 185–214. London: Equinox.

Foster, Benjamin R. 2005. *Before the Muses. An anthology of Akkadian Literature*. Bethesda, MD: CDL Press.

Franks, Bradley. 2003. "The Nature of Unnaturalness in Religious Representations: Negation and Concept Combination." *Journal of Cognition and Culture* 3(1): 41–68.

Gonce, L. O., M. Afzal Upal, D. Jason Slone, and R.D. Tweney. 2006. "Role of context in the recall of counterintuitive concepts." *Journal of Cognition and Culture* 6(3): 521–547.

Guthrie, Stewart. 1993. *Faces in the Clouds: A New Theory of Religion*. Oxford: Oxford University Press.

Heimpel, Wolfgang. 1968. Tierbilder in der sumerischen Literatur. Rome: Päpstliches Bibelinstitut.

Hirschfeld, L.A. and Susan A. Gelman. 1994a. *Mapping the Mind: Domain Specificity in Cognition and Culture*. Cambridge: Cambridge University Press.

Hirschfeld, Lawrence A. and Susan A. Gelman. 1994b. "Toward a topography of mind: An introduction to domain specificity." In *Mapping the Mind: Domain Specificity in Cognition and Culture*, L. A. Hirschfeld and S. A. Gelman, 3–35. Cambridge: Cambridge University Press.

Jacobsen, Thorkild. 1976. *The Treasures of Darkness*. New Haven, CT: Yale University Press.

Jastrow, Morris. 1898. *The religion of Babylonia and Assyria, Handbooks of the History of Religions*. Ginn and Company / Athenæum Press.

Johnson, Mark, and George Lakoff. 1980. *Metaphors We Live By*. Chicago, IL: University of Chicago Press.

Keil, Frank C. 1979. *Semantic and Conceptual Development: An Ontological Perspective*. Cambridge, MA: Harvard University Press.

———. 1994. "The birth and nurturance of concepts by domains: The origins of concepts of living things." In *Mapping the Mind: Domain Specificity in Cognition and Culture*, edited by L.A. Hirschfeld and S.A. Gelman, 234–254. Cambridge: Cambridge University Press.

Kramer, Samuel Noah. 1948. "Review of The Intellectual Adventure of Ancient Man." *Journal of Cuneiform Studies* 2: 39–70.

Lambert, W. G. 1971. Gott: Nach Akkadischen Texten. In *Reallexikon der Assyriologie und Vorderasiatischen Archaologie,* vol 3, edited by D.O. Edzard, 543–546. Berlin: de Gruyter.

———. 1975. "The historical development of the Mesopotamian pantheon: A study in sophisticated polytheism." In *Unity and Diversity. Essays in the history, literature and religion of the Ancient Near East*, edited by H. Goedicke and J.M.M. Roberts, 191–200. Baltimore, MD: Johns Hopkins University Press.

————. 1990. Ancient Mesopotamian Gods. Superstition, philosophy, theology. *Revue de l'Histoire des Religions* 207(2): 115–130.

Landsberger, Benno. 1974. *Three essays on the Sumerians, Monographs on the ancient near east.* Los Angeles, CA: Undena Publications.

Lisdorf, Anders. 2004. "The spread of non-natural concepts: evidence from the Roman prodigy lists." *Journal of Cognition and Culture* 4(1): 151–173.

————. 2007. *The Dissemination of Divination in the Roman Republic: A Cognitive Approach, History of Religions.* Copenhagen: University of Copenhagen.

McCauley, Robert N. 2000. "The Naturalness of Religion and the Unnaturalness of Science." In *Explanation and Cognition*, edited by R.N. McCauley, R. Wilson and F.C. Keil, 61–86. Cambridge: MIT Press.

Murphy, Gregory L. 1996. "On metaphoric representation." *Cognition* 60: 173–204.

Oppenheim, Leo. 1964. *Ancient Meopotamia, portrait of a dead civilization.* Chicago, IL: University of Chicago Press.

Postgate, J.N. 1992. *Early Mesopotamia. Society and economy at the dawn of history.* London: Routledge.

Pyysiäinen, Ilkka. 2003. *How religion works.* Leiden: Brill.

Roaf, Michael. 1990. *Cultural atlas of Mesopotamia and the ancient Near East.* New York: Facts on File

Selz, Gebhard. 1997. "The holy Drum. the Spear, and the Harp. Towards an understanding of the problems of deification in the third millenium Mesopotamia." In *Sumerian Gods and their Representations*, edited by I.L. Finkel and M.J. Geller, 167–213. Groningen: Styx Publications.

Sperber, D. 1985. "Anthropology and Psychology. Towards an Epidemiology of Representations. "*Man* (New Series) 20: 73–89.

Starr, Ivan. 1983. *The Rituals of the Diviner.* Malibu, CA: Undena Press.

Sørensen, Jesper. 2007. *A Cognitive Theory of Magic.* Edited by L. H. Martin and H. Whitehouse, Cognitive science of religion series. Plymouth: Rowman Altamira.

Tallqvist, Knut. 1938. *Akkadische Götterepitheta, Studia Orientalia.* Helsinki: Societas Orientalis Fennica.

Westh, Peter. 2001. "Gods and natural phenomena in Mesopotamian religion" (in Danish). Unpublished M.A. thesis, University of Copenhagen.

# — 5 —

## Connecting Cultural Stability and Experience of Landscape: A Cognitive Approach in the Study of Tree Symbolism with Special Reference to Mesoamerica and Prehispanic Maya Culture

### Christian M. Prager

The experience of landscape, be it perceived directly or virtually, triggers a tacit affective appraisal in the cognitive apparatus of the human mind (cf. Appleton 1975; Dewey 1925; Orians and Heerwagen 1992). In many regions of the world, a landscape's most salient features are forest and shrub vegetation (Kaplan and Kaplan 1989, 572). It is thus not surprising that, throughout cultural evolution, forests and trees have become major symbols, and as such they are commonly used as designs or motifs in literature, art and other forms of cultural representations (Bloch 2001; Crews 2003; Thompson 1958). I would like to present a cognitive framework in order to understand the evolution and effectiveness of the human symbolic device—most likely a mental tool (cf. Sperber 1975)—as exemplified by tree symbolism. This paper examines the mental mechanisms and the evolutionary origins that contribute to the generation and transmission of tree symbolism in ancient and modern human cultures. Sources that allow a glance into past minds are usually limited and incomplete. Where historical (i.e. material) sources are missing or reach their explanatory limits, both evolutionary psychology and cognitive science of culture may bridge this gap and provide a methodological framework in order to open a window into past minds.

### Introduction

Woodlands, groves or trees in general are highly visible and salient attributes of a landscape and throughout human history they have provided both an essential material and a symbolic resource (Rival 2001b). In the evolutionary landscape of *Homo sapiens,* trees most likely both afforded refuge and provided a strategic locus from which to appraise the surrounding environment. While the pragmatic aspect of wood and its daily use is not under discussion, the metarepresentational facet of trees and the question of why they are used as symbols all over the world (cf. Bloch 2001; Ladner 1979) will be the focus of the present paper. I will discuss the impact of human environmental aesthetics and landscape preference on "cultural stability" (cf. Sperber and Hirschfeld 2004) of tree symbolism.

Given the independent cultural and historical development of the American civilizations before the Spanish conquest in the early sixteenth century, the topic will be exemplified by tree representations in New World societies in order to underline its old, wide and stable distribution throughout the world.

In the first place, the term *symbol*, often loosely used in different contexts, requires closer consideration. Cognitively, a symbol is a metarepresentational causal-relational tool that is activated when "a rational interpretation is unavailable or insufficient" (Boyer 1999, 216). It is an "interface" or a thinking device (cf. Sperber 1975) connecting the human mind with both the stimuli of the external world and with superstimuli (Sperber and Hirschfeld 2004, 45) that are produced by culturally shaped worlds in order to explain and interpret the social and physical surroundings of people. In the cultural world, natural features, innate psychological dispositions, and human behaviour are often hyped or exaggerated and provide what ethologists call "superstimuli" for human cognition (Sperber and Hirschfeld 2004, 42). Also known as supernormal stimuli, they are the result of the so-called "peak shift" principle, a psychological phenomenon underlying any sensory aspect of human life, including art, music or verbal utterances. This principle exaggerates physical objects, psychological features or human practices in order to focus super-attention and to attach a special importance to these items (Ramachandran and Hirstein 1999, 17ff.).

In social anthropology, a symbol is often described as a *thing* or as an *artifact* (LeCron Foster 1994, 366), or as a public representation that represents or stands for something other than itself (Sperber 1993). Anthropologists usually differentiate between, on the one hand, a world of self-evident or natural meanings and, on the other hand, "shifted" meanings, the latter standing for something but not itself (Haviland 1997, 370). The ways in which people understand and interpret their physical and social environment became the focus of symbolic anthropology. According to William Haviland for example, a "symbol [...] means any kind or sound or gesture to which cultural tradition has given meaning as standing for something, and not one that has a natural or self-evident meaning" (1997, 370). In contrast to signals that have a natural or self-evident meaning, symbols are regarded as a kind of vehicle transporting meanings and values between like-minded people. The meaning of a symbol comes from the "larger structure of knowledge, associations, and practices in which it is embedded. Moreover, different viewers, with different histories and experiences, might draw from it very different interpretations and associations" (Bowen 1997, 142).

So, the term 'symbol' and its use is strongly interwoven with cultural representations like art, belief, language, literacy, writing and other forms (cf. LeCron Foster 1994). For the cognitive anthropologist Dan Sperber, the term *culture* refers to mental representations of relative similarity, which are attention-grabbing, easily memorable and, consequently, readily transmitted between the members of a community (cf. Sperber 1993). For the present paper, I follow Sperber's cognitive understanding of symbolism as a human capacity, an innate mechanism conceptualized as a "mental device coupled to the conceptual mechanism" (Sperber 1975, 140ff) whose function is to *focus* attention, to *elicit* representations from memory, and to *reify* hard-to-process beliefs.

## Landscape Signals

"Trees and forests, probably because of their great size and sometimes longevity, vividly affected the imagination of preliterate societies" (Crews 2003, 37). Human conceptions of trees are indeed multi-faceted and have their foundations in the evolutionary landscape of the African savannahs in which the modern human mind and its capacities is thought to have evolved (cf. Orians and Heerwagen 1992). Over the past 30 years, evolutionary psychologists have provided evidence that affairs closely linked to human survival and reproduction are likely to engage positive affective appraisal (Buss 2004, 130ff.). Speaking generally, the natural world is the focus of cultural attention because it is closely linked with survival and reproductive success (cf. Hirschfeld and Gelman 1994). As we will see throughout the paper, trees are as often the object of cultural representation as of pragmatic interest. As a representative subject, tree symbolism has been the focus of a vast amount of cultural narratives (cf. Brosse 1989; de Souzenelle 1984; Deleuze and Guattari 1976; Demandt 2002; Hageneder 2001; Harrison 1992; Lévi-Strauss 1971; Rival 2001a; Ward 1977). In such narratives, forests serve as habitats of witches, gnomes, or trolls; and they are often represented as places to avoid because they are intuitively associated with fear, misery and with the possibility of harm (Thompson 1958, 308ff.). The other side of the coin is that people are attracted to nature and its multiple features. Trees, flowers, and the view of 'beautiful' landscapes support psychological and physiological well-being (cf. Pinker 1994, 443ff.; Wilson 1991).

Humans' encounter with unfamiliar natural settings appear along with their intuitive assessment about, whether to explore and settle in a novel environment or avoid it and move on to another terrain (cf. Orians and Heerwagen 1992). To enhance survival and reproductive success people must explore, understand and draw inferences about their living space (Kaplan 1992, 587). The selection of habitat therefore involves an emotional response to key elements of the natural setting. Landscapes and natural features that promise to satisfy basic human biological needs evoke a tacit aesthetic pleasure and preference. Preferred environments cause positive feelings and incite an approach behavior (Ruso *et al.* 2003, 280). On a more general level, environmental stimuli arouse tacit feelings like well-being and evoke affective states, such as like or dislike. As argued by renowned sociobiologist Edward O. Wilson, people are likely to prefer "natural settings in which the human mind almost certainly evolved and in which culture has developed over these millions of years of evolution" (Wilson 1991).

A landscape, whether viewed directly or through an artistic or verbal medium (Appleton 1975), thus induces negative or positive appraisal, and people usually do not reflect on why they prefer or dislike a natural setting (Orians and Heerwagen 1992, 555). Landscapes, however, consist of an apparently countless number of natural elements, features or attributes and for human cognition they provide a myriad of stimuli. Gordon Orians and Judith Heerwagen explain that this emotional appraisal is activated by both spatial and temporal factors that motivates rejecting, selecting, exploring or settling a new habitat (Orians and Heerwagen 1992, 561–565). In his seminal book on landscape appreciation, Jay Appleton (1975) addresses two questions: *what* is it that humans like about landscapes, and *why* do they prefer it? Appleton observes that humans are perceptually attuned to landscape configurations like shapes, colours and spatial arrangements to which they spontaneously respond (1975, 69). He further argues that the experience of a landscape incites both a behavioral and an affective response because certain attributes are seemingly perceived by humans as optimum prospects and refuges, both of which are key to self-preservation (Appleton 1975, 70–74). According to Appleton's prospect-refuge theory, elevated, open and visually unrestricted landscapes constitute prospects that enable an organism to survey its environment for predators, while complex, visually impeded, or gloomy and hidden environments constitute refuges in which predators might hide. Appleton thus concludes "that aesthetic pleasure in landscape derives from the observer experiencing an environment favorable to the satisfaction of his biological needs" (1975, 73).

Beginning with John Dewey's classical study of landscape experience and environmental aesthetics (1925), empirical testing has shown that *coherence, complexity, legibility,* and *mystery* determine the emotional attractiveness or the aesthetic value of a landscape (Kaplan 1992, 586ff.). Human aesthetic responses to physical settings are predominantly determined by so-called legible environmental key-features. One must not forget that for survival and reproductive success the human mind is designed to perceive, assess and interpret the social and natural "signals" surrounding him. According to Stephen Kaplan's model, *legibility* signifies that a landscape is open to allow visual access and that the physical environment is patterned by a set of distinctive and salient landmarks or natural signs (Kaplan 1992, 588). Commonly valued contents of a landscape include rock formations, caves, elevations, mountains, bodies of water, plant cover, forest or trees (cf. Ruso, *et al.* 2003, 288). They are independently perceived "signals" that serve as landmarks for orientation. Especially trees (Kaplan 1992, 589) give the scene depth and according to empirical testing evoke both short-term emotional states and long-term experience, such as mood, affective appraisal and emotional disposition (Kaplan 1987; Paz Galindo Galindo and Corraliza Rodríguez 2000; Ruso, *et al.* 2003, 288). Salient landscape features like trees are thus cognitively optimal, because they are interpreted by humans as powerful signals that focus attention, elicit knowledge and increase emotional arousal. Another important key feature in the spatial preference matrix is *mystery* (Kaplan 1987). Mystery in landscape implicates the presence of hidden or additional information and drives humans to further explore a novel environment. Information is the basic need for survival (Boyer 2001, 120); a second is co-operation and communication which enables the exchange of relevant information (cf. Sperber and Wilson 1986).

## Tree Signals

To summarize: a habitat that represents conditions conducive to survival evokes innate biological preferences and, as such, its salient, legible and mystic attributes have a high aesthetic value and positive appraisal (Appleton 1975, 48ff.). In an optimal environment, humans could both retreat in safety and observe the setting for potential predators or promising prey. It follows that knowledge and the communication of information about the physical landscape is likely to spread and become cultural because it is attention-grabbing, highly memorable and strongly linked with survival (Hirschfeld and Gelman 1994, 20). Hirschfeld and Gelman emphasize the importance of vegetation in general and state that the biological world is very often a focus of cultural interest (1994, 21).

A cross-cultural survey by Gerhart Ladner (1979) has shown that cultural representations such as works of art, myths, or narratives, generally exhibit elements that have natural appeal, especially tree and plant motifs. According to Ladner, tree symbolism is a major example since it is an old and widespread cultural representation (cf. 1979). Scanning the folkloristic record (cf. Thompson 1958), one notices that the natural environment and biological diversity are indeed a focus of symbolic attention all over the world and throughout the history of humankind (Appleton 1975, 238–256; Bloch 2001, 1). Furthermore, research findings indicate a special preference for landscapes containing trees and other forms of vegetation (Ulrich 1986, 29). A tree naturalizes possession, marks space, measures time, functions as a genealogical reference point, and ties humans to nature (Crews 2003). Surveying tree symbolism in different societies and cultures, Laura Rival observes that trees are very often represented in order to reify the hard-to-process concept of life because of their status as natural category, or living form (Crews 2003; Rival 2001b, 3). This accords with Scott Atran's conclusion that trees are intuitively assumed to be a living kind which "[p]eople naturally tend to find ... phenomenally compelling because of their evident ecological role in determining local distributions of flora and fauna" (Atran 1990, 35). Cross-cultural data indeed suggests that "tree", like "table" or "mountain," is a kind-concept that intuitively activates higher-level categories of the ontological kinds in the world (Boyer 2000, 196-197). The representation of a "tree," be it viewed directly or through a medium, thus evokes not only semantic knowledge, but also experiences and emotional appraisal linked both to the kind-concept and the associated higher-level category.

## Cultural Stability and Aesthetics Evaluation

The interpretative term "cultural" distinguishes public representations and behaviors that are transmitted from person to person and are widely and durably distributed with minor variation in a social group (cf. Boyer 2000; Sperber 1985). Members of a group share ideas and practices through which they recognize themselves as "performing the same ritual, endorsing the same belief, or eating the same food" (Sperber and Hirschfeld 2004, 40). For group identity to be maintained, only slight alterations are allowable. To become cultural in this sense, a representation or an action must be "naturally easier to generate and to acquire than others" (Whitehouse 2004, 188).

Sperber and Hirschfeld underline the abundance of stable cultural contents in cross-cultural perspective and scrutinize the mental mechanisms that contribute to their stability (Sperber and Hirschfeld 2004, 40). The authors claim that cultural concepts "rely on and exploit a natural disposition" by over-emphasizing specific features that attract attention (Sperber and Hirschfeld 2004, 42). Representations that are linked to survival and reproductive success, like avoiding predators, eating the right food, forming alliances or reading other people's minds, intuitively evoke attractions towards these representations. Using the historical example of tree symbolism in Classic Maya art, I would like to extend this idea and assert that the motif selection of the human symbolic mechanism involves an affective response to natural environment and landscape aesthetics in particular. This is again in accord with Sperber and Hirschfeld claiming that psychological factors play an essential role in cultural diversity and stability. Humans for example assess as "beautiful" those landscapes that include attributes that in the course of phylogenesis have proved to be beneficial for survival. And Sperber further spells out that humans are susceptible to particular types of representations that can be organized taxonomically, especially animals and plants.

I suggest further that the psychological mechanisms governing environmental preference and aesthetics may also affect processes of the evolution, the stabilization, and the transmission of cultural representations. As suggested by Sperber and Hirschfeld, affective responses are central to the stability of thought, meaning and behavior and, thus, should be considered as a variable that effects the spread and endurance of cultural representations. Hirschfeld further argues that the relation between environmental knowledge and human survival may be seen as the foundation for the use of biological diversity in symbolic representation.

## Cross-cultural Perspective of Tree Symbolism

A cross-cultural comparison of folklore and imagery reveals that trees symbolically represent the life processes of living things and stand for the perpetuity and inexhaustibility of the life essence (cf. Crews 2003). Its natural growth phases seemingly reify the hard-to-process concepts of growth, development and death of living things in the most general sense. In many cultures, the vertical morphology of trees, with its roots underground, a single main stem above ground, and foliage stretching toward the sky suggest the concept of a central pole or world-axis standing at the center of the world and supporting the heavenly canopy (Eliade 1958, 77–78). Such "world trees" are believed to run like a pole through this world, often represented as a middle world, with a lower underworld and an upper world or heaven in which supernatural beings reside. Trees thus represent a connection between a lower, middle and upper world by which supernaturals climb up and down to travel from one sphere to another. The tree of life concept is a widespread and old motif in many narratives around the world. In ancient Egyptian mythology, for example, the sycamore fig, *Ficus sycomorus*, was regarded as central tree of life (Bergmann 1979). This genus was the only tree of useful size and hardiness in Egypt and it most often grew along the edge of the desert. Because of its close symbolic relation to the maternal and tree goddesses Nut, Isis, and especially the goddess of life and afterlife, Hathor, fig trees were often placed near tombs and necropolises and many coffins were made of the same wood. Another example of the tree of life comes from Norse mythology. According to the mythological record the central tree was a giant ash tree, *Yggdrasil* whose canopy sheltered the whole world. It nourished gods, humans and all animals and it connected all living things and represented all life processes, like growth and development.

Beliefs in cosmic trees, supporting the sky and being the source of life and prosperity are also found in the Abrahamic religions, as well as in Greek, Persian, Scandinavian, Haitian, Hungarian, Indian, Chinese, Japanese, Siberian folklore (cf. Crews 2003). Among past and present New World societies, the representation of an *axis mundi* is also very common and widespread. In many South American religions related to Shamanism, a mountain or other elevated places, a hollow tube, post or a ladder, where earth surface and sky are perceived to come closest, represent the axis that connects the levels of the cosmos (Cipolletti 1991, 270). This axis is the means by which religious specialists or supernatural beings may transverse the different levels of the cosmos (Townsend 1997, 437). In most modern South American traditions it is explicitly stated that a tree representing the *axis mundi* existed only in ancestral times (Cipolletti 1991, 270). The Maká of Paraguay and the Matako of Argentina, for example, believed that in ancient times people climbed up a large tree in order to go hunting in the profitable hunting grounds of the moon. According to the Maká, the moon defended his possession and cut down the tree. The Matako version of the story explains that the tree was felled by an aged man who felt that the allocation of meat to him was too meager (Cipolletti 1991, 270–271). Cipolletti emphasizes that many modern South American societies still hold a wistful memory of an alleged lost *axis mundi*. It is obvious that this concept represents a form of a "collective regret," a yearning for a lost paradise-like life on earth (Cipolletti 1991, 270).

## Prehispanic Tree Symbolism in Mesoamerica

The generation and distribution of similar ideas, values, norms, techniques and practices throughout time and continents begs for explanations and has been the subject of many studies in anthropology and sociology (Brown 1991). Only few studies of the Americas, however, include in their discussion of cultural processes and dynamics examples from pre-contact societies. Without question, the civilizations of the American continent experienced an independent cultural and historical development before the European conquest that began in the early sixteenth century. Precolumbian civilizations thus enable the examination of cultural mechanisms from a perspective that is definitely independent of Old World influences. This is important for our discussion of the evolution, spread and use of tree representations in New World societies in order to emphasize their universal and stable distribution throughout history and cultures around the world. Among the Pre-Columbian cultures of Mesoamerica the symbolic representation of vegetation in literature and imagery is very common (Heyden 1994; Miller and Taube 1993; Woodford 1953). The symbolic use of trees, shrubs, herbs, maize or fruits is strongly tied to their society and religion (cf. Flores and Kantun Balam 1997; Martin 2006; Peterson 1983; Taube 2001; Woodford 1953). Trees are usually associated with the origin of the cosmos and its organization (cf. Freidel, *et al.* 1993) and with the life cycle (La Farge 1947). And trees form an essential part of the narratives and imagery related to the creation of humankind and to their view of the cosmos (Thompson 1965; Thompson 1967).

Mesoamerica is a cultural area consisting of Belize, Guatemala, El Salvador, Honduras, Nicaragua, Panama, Costa Rica and all but the northern parts of Mexico (Kirchhoff 1943). This area was first populated about 13,500 years ago (Toby Evans and Webster 2001, xiii) and served as habitat to some of the most complex and advanced cultures of the Prehispanic Americas—for example, among many other groups in that area, those related to the Olmec (1200–500 B.C.), the Zapotecs (500 B.C–A.D. 1521), the Mixtecs (A.D. 300–800), the Maya (A.D. 200–900) or the Aztec people (A.D. 1200–1520) (Toby Evans and Webster 2001, ix–xv). These people developed complex sociopolitical structures, reached a high intellectual and technological level, and took part in short and long-distance interaction systems that resulted in the generation and transmission of a great variety of cultural representations that are comparable to Old World civilizations (Coe 2002).

At the end of the Pleistocene and beginning with the arrival of the first hunter-gatherer Paleo-Indians, the climate was mild and the evolutionary landscape was dominated by a savannah-like landscape with thorn-scrub vegetation and some forest cover (Sharer and Traxler 2006, 153ff.). The Archaic period, or the transition from the Pleistocene to Holocene geological epoch at about 8000 B.C. is marked by a gradual, but rapid growth of dense tropical vegetation; this period also saw the beginning of agriculture and the origin of social stratification (Miller and Taube 1993, 9ff.). The Preclassical period from between 2000 B.C. to A.D. 200 is marked by the rise of complex social and political hierarchical organizations. Script, calendar systems, pyramidal platforms, specific ways of subsistence farming and other cultural representations characteristic to the area are materially attested by 500 BC (Coe 1999). Dating to this period, the iconography from San Bartólo in the Central Peten of Guatemala contains the first symbolic representations of trees serving as *axis mundi*. Around A.D. 150 a rapid growth of population occurred in the Maya Lowlands of the Yucatan Peninsula with cultural markers associated with the ancient Maya *per se*. In the Classic Period (A.D. 250–900) the essential political entity was the city-state consisting of a ceremonial center and its surroundings. At the head of state was the hereditary sovereign or *k'uhul ajaw* (Grube 2000) whose bodily attendance was believed to represent the incarnated *axis mundi*. The monumental center was the regal and ritual center of a city-state. It was supported by its surrounding lands inhabited mainly by farmers who had to render tribute to the court (Sharer and Traxler 2006). Without doubt, the invention of writing and its widespread and long use prior to the arrival of the Spaniards is deemed to be one of the most remarkable cultural representations of the Classic Maya. The script was primarily carved on monumental sculptures as well as on portable objects, and painted on ceramic vessels. The hieroglyphic texts and imagery, complemented by archaeological data, colonial period reports and modern ethnographic fieldwork, are thus the principal means of reconstructing the ancient Maya world and the peoples' minds.

Maya iconography abounds in anthropomorphisms (cf. Benson 1988; Houston, *et al.* 2006). It also features flora and fauna exhibiting a multiplicity of animal representations (Tozzer and Allen 1910), as well as vegetation like flowers, maize, watery plants or tree motifs in particular (Kubler 1969; Robicsek 1978; Spinden 1913). The abundant botanical imagery reflects the stupendous vegetation of the tropical environment which stands out for its rich variation (Marcus 1982; Miller and Taube 1993). As for the meaning of trees in the daily life the Classic Maya, Linda Schele explains that "for the Maya, trees constitute the ambient living environment, the material from which they fashioned homes and tools, the source of many foods, medicines, dyes, and vital commodities such as paper. They provided the fuel for cooking fires and soil-enriching ash that came from the cutting and burning of the forest. Trees were the source of shade in the courtyards and public places of villages and cities, and the home of the teeming life of the forest" (Schele and Freidel 1990, 90).

Like many other botanical representations in Classic Maya art, trees are stylized and in most cases their rendering resembles a capital Y or T. Sometimes they are even depicted as cross-shaped (Beauvois 1902). The morphology of the leaves, buds, fruits, blossoms, bark or other diagnostic features usually help to identify the species of the individual tree depicted (Zidar 2006). An iconographical survey shows that the first complex appearance of the tree motif can be traced back to around 200 B.C. to the newly discovered murals of the Early Classic Maya site of San Bartólo (cf. Saturno and Taube 2004; Stuart 2005). Thenceforward, trees are of crucial importance to Mesoamerican and Maya worldviews (Miller and Taube 1993, 57). According to various Maya cosmological beliefs, the shape of the cosmos resembles a Maya apsidal house with four poles and palm thatch on a timber frame and with fairly straight front and rear walls (cf. Freidel, *et al.* 1993). The main posts consist of four stout, forked posts, one driven into the ground at each corner of a rectangle. Similarly, altars, which form the center of most rituals among the Yucatec Maya, are made of four poles and vines resembling a small, rustic and rectangular table. Many Maya groups believe that the cosmos has a similar structure, a notion that is also portrayed on polychrome murals in an Early Classic tomb from Rio Azul (Adams 1986). Each wall of this rectangular-shaped cosmos is associated with a specific cardinal direction. According to the Prehispanic, colonial and modern sources, cardinal directions were and still are associated with a broad spectrum of things from the natural and cultural world (Miller and Taube 1993, 78ff). One of the most important and pervasive of these embodiments of the cardinal directions was world trees, each oriented to a specific direction and associated with a specific color.

Among the modern Maya, trees are regarded as focal points in landscape (Lamb 1995). In the dense tropical forests the indigenous people get their bearings by trees in particular, and by other focal points, such as rock formations, depressions or caves. With the Spanish military, political and religious conquest in the sixteenth century, the tree motif became assimilated to the Christian cross, although it is still retained its function as a marker of the world corners and as a boundary between the wild or uncivilized on one side and the cultivated or civilized world on the other side. The Mam or Kanjobal Maya, for example, viewed crosses as conventionalized trees (Oakes 1951). In the Kanjobal community of Santa Eulalia a set of functionally different crosses were erected and revered (La Farge 1947). The great cross right next to the Catholic church marks the center of the village and was venerated as a local deity.

## Conclusion

It has been argued in this paper that tree symbolism is indeed a widespread and stable cultural representation through space and time. On the basis on Sperber's and Hirschfeld's ideas on the mechanisms constraining the stability of cultural representations (Sperber and Hirschfeld 2004), it has been explained that psychological factors like aesthetic evaluation and affective appraisal are essential for the spread and cultural stability of tree symbolism around the world. Experimental studies by Gordon Orians show that landscape or habitat preferences are both biological adaptations and behavioral responses molded by evolution of which humans are not aware (Orians and Heerwagen 1992). Orians claims that humans are capable of processing innately environmental events as positive or negative and/or good or bad for their interest. Landscape psychology and studies of evolutionary aesthetics indicate that humans have an innate preference for savannah-like environments (cf. Orians and Heerwagen 1992; Ruso, *et al.* 2003), a preference for bodies of water, for trees as structural and patterning components, for focal points, semi-open spaces, changes in elevations, unobstructed view of the horizon, plant growth and moderate complexity. According to Ruso, Renninger and Atzwanger (2003), this type of landscape is related to a feeling of safety and establish one landscape as more attractive than another. As for trees, bole height and crown configuration are indeed important attributes in the aesthetic assessment (Coss 2003). Furthermore, Ulrich shows that trees and plants in general have a positive effect on psychological and physiological well-being (Ulrich 1986). The apparent preference for savanna-like environments and the positive judgment of trees may be a key for understanding its stable and widespread use as a representation in the symbolic mechanism of the human mind.

## References

Adams, Richard E.W. 1986. "Río Azúl: Lost City of the Maya." *National Geographic Magazine* 169(4): 420–451.

Appleton, Jay. 1975. *The Experience of Landscape.* Chichester: John Wiley and Sons.

Atran, Scott. 1990. *The Cognitive Foundations of Natural History: Towards an Anthropology of Science.* Cambridge: Cambridge University Press.

Beauvois, Eugène. 1902. "Les croix précolombiennes chez les Mayas du Yucatan et des contrées voisines." *Revue des Questions Scientifiques* 2: 93–124.

Benson, Elizabeth P. ed. 1988. *Maya Iconography.* Princeton, NJ: Princeton University Press.

Bergmann, Jan. 1979. Nut - Himmelsgöttin - Baumgöttin - Lebensgeberin. In *Religious Symbols and Their Functions,* edited by H. Biezais, 53–59. Scripta Instituti Donneriani Aboensis vol. 10. Stockholm: Almqvist and Wiksell International.

Bloch, Maurice. 2001. "Why Trees, Too, Are Good to Think With: Towards an Anthropology of the Meaning of Life." In *The Social Life of Trees: Anthropological Perspectives on Tree Symbolism.* L. Rival, 39–56. Oxford: Berg.

Bowen, John R. 1997. *Religions in Practice: An Approach to the Anthropology of Religion.* Needham Heights: Allyn and Bacon.

Boyer, Pascal. 1999. Cultural Symbolism. In *The MIT Encyclopedia of the Cognitive Sciences,* edited by R.A. Wilson and F.C. Keil, 216–217. Cambridge, MA: The MIT Press.

———. 2000. "Functional Origins of Religious Concepts: Ontological and Strategic Selection in Evolved Minds." *The Journal of the Royal Anthropological Institute Incorporating Man* 6 (2): 195–214.

———. 2001. *Religion Explained: The Evolutionary Origins of Religious Thought.* New York: Basic Books.

Brosse, Jacques. 1989. *Mythologie des arbres.* Paris: Plon.

Brown, Donald E. 1991. *Human Universals.* Philadelphia, PA: Temple University Press.

Buss, David M. 2004. *Evolutionäre Psychologie.* Munich: Pearson Studium.

Cipolletti, María Susana. 1991. "Schamanismus und die Reise ins Totenreich—Religiöse Vorstellungen der Indianer des südamerikanischen Tieflands." In *Geschichte der religiösen Ideen,* III/2: Vom Zeitalter der Entdeckungen bis zur Gegenwart. edited by M. Eliade and I.P. Cilianu, 265–290. Freiburg: Herder.

Coe, Michael D. 2002. *Mexico: From the Olmecs to the Aztecs.* London: Thames and Hudson.

———. 1999. *The Maya.* London: Thames and Hudson.

Coss, Richard G. 2003. "The Role of Evolved Perceptual Biases in Art and Design." In *Evolutionary Aesthetics.* edited by Eckart Voland and Karl Grammer, 69–130. Berlin: Springer.

Crews, Judith. 2003. "Forest and Tree Symbolism in Folklore." *Unasylva* 54(213): 37–43.

de Souzenelle, Annick. 1984. *Le symbolisme du corps humain: De l'arbre de vie au schéma corporel.* St. Jean de Braye: Édition Dangles.

Deleuze, Gilles and Félix Guattari. 1976. *Rhizome: introduction.* Paris: Les Editions de Minuit.

Demandt, Alexander. 2002. *Über allen Wipfeln: Der Baum in der Kulturgeschichte.* Cologne: Böhlau.

Dewey, John. 1925. *Experience and Nature.* London: Allen and Unwin.

Eliade, Mircea. 1958. *Rites and Symbols of Initiation.* New York: Harper.

Flores, José Salvador and Jesús Kantun Balam. 1997. "Importance of Plants in the Ch'a Chaak Maya Ritual in the Peninsula of Yucatan." *Journal of Ethnobiology* 17(1): 97–108.

Freidel, David, Linda Schele and Joy Parker. 1993. *Maya Cosmos: Three Thousand Years on the Shaman's Path.* New York: William Morrow.

Grube, Nikolai. 2000. "The City-States of the Maya." In *A Comparative Study of Thirty City-State Cultures.* edited by M.H. Hansen, 547–565. Historisk-filosofiske Skrifter, vol. 21. Copenhagen: Det Kongelige Danske Videnskabernes Selskab.

Hageneder, Fred. 2001. *The Heritage of Trees: History, Culture and Symbolism.* Edinburgh: Floris Books.

Harrison, Robert P. 1992. *Forests: The Shadow of Civilization.* Chicago, IL: University of Chicago Press.

Haviland, William A. 1997. *Anthropology.* Fort Worth, TX: Harcourt Brace College Publishers.

Heyden, Doris. 1994. "Trees and Wood in Life and Death." In *Chipping Away on Earth: Studies in Prehispanic and Colonial Mexico in Honor of Arthur J. O. Anderson and Charles E. Dibble.* edited by E. Quiñones Keber, 143–152. Lancaster: Labyrinthos.

Hirschfeld, Lawrence A. and Susan A. Gelman. 1994. "Toward a Topography of Mind: An Introduction to Domain Specificity." In *Mapping the Mind: Domain Specificity in Cognition and Culture.* edited by L.A. Hirschfeld and S.A. Gelman, 3–35. Cambridge: Cambridge University Press.

Houston, Stephen D., David Stuart and Karl A. Taube. 2006. *The Memory of Bones: Body, Being, and Experience Among the Classic Maya*. Austin: University of Texas Press.

Kaplan, Rachel and Stephen Kaplan. 1989. *The Experience of Nature*. New York: University Press.

Kaplan, Stephen. 1987. "Aethetics, Affect, and Cognition: Environmental Preference from an Evolutionary Perspective." *Environment and Behavior* 19(1): 3–32.

———. 1992. "Environmental Preference in a Knowledge-Seeking, Knowledge-Using Organism." In *The Adapted Mind: Evolutionary Psychology and the Generation of Culture,* edited by J.H. Barkow, L. Cosmides and J. Tooby, 581–598. Oxford: Oxford University Press.

Kirchhoff, Paul. 1943. "Mesoamérica, sus límites geográficos, composición étnica y carácteres culturales." *Acta Americana* 1: 92–107.

Kubler, George. 1969. *Studies in Classic Maya Iconography,* vol. 18. New Haven, CT: Academy of Arts and Sciences.

La Farge, Olivier. 1947. *Santa Eulalia: The Religion of a Cuchumatán Indian Town*. Chicago, IL: University of Chicago Press.

Ladner, Gerhart B. 1979. "Medieval and Modern Understanding of Symbolism: A Comparison." *Speculum* 54(2): 223–256.

Lamb, Weldon. 1995. "Tzotzil Maya Cosmology." *Tribus* 44: 268–279.

LeCron Foster, Mary. 1994. "Symbolism: The Foundations of Culture." In *Companion Encyclopedia of Anthropology: Humanity, Culture and Social Life,* edited by T. Ingold, 366–395. London: Routledge.

Lévi-Strauss, Claude. 1971. *Mythologiques 4: l'homme nu*. Paris: Plon.

Marcus, Joyce. 1982. "The Plant World of the Sixteenth and Seventeenth-Century Lowland Maya." In *Maya Subsistence. Studies in Memory of Dennis E. Puleston,* edited by K.V. Flannery, 239–274. New York: Academic Press.

Martin, Simon. 2006. "Cacao in Ancient Maya Religion: First Fruit from the Maize Tree and Other Tales from the Underworld." In *Chocolate in Mesoamerica: A Cultural History of Cacao,* edited by C.L. McNeil, 154–183. Gainsville: University Press of Florida.

Miller, Mary and Karl A. Taube. 1993. *The Gods and Symbols of Ancient Mexico and the Maya: An Illustrated Dictionary of Mesoamerican Religion*. London: Thames and Hudson.

Oakes, Maud. 1951. *The Two Crosses of Todos Santos: Survivals of Maya Religious Ritual,* vol. 27. New York: Pantheon Books.

Orians, Gordon H. and Judith H. Heerwagen. 1992. "Evolved Responses to Landscapes." In *The Adapted Mind: Evolutionary Psychology and the Generation of Culture,* edited by J.H. Barkow, L. Cosmides and J. Tooby, 555–579. Oxford: Oxford University Press.

Paz Galindo Galindo, Maria and José Antonio Corraliza Rodríguez. 2000. "Environmental Aesthetics and Psychological Wellbeing: Relationships Betweenn Preference Judgments for Urban Landscapes and Other Relevant Affective Responses." *Psychology in Spain* 4(1): 13–27.

Peterson, Jeannette F., ed. 1983. *Flora and Fauna Imagery in Precolumbian Cultures: Iconography and Function,* vol. 171. Oxford: John and Erica Hedges.

Pinker, Steven. 1994. *The Language Instinct: How the Mind Creates Language*. New York: William Morrow.

Ramachandran, Vilnayapur S. and William Hirstein. 1999. "The Science of Art: A Neurological Theory of Aesthetic Experience." *Journal of Consciousness Studies* 6(6–7): 15–51.

Rival, Laura, ed. 2001a. *The Social Life of Trees: Anthropological Perspectives on Tree Symbolism*. Oxford: Berg.

———. 2001b. "Trees, from Symbol of Life and Regeneration to Political Artefacts." In *The Social Life of Trees: Anthropological Perspectives on Tree Symbolism,* edited by L. Rival, 1–36. Oxford: Berg.

Robicsek, Francis. 1978. *The Smoking Gods: Tobacco in Maya Art, History, and Religion*. Norman: University of Oklahoma Press.

Ruso, Bernhard, LeeAnn Renninger and Klaus Atzwanger. 2003. "Human Habitat Preferences: A Generative Territory for Evolutionary Aesthetics Research." In *Evolutionary Aesthetics,* edited by Eckart Voland and Karl Grammer, 279–294. Berlin: Springer.

Saturno, William A. and Karl A. Taube. 2004. "Hallazgo: las excepcionales pinturas de San Bartolo, Guatemala." *Arqueología Mexicana* 11(66): 34–35.

Schele, Linda and David Freidel. 1990. *A Forest of Kings: The Untold Story of the Ancient Maya*. New York: William Morrow.

Sharer, Robert J. and Loa P. Traxler. 2006. *The Ancient Maya*. Stanford: Stanford University Press.

Sperber, Dan. 1975. *Rethinking Symbolism*. Cambridge: Cambridge University Press.

———. 1985. "Anthropology and Psychology: Towards an Epidemiology of Representations." *Man* 20: 73–89.

———. 1993. "Interpreting and Explaining Cultural Representations." In *Beyond Boundaries: Understanding, Translation and Anthropological Discourse,* edited by G. Pálsson, 162–183. Explorations in Anthropology. Oxford: Berg.

Sperber, Dan and Lawrence A. Hirschfeld. 2004. "The Cognitive Foundations of Cultural Stability and Diversity." *Trends in Cognitive Sciences* 9(1): 40–46.

Sperber, Dan and Deirdre Wilson. 1986. *Relevance: Communication and Cognition*. Oxford: Blackwell.

Spinden, Herbert Joseph. 1913. *A Study of Maya Art: Its Subject Matter and Historical Development,* vol. 6. Cambridge: Peabody Museum of American Archaeology and Ethnology, Harvard University.

Stuart, George E. 2005. *The Murals of San Bartolo, El Petén, Guatemala—Part 1: The North Wall,* vol. 7. Barnardsville: Center for Ancient American Studies.

Taube, Karl A. 2001. "Maize: Iconography and Cosmological Significance." In *The Oxford Encyclopedia of Mesoamerican Cultures: The Civilizations of Mexico and Central America*, vol. 2: edited by D. Carrasco, 150–152. Oxford: Oxford University Press.

Thompson, J. Eric S. 1965. "Maya Creation Myths: Part 1." *Estudios de Cultura Maya* 5: 13–32.

———. 1967. "Maya Creation Myths: Part 2." *Estudios de Cultura Maya* 6: 15–43.

Thompson, Stith. 1958. *Motif-Index of Folk-Literature: A Classification of Narrative Elements in Folktales, Ballads, Myths, Fables, Mediaeval Romances, Exempla, Fabliaux, Jest-Books, and Local Legends,* vol. 6, Index. Copenhagen: Rosenkilde and Bagger.

Toby Evans, Susan and David L. Webster, eds. 2001. *Archaeology of Ancient Mexico and Central America: An Encyclopedia*. New York: Garland Publishing.

Townsend, Joan B. 1997. "Shamanism." In *Anthropology of Religion: A Handbook,* edited by S.D. Glazier, 429–470. Westport, CT: Greenwood Press.

Tozzer, Alfred Marston and Glover M. Allen. 1910. *Animal Figures in the Maya Codices,* vol. 4(3). Cambridge: Peabody Museum of American Archaeology and Ethnology, Harvard University.

Ulrich, Roger S. 1986. "Human Responses to Vegetation and Landscapes." *Landscape and Urban Planning* 13: 29–44.

Ward, Donald. 1977. "Baum." In *Enzyklopädie des Märchens: Handwörterbuch zur historischen und vergleichenden Erzählforschung,* vol. 1, edited by K. Ranke, W. Brückner, M. Lüthi, L. Röhrich and R. Schenda, 1366–1374. Berlin: Walter de Gruyter.

Whitehouse, Harvey. 2004. "Toward a Comparative Anthropology of Religion." In *Ritual and Memory: Toward a Comparative Anthropology of Religion,* edited by H. Whitehouse and J. Laidlaw, 187–205. Walnut Creek, CA: Altamira.

Wilson, Edward O. 1991. "Arousing Biophilia: A Conversation with E. O. Wilson." *Orion Magazine*, Winter 1991

Woodford, Irene B. 1953. "Tree of Life in Ancient America." *Bulletin of the Brigham Young University Archaeological Society* 4: 1–18.

Zidar, Charles. 2006. *Ancient Maya Botanical Research.* http, //research.famsi.org/botany/index.php.

## — 6 —

## No Time to Philosophize? Norwegian Oral Tradition and the Cognitive Economics of Belief

Dirk Johannsen

### Introduction: The Oral Tradition

In Norway, the oral tradition with its legends, fairy tales and ballads has been collected extensively since the 1830s. In the broader context of the nation-building programme following Danish rule, the narrative skills of the traditional storytellers, the richness of their repertoires, and their knowledge of the local history were discovered as a national treasure (Hodne 1995). The mind that found its expression in the stories told, however, remained suspect. Greeted as the heritage from the kingdoms period of independence and power during the Middle Ages, it came with a pagan and superstitious imprint that seemed opposed to the pursuits of a progressive nation (Dorson 1964). With the growing number of legends about spirits and ghosts, divination and witchcraft, the questions concerning the age, nature, and social relevance of this type of tradition grew as well. The connection between an elaborate and ingenious storytelling culture and a seemingly primitive "folk belief" became the subject of debate.

The supernatural entities receiving most of the attention within this debate were the Hidden People (*huldrefolk*), who were known by various names all over the country and dominated a large number of the stories told. Closely related to the *vættir* and elves of the Old Norse literature, they were said to look like humans, only that they would rarely be seen, as they live within the mountains, under the ground, or on invisible farms. Turning up every now and then, the legends give broad accounts of how they abducted people from the local community or caused some other sort of mischief. Still, they were in no way solely depicted as negative. The legends articulate a fascination about their beauty and power that would provide a positive reason for the routinized food offerings which, much to the displeasure of the established church, had been a widespread custom among the peasants for several centuries.

The church started fighting this type of commitment as early as in the thirteenth century, with the oldest Norwegian legal texts prohibiting offerings or contact to "the spirits of the woods, hills and rivers" as part of a larger package of laws directed against pagan forms of worship.[1] During the period of witch-hunts in the sixteenth and seventeenth centuries, contact with Hidden People sometimes became a topic, as it was thought of as a way to obtain magical powers.[2] The evidence concerning the social significance of such concepts in former times, however, remains somewhat unclear, as the Catholic Church in the late Middle Ages referred to it only in demonological categories and as the early Lutheran church did not make much of the differences between Pre-Christian beliefs and remainders of Catholic piety. Both were categorized as pagan superstition and considered of no interest other than something to be disposed of. The idea of a prevalent "folk belief" emerged only by the end of the seventeenth century, when pietism became a major current in the Danish Church. With its new criterion of an inward understanding of Christianity, the Norwegian peasants were soon identified as merely "baptized pagans" (Amundsen 2005). Key persons like Bishop Erik Pontoppidan (1698–1764) began to take an interest in what appeared to be the source of persistent rumours or even heresy. Comprehensive lists of different species of supernatural entities were compiled, summarizing their characteristics and typical episodes were told about them. In this way, "folk belief" was invented as a broad and doctrinal system in opposition to the Christian faith.

Recent cultural studies have emphasized the artificial character of the notion of "folk belief" by pointing out that the tradition as found in the eighteenth and nineteenth centuries was deeply interwoven with Christianity. To capture its dynamic character, the concept of "folk religiosity" was introduced (Eriksen 1993), denoting a form of religiosity "more open and capable of variation than the different forms of institutionalized religion would facilitate" (Skjelbred 1995, 68). Concerning the supernatural entities, Arne Bugge Amundsen recently argued that when looking at the tradition in its historical context, it "becomes relevant to ask if it makes sense to speak of 'belief' in relation to such concepts" (Amundsen 2005, 270). Although there was a broad consensus that entities and powers other than those represented by the Christian faith existed, most people probably just took them for granted and dealt with them as good Christians.

With the identification of supernatural entities as counterintuitive concepts (see below), a similar debate originated in the cognitive science of religion. Why some counterintuitive agents become the object of serious commitment, while others are seen as less relevant or are not even considered to be real is the question referred to as the "Mickey Mouse problem"; the anthropomorphic mouse being a counterintuitive agent evoking rather little religious commitment (cf. Tremlin 2006, 107–142).

In the following, I will use related findings of the cognitive science of religion to analyze the oral tradition and the belief in the Hidden People as it was documented in the Norwegian province Telemark.[3] As the legends are the only comprehensive source of the historical tradition and beliefs, and were the basic vehicle for the transmission and eventual formation of related concepts and ideas, my approach is one of cognitive narratology. Looking at the narrative context rather than distinct concepts allows us to see how the supernatural

---

1.  *Gulatingslov* c. 32, *Frostatingslov* c. 45, *Landslov* IV.4 . All translations are mine.

2.  A well documented example from the Telemark is the trial against the 'wise woman' Ragnhild Ohls-datter in 1662 (*Bratsberg Amt, dok. 1564–1789, pk. 352; Byregnskaper Skien, J 10, 1655–1727,* Norsk Riksarkivet).

3.  This article is based on research of published and unpublished material collected from the Telemark municipalities Seljord, Hjartdal, Sauherad, and Notodden.

was presented and what possible meanings might be deduced from the stories. Identifying mental systems and cognitive mechanisms utilized by the tradition allows accounting for dominating and recurring traits in mythical folklore.[4]

It is necessary to emphasise that, in the local context, telling legends was considered an art. Although storytelling "seems to be a fundamental feature of human existence" (Sjöblom 2005, 235) and legends are often referred to as a typical example of everyday narrative discourse, it was mainly in the hands of some local specialists to constitute the basic forms and to set up or refresh the basic parameters of the narrative tradition (Bø, Grambo, B. Hodne, Ø. Hodne 1995: 11–60). To focus the analysis accordingly, the collection *Tussar og Trolldom* (roughly: *Hidden People and Sorcery*) by Kjetil A. Flatin (1881–1916) is used as the basic reference (Flatin 1930). Born in Seljord, Flatin was a storyteller himself and locally acknowledged as a master in his field. He was praised for having "captured the characteristics of elocution in writing," creating a "precise and good reproduction" of the traditional style (Flatin 1917, iii; Flatin 1930, 5–7). Both his mastery of the art as well as his reliability concerning phrasing and content is confirmed by comparisons to materials from other collections as well as historical documents.

## Domain Violations and their Narrative Context

Both the richness of the tradition as well as the technical skills of the narrators can be illustrated by applying Pascal Boyer's conceptual "catalogue of the supernatural" (Boyer 2003) to the collections of local legends. Boyer's underlying theory proposes that in the course of evolution the human cognitive system was equipped with a sort of "mental catalogue of the things that are around us" (Boyer 2002, 114). Instead of starting from zero with every sensory stimulus we get, we come equipped with certain ontological expectations. This "intuitive ontology" prestructures our perception, directs our attention and prepares for adequate behaviour. Boyer suggests the ontological categories "person," "animal," "plant," "artefact," and "natural object," each allow some "default inferences" concerning their basic physical, biological and psychological properties. If, for example, we see a resting mammal, even of a kind we have not seen before, we expect—different from seeing a plant—that it could jump up and move. The same goes for persons, except that we instantly attribute differentiated mental states to them as our hardwired social interaction schemes become activated. A violation of these type expectations is always attention demanding and worth a story:

> Every summer, the wife and daughters of the old Leidulv Meaas were out on the Tjønn-pasture with their cattle for a long time. One evening, an ugly old woman nobody knew scrambled through the door of the chalet. She had a small basket in her hands, with silver jewellery and other oddities she asked the women to buy. But they wouldn't bargain with her. 'Where do you live?' they asked. 'I live down in the crowberry mount', she answered, whereupon she vanished right before their eyes. (Flatin 1930, 62)

The old woman is thought of and dealt with as a person with intentional states of mind and an ordinary biology (e.g., we would assume that if somebody stabbed her she would

---

4. The lack of the performative aspects in written collections, in folklore studies often referred to as a major obstacle to narratological approaches, is at least to some extend ignorable when concerned with basic mechanism of story processing, as higher level word processing has been shown to work rather similar in reading and listening (Chee *et al.* 1999; cf. Eysenck and Keane 2005, 359).

| Ontological categories | Intuitive-knowledge-domain violations | | |
|---|---|---|---|
| | Psychology | Biology | Physics |
| **Person** | Diviners | A girl with a horsetail (*Guro Rysserova*) | Invisible People (*huldrefolk*) |
| **Animal** | A talking cat | A pig-headed chicken | A bird that can't be shot (*troll*-bird) |
| **Plant** | A tree protecting a farm | A tree bleeding (after being shot at) | Trees floating upside down in the air |
| **Artefact** | An evil book, creating misfortunes (*Svartebok*) | Bleeding butter (*trollsmør*) | Coins duplicating (*tussepenger*) |
| **Natural Object** | A whispering fjord | A stone formed like a chair jumping around | A mountain opening up |

Table 6.1   Examples of domain violations in *Tussar og Trolldom* by Kjetil A. Flatin. Layout adapted from Barrett 2000.

bleed). By vanishing in the middle of the room, however, she counters our intuition concerning her physical properties. Taken out of its narrative context, when reported as true, the incident gives rise to serious theological and philosophical questions, as they were often addressed in clerical critiques of popular beliefs. But while processing the story, our on-line thinking is not concerned with them as it stays attached to the scheme with intuitions of folk psychology, folk biology and folk physics processed separately. Still, after her vanishing, we tend to think of the woman as being biologically alive (e.g., a knife thrown into midair would still harm her, as several other legends report) and attribute coherent mental states to her (e.g., we could suspect her of being disappointed or angry not to have sold something). The concluding domain violation is, therefore, conceived not as a breach with the given situation but only as increasing the amount of possible inferences that might be drawn from the episode dramatically. Invisible, the Hidden People might be around at any time, knowing what is said and done. They have full access to strategic social information and thus there will always be a reason for them to cause mischief or to do a good deed—and they always have the possibility to carry it out unnoticed (Boyer 2002b). In this way, the everyday ups and downs of life find a universal explanation. All sorts of events can be related to each other, and an infinite number of stories can be told. The story of the rejected hawker soon connects to a burning barn, while in another story a person's heartiness and sincerity might ensure a good harvest, with the Hidden People helping unseen. With their counterintuitive properties, the Hidden People become "immediately salient and especially relevant to human life," as they have "unique access to what matters most to minds like ours—strategic information and personal moral qualities" (Tremlin 2006, 120).

Counterintuitiveness produced by breaches or transfers of expectations in the intuitive domains of knowledge have been identified as the common denominator of supernatural concepts in their entirety (Pyysiäinen 2002). Table 6.1 shows that the Norwegian oral tradition makes regular use of the full spectrum: a collection like Kjetil A. Flatin's *Tussar og Trolldom* alone includes every possible domain violation. The narrators were adept at diversifying attention-gripping ideas throughout the legends, and neatly confining them to minimally counterintuitive concepts, violating only one intuition at a time.

Domain violations that concern intentional agents and furthermore lead to an increase in the agent's access to social strategic information are the most common. Flatin's collection *Tussar og Trolldom* consists of 122 subchapters, all of which are concerned with several episodes about a certain farm, an individual, or a concept. In total, I counted 213 domain violations made explicit:[5] 72% belong to the person category, with 60% of the total domain violations leading to an increased access to social strategic information, mostly by thought-reading or invisibility in the way described above. Connected concepts like the invisible cattle and farms of the Hidden People account for another 10%, leaving 18% to sporadic or unique concepts. Slightly more than one third of the episodes (35%) contain no domain violation at all.

As can be seen from this distribution, not all types of counterintuitivity are used equivalently in the oral tradition. In the narrative context, domain violations are utilized as a multi-purpose tool. They provide not so much a diversity of independent concepts but a golden thread and serve as a reason for conflict or its climax. Especially, types from the ontological categories plant, artefact, and natural object are often introduced as a sensational climax, something to make otherwise very similar motifs recognizable. Dancing furniture or forests suddenly teeming with intestines only illustrate the unfathomable might of a special sorcerer. Their incredibility is even underlined, as they are meant to highlight the episode as unique. Other counterintuitive concepts are basically used as an interchangeable narrative aid. Survey articles about Norwegian folk belief generally state that *huldra* (or the female *tusse*) is thought of as a woman with a cow's tail. This catchy blending of ontological categories was first accentuated by some of the early folklorists and, later on, made a favoured motive for painters like Theodor Kittelsen and, finally, became a sort of symbol for the Norwegian folk tradition. However, in the more authentic collections we find the tail to serve less as an attribute than an artifice necessary for certain plot structures. The moment a protagonist catches a glimpse of the tail on an otherwise perfectly normal person, he realizes whom he is dealing with and thus a dramatic conflict is initiated. Any further interaction would mean risking one's humaneness and eternal beatitude. If not needed for the plot, it is not mentioned, and the protagonist might even have intercourse with a *huldre* but remain clueless until one day his own child vanishes right before his eyes.

In this way, most types of counterintuitivity become meaningful only within their specific narrative context. As the title of Flatin's collection already indicates, the Hidden People (*tussar*) and magic or sorcery (*trolldom*) are the only discrete concepts already postulated by the local tradition he reproduces. For the legends to be conceived as factual truth, the audience must only believe in this substrate. The rich variety of domain violations is only a subordinate consequence of the narrative form, its constraints and ornamentations, and might be the subject of discussion, but does not affect the credibility of the tradition in general. Accordingly, the Hidden People and sorcery received the most attention in how they were depicted and argued for. Their existence is crucial to the oral tradition.

## The Case of the Hidden People

The existence of the Hidden People was subject to a well-documented historical debate originating in the late eighteenth century, when enlightenment became the major intellectual current within the Danish Church. The system of folk belief invented during the pietistic period was more and more interpreted as a systematic misunderstanding of the laws of nature. Ignorance took the place of pagan depravity as the primary cause for the-

---

5.  Parenthetical mentions of concepts like the *huldrefolk* were ignored, as long as no damain violation occurred. All instances are told as if facts. Percentage given is rounded to the nearest whole percent.

ological incorrectness. Outstanding in this line of argument was bishop Peder Hansen (1746–1810), who by the end of the eighteenth century asked his priests to write down the folk stories they heard, so that he could comment on them in his *Archiv for Skolevæsenets og Oplysnings Udbredelse i Christiansands Stift* (Archive for the Propagation of Education and Enlightenment in the Kristiansand Diocese). He formulated what can be seen as an early attempt to rationalize rather than to judge the tradition: "What is more natural," he asked, than seeing Hidden People? A "heated imagination and a heated blood lead us to hear and see, both awake and while dreaming, what occupies our thoughts. Is there any need for other entities?" Both hopes and fears would trigger misperceptions that reconfirm the legends and ensure that "there is never a lack of something to talk about."[6] Equipped with this type of argument, Hansen hoped his priests would get rid of the "laughable superstitions" by using the catechisation (i.e., the examination of the congregation following the service) as a stage for continuing education in these matters. How successful the objections were communicated becomes obvious by a look at the legends collected a few decades afterwards. The overconfident priest or schoolmaster giving a derogatory speech to rationalize the supernatural entities had become a frequent motif. Only a terrifying encounter would finally "convert" him and lead him to confess that there is more than meets the eye. Besides these comic episodes, several more surprising responses were given as well: "Fair enough," sensory perception was prone to error, "but what is gained by not believing in Hidden People?" Creatures produced by the mind, however natural, seemed even harder to deal with: "those fantasmata, as the schoolmaster called them, seem terrifying beasts nobody can protect themselves from" (Landstad 1926, 65). Or as phrased in the account of a man who ran into a whole group of "real Hidden People" one day: "There was no time to philosophize." (J. Særsland in Nes 1991, 15). Agents could be interacted with immediately, nature and fantasy must be explained.

From this extract of the early debate concerned with the nature of folk belief, a very simple type of experience is suggested to reconfirm and stabilize the oral tradition. If at least some people, while taking part in the tradition, were able to rate the belief in supernatural entities as an act of cognitive parsimony, it indicates how common they thought the related experiences to be. There was no need for extraordinary events, ecstatic visions or traumatic encounters. Very similar to Hansen's argument, a natural bias for "hyperactive agency detection," that is, for an over-attribution of agency to the surroundings, has been identified in the cognitive science of religion as a significant factor for producing or reconfirming concepts of counterintuitive agents (Barrett 2004). From an evolutionary perspective, detecting agents, which could turn out to be predators, as early as possible is a cognitive capacity crucial for the survival of the species (Guthrie 1993). Non-reflective interpretations of ambiguous sensory input as "caused by or being an agent" (Barrett 2004, 31) are, in other words, ordinary cognitive mechanisms that, however, eventually produces mistaken attribution of agency to natural phenomena and objects as well. Out in the dark woods, with cracking branches, squalls, and leaves rustling, it would require a notable cognitive effort to verify all evidence for the detection of possible agents. In many cases, assuming Hidden People may serve as the more economic cognitive strategy to coordinate attention and behaviour, as it requires notably less computational effort: "we spontaneously create these interpretations anyway" (Boyer 2002b, 75). First hand accounts (memorates)

----

6.    Reprinted in Amundsen and Eriksen (1999, 9–15). The Telemark was a part of Kristansand Diocese until 1925.

from people who claimed an encounter with the Hidden People in many cases conform to this mechanism. Typically, we hear little to nothing about the entities involved, but much about the perceptual processing:

> One autumn, I was out hunting and spent the night beneath Skarfjell. [...] Suddenly I awoke to a horrible noise, coming from Verheim or Vomstul, coming closer and closer. Sometimes it sounded higher, sometimes deeper, screaming, howling, roaring. I took my rifle—now I was in midst of that noise, but I didn't shoot. It went over to Meheidfjell and vanished. I think it was the oskorei. (Stranna 1925, 563; translation by the author)

The *oskorei* is the Norwegian variant of the Wild Host, mostly identified as a host of Hidden People riding through the air. The narrative focus is strictly on recreating the sensory input by connecting landmarks to a diffuse auditory image. It is "show, don't tell." The supernatural concept serves merely as a lexical label, subsuming this kind of experience and its complex impression. In the legends, similar principles are utilized to create a similar experience just listening to the story.

## To Lift the Weight of Disbelief: The Economics of Narrative Processing

The oral tradition is not based on individual cases of misperception or a hyperactive attribution of agency, however common, but it makes use of analogous cognitive mechanisms. Misperceptions may function as evidence but they are in no way necessary since the stories told already provide the experiences to be explained. They produce the cognitive effort that counterintuitive agents are appropriate to resolve, and by that they create credibility within their narrative structure.

Most cognitive theories of story processing propose that the reader or listener constantly constructs coherence, either by matching the information given to a prototypical script for similar situations or by forming propositions from the text and continually integrating them into a more general statement that sums up the meaning deduced (Schank and Abelson 1977; Kintsch and van Dijk 1978). Further, it has been shown that in language comprehension the mental representation of a situation described includes the activation of analogous perceptual symbols (Zwaan, Stanfield, and Yaxley 2002). Text comprehension is achieved not by constructing a mental representation of the text itself but of the situation described (Zwaan and Radvansky 1998). According to perceptual simulation theory, reading or listening to a story is, thus, an experience in itself (Eysenck and Keane 2005). Therefore, the spontaneous search for meaning when confronted with a story may activate similar or identical cognitive mechanisms as those activated by the situations described. As specified above, in states of confusion and cognitive dissonance, especially when alone and in the wilderness, search for intentional agency is prioritized. Listening to a narrative recreating such a situation triggers the same mechanism. In the context of the tradition, a concluding statement like "I think it was the *oskorei*" does not first reveal there was agency involved, as the audition will tend to this conclusion anyway. It just identifies the concept with the broadest range of applicability and inferential potential, thus the one most economic with which to think.

In Flatin's collection, 35% of episodes concerned with the Hidden People do not include any explicit domain violation. Instead, Flatin utilizes several narrative techniques to create impressions that require a strong processing effort. Vividly presented cognitive dissonances, like those in the first-hand account quoted above, are but one example ("There was turmoil throughout the night [...] It scuffled and shuffled at the walls, a gnawing and going at the floor [...]," Flatin 1930, 54). In reproducing distinct and confusing situations, further frequently used narrative devices include alternations of descriptive airiness and hyperrealism, fractures in the narrative thread and, most important, the character of the protagonist.

Already the first subchapter in *Tussar og Trolldom*, an elaborate saga of the local Lonar family, thoroughly illustrate the general principle. According to this story, young Olav Lonar, while walking through a dark forest, one day "suddenly" stumbled into a cosy parlour. An elderly couple sits by the fireplace, smiling at him, and a beautiful girl enters and offers Olav a meal. He stands stunned, only able to think that "something is not really fitting together". Soon, as suddenly as he had entered, he finds himself out in the woods again. Seeing his campfire fire burned down to embers, he realizes that what seemed to be but a few minutes had been many hours. He went back to the farm but from now on, "he was almost unrecognisable," always longing for that girl. A year later, the experience repeats itself, and this time the elderly couple introduces themselves as the parents of the girl – who he is meant to marry. Thus, he comes back home with his new fiancée, who in the years to come will lead the farm to prosperity. And only now, after two closely printed pages and no domain violation made explicit, is the girl casually named a *tusse* (Flatin 1930, 9ff.).[7]

In their survey of situation models in text comprehension, cognitive psychologists Zwaan and Radvansky identify five basic situational dimensions that are monitored while reading a story: time, space, causation, intentionality, and protagonist. As shown experimentally, for every discontinuity in one of these aspects a higher processing effort is required for a mental representation of the evolving story (Baker and Anderson 1982; Zwaan and Radvansky 1998). In the legend summarized, discontinuity is maximized in a most direct way. The spatiality changes from one sentence to the other as Olav stumbles through the dark forest into a parlour. No causal relationship is given and no intentionality can be deduced to explain this; only later do we learn that Olav is meant to marry the girl. Before he discovers this, however, he is stumbling through the wilderness again, and we are informed that more time has passed than the event took. Coming home to his family, he seems as a different person than before.

None of these breaches in the narrative thread is accidental or a feature of Flatin's distinct narrative style. The sudden change of spatiality is one of the basic motifs in Scandinavian folklore: Olav Lonar was "taken in". The Hidden People sometimes take people, either for a short period or for eternity, to stay "within the mountain". Remarkably, in the Telemark material it never becomes quite clear if this was judged as a good or bad thing to happen for the person concerned. In legends where the abduction is noticed, church bells were rung, either as a way to guide the abducted back to the human world or to invoke God's power against the pagan forces. But as regularly as this is undertaken, it does not work out: the rope of the bell would break or a voice from underneath would threaten to kill the abducted person. And after all that struggle, the narrators will conclude by letting the abducted give a last, preferably heretical, message to his family stating something like: "to me, it is like Christmas every day". Connected to the idea of a mountain-realm, Flatin includes confusion about the lapse of time, which is an international motif in folktales (F377 in the Thompson-Index, "supernatural lapse of time in fairyland," cf. Thompson 1955–58). The changed character of Olav Lonar is a typical attribute as well and will follow any close

---

7. In a following paragraph the wedding is held and people notice a tail on her back, "and now they understood what they were dealing with".

encounter with the Hidden People. In Norwegian, there is even a technical term: people become *huldrin* or *tusset*, meaning they behave in a strange way, are withdrawn, and often seem to yearn for "the mountain." Normally, there is no explicit breach in causality but the nexus of events remains unclear: "something is not really fitting together," as the protagonist himself puts it. Most characteristic is the pronounced lack of intentionality: in virtually no legend do we get to know anything about the Hidden People's inner lives. While the human protagonists (as long as they are not *huldrin*, i.e. one of them) are reported to have inner monologues and rich feelings, the aims and motivations of the Hidden People remain a mystery.

The incoherent situation described raises a multitude of questions. To fill the gaps omitted by the author, a diversity of explanations is conceivable but, with the principle of parsimony guiding narrative processing, counterintuitive agents have a critical advantage. They are prone to transform nature's complexity into a social complexity. They activate our social mind, what corresponds to our natural bias: they allow richer inference with less computational effort; thus, they come to mind naturally. By being concluded rather than provided, credibility is gained.[8] Simultaneously, they give rise to new questions, now on a different level. After the story is naturally accepted, there is time to philosophize: not about the counterintuitive properties but about the intentions of the Hidden People, whether, for example, they are more of a threat or a promise to man, and how one should relate to them. In some legends, the *tusse* is depicted as a beautiful woman when seen from the front, but when she turns around she turns out to be hollow "like the stub of an ash tree" (Flatin 1930, 30). She is made up for the audience as a narrative facade to be filled with depth and meaning.

## Conclusions: Folk Legends as a Field of Discourse

In the mythical oral tradition of the Telemark, the supernatural entities were neither forthrightly referred to as something taken for granted nor as the object of a certain religious belief. The narrators applied a set of narrative techniques suitable to utilize basic cognitive mechanisms of sensory and narrative processing to first create credibility—an aura of significance and a need for the listener to react and position himself. In this way, the legends framed a dynamic field of discourse. Although mostly static in content and form, the tradition proved alive and able to adapt to changing religious and cultural contexts. In the legends, not only answers to the objections of the church are given, but an arena emerged in which values and an outlook on life could be negotiated. The individual understanding of the Hidden People served as a marker of identity in relation to the local community. We find introducing characterisations ("Gunleik Bakken did not want to have anything to do with the *tusser*," Flatin 1930, 48), self-proclaimed status identifiers ("Halvor was a good

---

8.   Another type of legend might further illustrate how one's own on-line reasoning compensates for contravened intuitions while processing a story. In one episode, Flatin tells about a stone formed like a chair, which is found by some people out in the woods. They carry it home to use it as a bench, but at night it starts hopping around, as if it tries to run off. Nobody can sleep with all that noise and people start getting upset, so it is decided to carry the stone back. The happening ends here. In the context of the tradition, however, there is no doubt that the chair belonged to the invisible Hidden People who tried to carry it back into the woods. The mysterious counterintuitive object of the episode is simply substituted for an equally mysterious counterintuitive agent. This conclusion, however, does not lead to new wonder or scepticism, but only to the admonition that one should not interfere with the Hidden People (Flatin 1930, 57).

friend of everything under the ground," J. Særsland in Nes 1991, 11), we find those who place their offerings for traditional reasons, and those who act out of serious commitment. We find those uninterested, but as well accounts of people with a yearning affinity and the hope to be "taken in" one day, and to live "much better than with Christian folk" (Landstad 1926, 92). The storytelling culture not only kept the belief in Hidden People alive but created it as an experiential reality.

Research on oral traditions, folklore and cultural studies has focussed on concepts and ideas in their historical context. A cognitive approach can provide additional insight as it allows conclusions about how the tradition worked. Thus, it becomes possible to identify and account for recurring patterns both in style and content, giving way to improved analyses of older and more fragmented material as well. In the case of the Norwegian tradition, especially the witch trials, including elements of the tradition in our research might reveal more of their inner dynamics. What is most often interpreted as a conflict between official doctrine, on the one side, and folk belief, on the other, might in many cases turn out to be a discourse with a collective search for meaning.[9]

# References

Amundsen, A. B. and A. Eriksen. 1999. *Folkloristiske klassikere 1800–1930*. Oslo: Norsk Folkeminnelag.

Amundsen, A.B. 2005. "Mellom inderlighet og fornuft." In *Norges religionshistorie*, edited by A.B. Amundsen, 243–294. Oslo: Universitetsforlaget.

Baker, L. and R. I. Anderson. 1982. "Effects of inconsistent information on text processing: Evidence for comprehension monitoring." *Reading Research Quarterly* 17(2): 281–294.

Barrett, J.L. 2000. "Exploring the Natural Foundations of Religion." *Trends in Cognitive Science* 4(1): 29–34.

———. 2004. *Why would anyone believe in God?*. Walnut Creek, CA: AltaMira Press.

Boyer, P. 2002a. *Religion explained*. London: Basic Books.

———. 2002b. "Why do Gods and Spirits matter at all." In *Current approaches in the Cognitive Science of Religion*, edited by I. Pyysiäinen and V. Anttonen, 68–92. London: Continuum.

———. 2003. "Religious thought and behaviour as by-products of brain functions." *Trends in Cognitive Sciences* 7(3): 119–124.

Bø, O., R. Grambo, B. Hodne and Ø. Hodne. 1995. *Norske segner*. Oslo: Det Norske Samlaget.

Chee, M.W., R.L. Buckner, K.M. O'Craven, R. Bergida, B.R. Rosen, R.L. Savoy. 1999. "Auditory and visual word processing studied with fMRI." *Human Brain Mapping* 7(1): 15–28.

Dorson, R.M. 1964. "Foreword." In *Folktales of Norway*, edited by R.T. Christiansen, v–xviii. Chicago, IL: The University of Chicago Press.

Eriksen, A. 1993. "Folkelig religiøsitet: forsøk til en avklaring." *Tradisjon* 23: 57–66.

Eysenck, M.W. and M. T. Keane. 2005. *Cognitive Psychology*. Hove: Psychology Press.

Flatin, K.A. 1917. *Rokkerova*. Skien: Norigs' Prenteverk.

———. 1930. *Tussar og Trolldom*. Oslo: Norsk Folkeminnelag.

Guthrie, S. 1993. *Faces in the clouds*. New York: Oxford University Press.

Hall, T. and H. Burhenn. 1988. "The Making of a Witch." *Scandinavian Studies* 60: 347–70.

Hodne, B. 1995. *Norsk nasjonalkultur. En kulturpolitisk oversikt*. Oslo: Universitetsforlaget.

---

9. An example seems to me the case of Elline Klokkers, which is the subject of an analysis by Hall and Burhenn 1988.

Kintsch, W. and T. van Dijk. 1978. "Toward a Model of Text Comprehension and Production." *Psychological Review* 85: 363–394.

Landstad, M.B. 1926. *Mytiske sagn fra Telemarken*. Oslo: Norsk Folkeminnelag.

Nes, T. 1991. *Haugety og trollskap*. Bø i Telemark.

Pyysiäinen, I. 2002. "Religion and the Counter-Intuitive." In *Current approaches in the Cognitive Science of Religion*, edited by I. Pyysiäinen and V. Anttonen, 110–132. London: Continuum.

Sjöblom, T. 2005. "Storytelling: Narratives of the Mind and Modes of Religiosity." *Historical Reflections / Réflexions Historiques* 31(2): 235–254.

Schank, R.C. and R.P. Abelson. 1997. *Scripts, plans, goals and understanding*. Hillsdale: Erlbaum.

Skjelbred, A.H. Bolstad. 1995. "Troens grenser." *Tradisjon* 25: 63–70.

Stranna, O. 1925. *Lundesoga*, vol. 2. Skien: Erik St. Nilssen.

Thompson, S. 1955–1958. *Motif-Index of Folk-Literature: A Classification of Narrative Elements in Folktales, Ballads, Myths, Fables, Mediaeval Romances, Exempla, Fabliaux, Jest-Books, and Local Legends*. Copenhagen: Rosenkilde and Bagger.

Tremlin, T. 2006. *Minds and Gods*. New York: Oxford University Press.

Zwaan, R.A. and G.A. Radvansky. 1998. "Situation Models in Language Comprehension and Memory." *Psychological Bulletin* 123: 162–185.

Zwaan, R.A., R.A. Stanfield and R.H. Yaxley. 2002. "Language Comprehenders Mentally Represent the Shapes of Objects." *Psychological Science* 13(2): 168–171.

# —7—

# Prisons of the *longue durée:*
# The Circulation and Acceptance of *prodigia* in Roman Antiquity

Anders Lisdorf

The use of cognitive theories for historiograpical research is a recent endeavor[1], but the idea that human psychology is necessary to explain long-term trends in history is not. Already 50 years ago Ferdnand Braudel argued for this:

> For us historians a structure is of course a construct, an architecture, but over and above that it is a reality which time uses and abuses over long periods. Some structures, because of their long life, become stable elements for an infinite number of generations: they get in the way of history, hinder its flow, and in hindering it shape it. Others wear themselves out more quickly. But all of them provide both support and hindrance. As hindrances they stand as limits (…) beyond which man and his experiences cannot go. Just think of the difficulties of breaking out of certain geographical frameworks, certain biological realities, certain limits of productivity, even particular spiritual constraints: mental frameworks too can form prisons of the *longue durée.*

Today we would probably not say that mental frameworks are prisons, but rather that human cognition imposes constraints on the long stretches of history. The last couple of decades the type of historiography championed by Braudel and the *Annales* school has sadly fallen into disuse.

In this article I will continue the project initiated by the *Annales* historians, a project of understanding long stretches of history by integrating knowledge of stable elements. Whereas earlier historians in this tradition have focused mostly on geography and other such external physical elements, recent developments in cognitive science has made it possible to say something more tangible about the stable elements of human cognition. I will therefore integrate contemporary knowledge of the stable elements of human psychology and try to show how this can aid us in understanding the long stretches of history. As an example of the utility of this approach, I will use the continuous report of prodigies in Roman republican times. By exploiting insights from the cognitive sciences I will argue

---

1. Examples of the recent growing interest in using cognitive theories in historiographical research include Beck (2006), Lisdorf (2005), Martin (2006), Whitehouse and Martin (2005).

that we can explain central features of the Roman prodigies that have not been properly understood before.

## Roman Culture

Before we can engage in the explanation we need to consider briefly some general features of Roman society and the Roman's conceptualization of prodigies. Roman society was based on a hierarchy. This was effectuated and held in place by a system of duties and favors: duties flowed upwards, and favors downwards.[2] The clients had duties toward their patron and the patron helped the client by doing favors. At the top of the Roman hierarchy was the gods. They were conceptualized as extensions of the perceptible society (Gradel 2002; Scheid 2005).

Acting in accordance with duties secured a positive outcome, while the contrary had the opposite effect. When this is joined with a conceptualization of the gods as masters of fortune and misfortune, the fulfilling of duties to the gods (*pietas*) becomes the cause of good fortune and the neglect of duties the cause of misfortune. The duties toward the gods were for the most part ritual, which is why ritual propriety is captured in the term *pietas*.

The gods, like other humans (and patrons), were also attributed the ability to communicate. They could express whether the duties had been fulfilled and the exchange relationship was in balance, that is, whether the individual was on a path towards fortune or misfortune. This sort of communication is what we know as omens.[3] The Roman omen vocabulary is extremely diverse and has many nuances. In Latin there are several different words, which would simply be rendered omen in English. The nouns are *augurium*, *auspicium*, *dirum*, *monstrum*, *portentum*, *ostentum*, *miraculum*. There are many adjectives denoting either a good omen (*faustus* and *bonus*) or a bad omen (*dirus*, *detestabilis*, *funestus*, *sinister*, *tristis*, *infaustus* and *adversus*).[4] The general sense of *omen* is a sign to an individual but it may also be directed towards a group signified by that individual, such as the army in the case of an army commander, or the state in the case of a consul. It signifies something that will happen in the future, either good or bad. To summarize: omens are indications of whether the person, to whom the omen is directed, has behaved in accordance with religious duty or not. Sometimes there was an indication of what could be done in order to re-establish the proper relation to the gods, who are above everything as exchange partners and givers of signs. It is possible to sketch a figure of the basic cultural model that will describe the various aspects of the most common terms (Figure 7.1).

A paradigmatic case illustrating this model can be seen in the story about Gaius Flaminius reported by Livy (Liv.21.62–22.6). It takes place at the height of the second Punic war in 217. Hannibal was threatening Rome from the North. Gaius Flaminius was elected to the consulship and was allotted the army lying near Placentia. Flaminius had already been consul once before, in 223, and had a history of disagreements with the senate. He therefore feared that they would falsify the auspices and use any means, such as obstruction of

---

2.  Strictly speaking they could both be described as favors merely differing in kind.

3.  Omens are not always described explicitly as stemming from the gods. There is, however, a Latin idiom used frequently by Cicero *quod omen di avertant* and other variants like *quod di immortales omen avertant* (Cic.*Har*.41) *quod Juppiter omen avertat* (Cic.*Brut* 1.12.1), *quod di omen obruant* (Cic.*Har*.20). This indicates that gods were indeed seen as the authors of omens. In the following, omen without italics will be used as a general analytical term capturing all different Latin terms, while the italicized *omen* will be reserved for the technical Latin term.

4.  For general accounts of the omen vocabulary in Latin, see Bloch (1963, 84f.); Riess (1995, 355–358); Wülker (1903, 1).

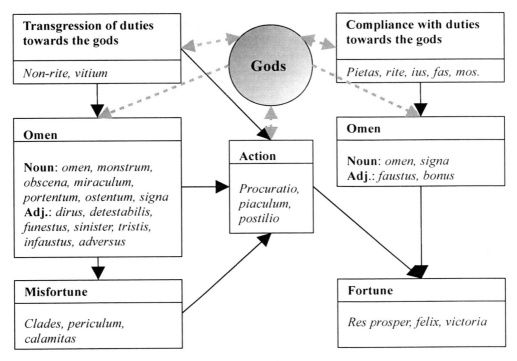

**Figure 7.1** *Cultural model for conceptualization of omen*

rituals, to detain him in the city.[5] Therefore he decided to disregard the religious duties in the city and travel to his army straight away. This meant that he would not enter office at the temple of Iuppiter Optimus Maximus, he would not sacrifice to Iuppiter Latiaris at the Latin festival, he would not receive the auspices and take his vow on the Capitol, as was customary. The senate recalled him in order that he might carry out these obligations to the gods but he did not comply. A few days later, he entered office with his army with the sacrifice of a calf. That much was performed according to custom. During the sacrifice the calf ran away and spattered many of the bystanders with blood. This was the worst possible sign in a sacrifice (Latte 1960: 388). He was advised to wait for his colleague before engaging Hannibal in direct battle but he did not like that advice and ordered them all to attack immediately. When he mounted his horse it stumbled and threw him over its head. This was seen as a bad *omen*. Further, the standard bearer reported that he could not pull up the standard. This was seen as another *omen*. Flaminius' army made it to Lake Trasumennus where Hannibal attacked the Romans by surprise. This is one of the most memorable defeats of the Romans. Livy tells us that 15,000 Romans and Flaminius himself perished in the battle. It can be seen that the omens almost literally suggested that Flaminius should wait for the other consul.[6]

There are not a lot of examples of positive omens but one example involves Publius Scipio Africanus, who finally conquered Hannibal (Liv.29.27.12–13). He was renowned

5. The consuls had many religious duties they had to carry out before they could leave the city. If a ritual was not performed properly it had to be carried out again.

6. There are many other stories like this one, see for example Verg.*A*. 3.358; Ov.*Ars*.1.212, Ov.*Met*.10.4; Cic.*Dom*.55; Cic.*Ver*.2.6.18.

for his religious reverence (Liv.26.19.3–4; Gel.6.1.6). At the close of the second Punic war, Scipio was sailing along the African coast looking for a place to disembark his troops. He asked what the nearest promontory was called and was told that it was called *pulchri promuntorium*, the promontory of beauty.[7] Scipio took this as an omen and landed the ship there. The troops disembarked without any problems and eventually Scipio celebrated many victories in Africa.[8]

These two stories both relate to probably the most central war in Roman self-consciousness, the second Punic war. Their value is not in whether they describe any historical realities but that they were told and express common assumptions among the Romans. The first shows how omens foretold the defeat at Lake Trasumennus because of the neglect of religious duties; the second shows how an omen foretells the eventual victory because of compliance with religious duties. We can fit the different components within the cultural model for omens we found above (Figure 7.2).

The model rarely includes all parts explicitly. Sometimes, the cause is not disclosed (Liv.9.14.8), sometimes the actual fortune or misfortune is missing (Pl.*Ep.*396–399, Ov.*Ep.*17.159, Ov.*Met.*5.546–550), and sometimes there is no action suggested (Cic. *Phil.*4.4.9). But omens in Roman culture are always related to the fortune or misfortune of the one it is perceived to be directed toward. They are never about neutral or irrelevant things, such as how many pigeons will be at the market next *nundinae*, but always related to the concerns of the interpreter. Sometimes this is an individual, sometimes a group and sometimes the state. They are conceived of as signs from the gods, and were integral parts of the most central narratives.

Prodigies differ only slightly from omens. Most notably they were directed towards the state in general and were always warnings of impending misfortunes. Often they contained the actions needed to get back on a path toward success. One document allows us to see this in great detail.

We are in the unique position of having, from Cicero, a *responsum* from one of the official colleges for interpreting prodigies, the *haruspices*, which gives us insight into how prodigies were interpreted by them. Let us take it line by line[9]:

1. *Loca sacra et religiosa profana haberi* (Cic.*Har.*9): "sacred and holy places have been profaned. That means that religious duties have been violated."
2. *in agro Latiniensis auditus est strepitus cum fremitu* ( Cic.*Har.*20): "in the Latiensis a groaning noise was heard." This is the prodigy.
3. *Exauditus in agro propinquo et suburbano est strepitus quidam reconditus et horribilis fremitus armorum* (Cic.*Har.*20): "a loud and groaning noise of weapons was heard."[10] This is also a *prodigium*, possibly a reiteration.
4. *Postiliones esse Iovi, Saturno, Neptuno, Telluri, dis caelestibus* (Cic.*Har.*20): "compensation is due to Jupiter, Saturn, Tellus the Gods of the Heavens."
5. *Ludos minus diligenter factos pollutosque* (Cic.*Har.*21): "the games have been celebrated

---

7. The Loeb edition has "Cape of the Fair God." This is because Polybius, in a parallel passage, makes reference to Apollon. The modern name is Ras Sidi Ali el Mekki situated in the North of modern day Tunisia.
8. Similar examples can be found in Ov.*Met.*10.277; *Ep.*17.159; Pl.*Per.*4.8.6; Hor.*S.*3.11.45
9. Translations are from Beard, North and Price 1998: II, 176. This is a reworking of a part of Lisdorf 2004.
10. This is my own paraphrase, since the line is not included in the translation of Beard *et al.* 1998: II, 176.

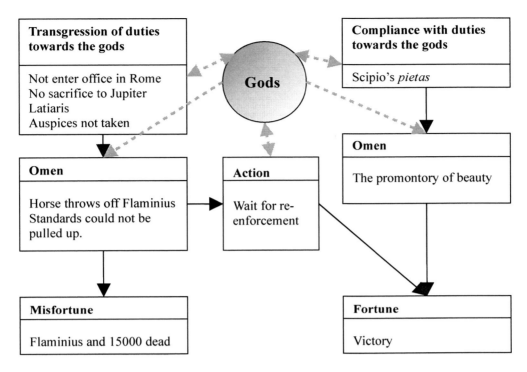

**Figure 7.2** *Cultural model of omens with examples*

without enough care and polluted." Games were also religious actions and dedicated to the gods.

6. *Oratores contra ius fasque interfectos* (Cic.Har.34): "envoys have been slain against all faith and right."

7. *Fidem iusque iurandum neglectum* (Cic.Har.36): "trust and sworn oaths have been neglected."

8. *Sacrificia vetusta occultaque minus diligenter facta pollutaque* (Cic.Har.37): "old and secret rites have been celebrated without enough care and polluted."

9. *Ne per optimatum discordiam dissensionemque patribus principibusque caedes periculaque. Creentur, auxilioque divinitus deficiantur, qua re ad unum imperium provinciae redeant exercitusque deminutioque accedat* (Cic.Har.40): "in order that murders and perils should not be caused by discord and dissension amongst the senators and the leading men; and that there should be no lack of divine help in preventing the power falling to a single man and the army from weakening and losing its strength."[11]

10. *Ne occultis consilis res publica laedatur* (Cic.Har.55): "in order that the Republic be not harmed by secret plans."

11. *Ne deterioribus repulsisque honos augeatur.* (Cic.Har.56): "in order that honor should not be increased for men of low worth and political failure."

12. *Ne rei publicae status commutetur* (Cic.Har.60): "in order that the basis of the Republic remain unchanged."

We can summarize this *responsum* in the following way. Religious duties have been violated:

---

11. The translation is awkward because the Latin text most probably is corrupt.

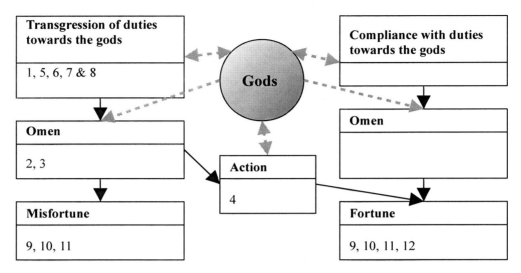

**Figure 7.3** *The cultural model of omens as seen in* De Responso Haruspicum.

sacred areas have not been respected (1), games have not been conducted with sufficient care (5), legates have been killed (6), oaths have been neglected (7), and ancient rites have not been properly carried out (8). There is a prodigy: noise and noise of weapons (2 and 3).[12] There is a description of the disasters that will happen if nothing is done: hostility will lead to killings, all power will fall into the hands of one man (9), secret plots will destroy the state (10), and unworthy people will increase their honor (11). There is a specification of what has to be done: compensatory sacrifice (4). What will happen if this is done: the status of the state will not change (12), and, by implication, killings will not occur (9) and power will not fall into the hands of one man (9), secret plots will not destroy the state (10), divine assistance will be achieved (9). This text fits with the cultural model we found for omens in general (Figure 7.3).

Now that we have reviewed the conceptualization of omens among the ancient Romans, we need to ask the basic question of why some things are seen as omens and others aren't. What qualities of an event make it an omen? Not much is known about this but recent research in developmental psychology conducted by Jesse Bering and Becky Parker may give us important clues as to how events become interpreted as omens (Bering and Parker 2006). Children from ages 4 to 7 were given the task of finding out in which of two boxes a ball was hidden. They were told to place their hand on the top of the box in which they thought the ball was and keep it there for 15 seconds. During the 15 seconds they could move their hand back and forth as many times as they wanted but by the end of the 15 seconds the position of their hand would count as the answer. The children were assigned to either an experimental group or to a control group. In the experimental group, the children were taken aside and shown a picture of "Princess Alice" after the explanation of the rules of the game. They were told that Princess Alice was a magical princess who could make herself invisible. They were also told that Princess Alice really liked them and that she would tell them when they picked the wrong box. In the control group, no story of Princess Alice was told. During some of the trials, one of two unexpected events would happen when the children had put their hand on the box. Either a picture of Princess Alice would fall from

---

12. This type of prodigies is not uncommon, noise: Obs. 45, 46, 48, 53, 57, 59; sound of weapons: Obs. 45; Liv. 24.44.8.

the door, or a table lamp would turn on and off twice in rapid succession.

The results of this research showed that the young children in the experimental group did not react to the unexpected events but the oldest children, who are closer to adults in performance, responded by moving their hand. This indicates that they had seen the unexpected event as an intentional sign related to their current concern, which was to win the game. It also shows how easily something unexpected can be interpreted as an intentional sign. We may here notice that the experimental group was primed with a story about a counterintuitive agent's interest in their concern to win the game and this counterintuitive agent was endowed with communicative abilities. This is very close to the situation we see in omens.

There is one difference from omens however; the children were explicitly told that Princess Alice would communicate in this way, which is not the case for omens. However, in Roman culture, where belief in omens is widespread, similar stories about the communicative abilities of a counterintuitive agent, and its interest in their concerns, are communicated in the type of omen stories mentioned above. It is possible that a constant sensitivity to omens is present because of frequent stories about them. These stories function as a "cultural prime" in much the same way as did the story of Princess Alice for the experimental group of children. Omens therefore seem to depend on a cultural prime and on some attention-demanding occurrence.

## Prodigies

Now let us look in more detail at the Roman prodigies. Prodigies were omens to the Roman state accepted by the senate. According to our sources, prodigies were accepted since the time of the kings but not until the end of third century BCE do they become frequent. Around the middle of first century BCE, the system seems to collapse and change. Therefore the period from 218–44 BCE has been singled out for analysis.

The sources we have are mainly from late Republican times or from the principate but they build on earlier sources and official archives. The Romans themselves had their theories of prodigies and especially Livy considered them shocking and attention demanding and used them to underline drama in his history. That said, there is consensus that the prodigies in Livy stem from official records though through intermediaries (Drews 1988; Rawson 1991).

## The Prodigy System

Now let us look in more detail at omens directed towards the state at large. These were termed *prodigia*. We have reasonably good sources concerning their character, identification and interpretation. Prodigies were a special kind of omen that circulated among the population and was eventually reported to a magistrate. This magistrate related it to the senate, which decided whether it should be accepted or rejected. If it was accepted it was given to one of three priestly colleges for interpretation. They produced a response on the basis of which the senate decided what to do.

## Brief Sketch of Acceptance Procedure

There are several distinct parts of what we could call the prodigy system.[13] The overall purpose of the prodigy system is to identify and interpret prodigies. The reason is that, as we saw in the previous section, prodigies are omens to the state in general. They are signs that

---

13. For descriptions see Bloch (1963, 120–129); Linderski (1995, 58); Rosenberger (1998); Wülker (1903, 26–50). For an analysis of the different parts of the prodigy institution as a distributed cognitive system see Lisdorf (2004a).

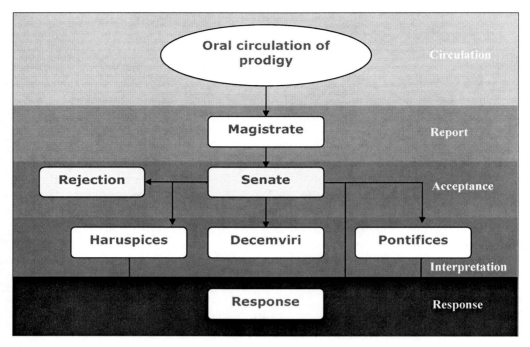

Figure 7.4   Acceptance procedure for prodigies

the state is on a path towards some future misfortune. It is therefore necessary to interpret what action is necessary to avert the impending misfortune and achieve a fortunate result. Prodigies were probably reported all year, but it was the duty of the consuls, after their assumption of office on the ides of March,[14] to expiate the prodigies according to the decisions of the senate (Bloch 1963, 120; Wülker 1903, 27). In a way prodigies resemble urban myths. Before they were reported they had probably gone through a period of oral circulation. This, at least, is the impression we get from Cicero. In *De responso haruspicum* we hear of a prodigy which has not been reported yet, but which is apparently widely known (Cic. *Har.*62). Another indication that oral circulation was prior to a report is the existence of doublets: sometimes we hear of a prodigy and just a couple of years later we hear it repeated (Rawson 1991a: 4–5). An example is the birth of a colt with five legs in Lucania in 200 BCE (Liv.31.12.7) and the same in Bruttium in 199 (Liv.32.1.11). It seems that some times the prodigy story kept circulating and was eventually reported again as a new prodigy. It was eventually reported to a magistrate, who then related it to the senate. The senate decided whether or not to accept the prodigy. If it was accepted, it was presented to one of the three priestly colleges: the *haruspices, decemviri* or *pontifices*. They would then make a response that formed the basis for further action. The acceptance procedure can be sketched as falling into five distinct sequences. The interrelation can be seen in Figure 7.4.

We have virtually no evidence regarding the reports and interpretation procedures. The few concrete interpretations can only be explained in light of the contemporary context, which is a subject for what Braudel called *l'histoire événementielle* in opposition to the *longue durée.* Consequently, what is of interest for the history of the *longue durée* is the

---

14.   We do occasionally hear about prodigies at the end of the year, for example Liv.39.56.6 and Liv.41.28.1. It is possible that the system changed or Livy moved the annalistic material.

| 0 | No perception of risk to Rome and her army |
| 1 | Minor problems; for example, rebellion in a remote region, or minor casualties in the Roman army |
| 2 | Larger problems; for example, limited military confrontations outside Italy, and some casualties in the Roman army |
| 3 | Major problems; major military confrontations outside Italy; substantial casualties |
| 4 | Serious problems; the enemy is in Italy or at its borders; Consuls killed or entire armies (the size of a legion or more) lost in battle |
| 5 | Acute problems; Rome is facing its demise, the city itself is threatened with capture (or perceived to be so), an unsustainable level of casualties in the Roman army. |

**Table 7.1** Crisis index

circulation and acceptance of prodigies. In the following I will sketch the conclusions previous research has reached, review cognitive theory pertinent to the problem, and then attempt another explanation.

## Circulation

Previous research has stipulated that fear fueled the circulation and report of prodigies. The central tenet of the fear thesis is that fear is the cause, in one way or another, of the report of circulation. Most often fear is produced by crises (Krauss, Bloch, Dumezil, Gladigow, and Rosenberger). The basic logic is that crises, such as wars, produce fear in the population[15], which produces a high number of prodigies in circulation, which are reflected in a high rate of prodigy reports to the senate. Fortunately we can test this theory against the historical record, since we have reasonably good evidence of the number of prodigies accepted per year and good evidence of the number of wars and other critical events per year in the period between 218–44 BCE.

Whereas information about the number of prodigies reported per year is relatively straightforward, we need to operationalize the degree of crisis. Such a measure will never be precise but we should still be able to see some rough correlation between degree of crisis and number of reported prodigies. A crisis index was devised according to which every year was assigned a value between 0 and 5[16] (Table 7.1).

Other things could be seen as the reason for crisis, most notably disease. The problem is that our sources speak of disease in general, and rarely gives us concrete historical information. Livy does occasionally inform us of plagues, but it is not clear in all cases how widespread they were. In order to have a fix-point, the chronological table in the *Cambridge Ancient History* Vol. VIII (524–541) and IX (780–798) can serve as a basis from which values for each year was assigned. Further, in order not to let theoretical preconceptions influence the individual ratings, values were assigned to each year before the count of prodigies per year was done.

For each reporting year we have a value designating the degree of crisis and another designating the number of prodigies and we end up with a list of paired values. To visualize the relation, a bubble plot was made. The size of the bubbles indicates the degree of crisis

---

15. It should be mentioned that some versions of the fear thesis stipulate that the cause was individual fear without any apparent outer reason (Dumezil 1970; Gladigow 1979; Krauss 1933), but there is no way we can test this. It remains a possibility, but should be considered speculation.

16. The index was devised by me, but was discussed with Ittai Gradel whom I thank for many fruitful suggestions and improvements. Any infelicities are naturally my responsibility.

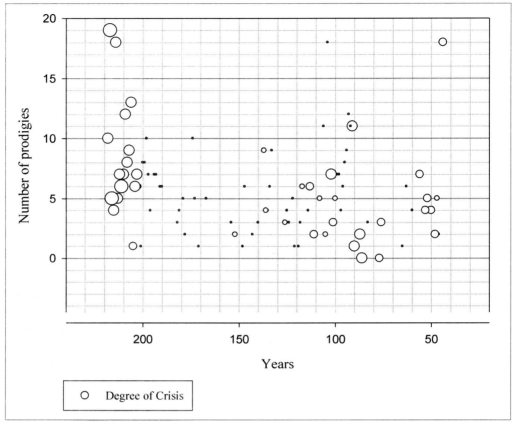

Figure 7.5    Relation between degree of crisis and number of prodigies

for the observation. If the fear thesis is correct we would expect big bubbles and no small ones at the top and small bubbles and no big ones at the bottom. The results can be seen in Figure 7.5.

Around the Punic war (from 218–202 BCE onwards), there are indeed some big bubbles at the top as expected but around 80–100 BCE, the big bubbles are at the bottom and the small ones at the top. We can see that there does not seem to be any big temporal difference, such as big bubbles at one end only, or high number of prodigies at one point. The fear thesis stipulates that there is a correlation between these two values whereas the null-hypothesis is that there is none. We can investigate which is most consistent with the observations statistically.

A box-plot was made and revealed the presence of four outliers. The first was from 217, which was at the height of the second Punic war, probably the greatest war in late republican memory. The only source for this is Livy. He sometimes uses prodigies to dramatize events in general (Levene 1993, 84–85). It is possible that he has here collapsed the prodigy lists for two years into one (Levene 1993, 38). The second observation is from 44. The explanation here is analogous. The year 44 was that in which Caesar was killed. Here we have more sources but they also seem to dramatize by listing a greater number of prodigies, where some on closer inspection more stringently could be called *omina*. *Omina* were directed towards private persons and not the state as were *prodigia*. There is, consequently, reason to doubt whether most of the prodigies for the year 44 are *prodigia* in the technical sense. The third observation stems from the year 104, where a serious attack of the Cimbri on North Italy took place at the same time as the second Sicilian slave war. It could therefore follow the pattern in Livy, where especially important events are dramatized with a higher number of prodigies by collapsing two years and counting *omina* as prodigies. Unfortunately we don't have Livy's history for this period, only the summary of Julius Obsequens.[17] Therefore we cannot investigate this in detail. The last observation is from the year 163, where, as far as we can see, nothing critical happened at all. Nevertheless 17 prodigies were reported. Unfortunately, again we only have the prodigy lists from Julius Obsequens so we cannot determine whether it is attributed to any dramatizing effect, but it can be seen that the prodigy lists from the previous year are missing. Consequently, it is probable, either by purpose or by mistake, that the lists from 164 and 163 were collapsed into one. These four outliers were eliminated from the data, since they were likely to skew the trend in the data.

The correlation coefficient for the trimmed data was 0,173 (r squared was 0,020), which is not a very good correlation.[18] A linear regression analysis was made with degree of crisis as the independent variable and number of prodigies as the dependent variable. This did not reveal any significant relationship between degree of crisis and number of prodigies— $F(1,102) = 3,151$, $P= 0.079$.[19] Other regression models were tried but the best fit was provided by the linear regression.

Based on the evidence available to us, the null-hypothesis cannot be rejected. Still we cannot say that fear can explain the number of prodigies reported in the Roman Republic in the period from 218–44 BCE. This period forms the bulk of our evidence of prodigies in the Roman republic. Previous theories explaining divination with recourse to fear, what I have called the fear thesis, is not consistent with the findings presented here. It should however be borne in mind that there are important uncertainties tied to the quantification of the number of prodigies and the degree of crisis and individual observations may be contended. The trend however, is reasonably clear. It should also be noted that I am not the first to reject this thesis. Susanne William Rasmussen also rejects the fear thesis because it is based entirely on "a very few vague passages from Livy taken from the period around the Second Punic War" (Rasmussen 2003, 29). The quantitative analysis presented here thus yields the same result.

Cognitive science may be able to throw some light on the circulation of prodigies. First of all, we can classify prodigies as micro-narratives. As mentioned above, the closest modern resemblance to prodigies is urban myths, although they are not integrated into a model of communication from the gods. Being narratives, we can apply important knowledge from studies of narrative comprehension and understanding. For a narrative to circulate it must be memorable. One way to be memorable is to be attention demanding. A growing body of research has demonstrated that certain types of concepts are more attention demanding than others (Boyer 1994; Boyer and Ramble 2001). All concepts belong to an ontological category. This category is connected to intuitive domains of physics (objects),

---

17. Julius Obsequens was an historian who extracted the prodigy lists and other portentous events from Livy and made them into a separate work (Schmidt 1968)

18. For the untrimmed data, r= 0.18 and r squared= 0.025.

19. The result for the untrimmed data was $F(1,106)= 3.730$, $p= 0.056$. This is actually slightly better than the trimmed data, but still not significant.

biology (plants and animals), or psychology (humans) from which normal expectations are generated (Atran 1990; Hirschfeld 1996; Keil 1979; Keil 1989; Sperber, Premack, and Premack 1995). If we know that something breaths, we automatically know that it will need nourishment, and sleep, and give birth to offspring of the same kind. Further, the former domains are embedded in the latter. Consequently, something that breaths, because it is also a physical entity, will also be subject to gravity and be visible. It will not, however, necessarily have a mind (plants breathe too). A concept, which falls into the biology domain, also falls into the physics domain, but not vice versa. According to Pascal Boyer, one violation of knowledge at the domain level makes a concept counterintuitive. This type of concept is the most attention demanding (Boyer, Bedoin, and Honore 2000; Boyer and Ramble 2001).

Justin Barrett and Melanie Nyhof demonstrated the existence of an intermediate category, which they termed "bizarre": "bizarre items possessed a highly unusual feature that violates no category-level assumptions but may violate basic-level regularities (e.g., a living thing that weighs 5000 kilograms may be unusual for a dog, but weighing 5000 kilograms does not violate assumptions about living things in general)" (Barrett and Nyhof 2001, 78). A bizarre feature is consequently a feature, which is highly irregular for any given kind, but not counterintuitive.[20] Although recent research has nuanced the picture somewhat (Alles 2006; Atran and Norenzayan 2004; Norenzayan, Atran, Faulkner, and Schaller 2006), these basic conclusions still stand. Narratives involving a few minimally counterintuitive features also seem to have a transmissive advantage (Barrett and Keil 1996; Gonce, Upal, Slone, and Tweeney 2006, 544). A recent study shows that the most widely circulated folktales are also characterized by minimally counterintuitive elements (Norenzayan, Atran, Faulkner and Schaller 2006, 546).

Based on such research, we should not expect there to be any difference in the number of prodigies in circulation based on the degree of crisis, which of course is what we found, but we should expect their circulation to depend on the involvement of counterintuitive and bizarre concepts in the narrative frame of the prodigy. To put it more clearly, we should expect that most prodigies will involve one minimally counterintuitive element, a lower number would involve a bizarre element, and the least number will only involve normal elements.

In an earlier article I carried out such an analysis (Lisdorf 2004b). This showed that 56 percent of all known prodigies (605) in the period from 218–44BCE involved one minimally counterintuitive element, 41 percent involved a bizarre element, and only 4 percent were entirely composed of normal elements. It was also possible to demonstrate that there were no temporal fluctuations in this pattern: All periods had the same distribution with most prodigies involving one minimally counterintuitive element, a smaller amount involving one bizarre element and virtually no prodigies with only normal elements. The circulation of prodigy stories thus seems adequately explained by insights from cognitive science

We saw that the theories proposed in previous research were not consistent with the empirical observations. The alternative hypothesis that the preference of the human cognitive system for attention demanding concepts to accurately predict the observed character and frequency of prodigies in circulation seems more precise: We here have an example of how knowledge of human cognition and constraints on the human mind can help us understand patterns in the *longue durée* of Roman history.

---

20.  For research along these lines see (Boyer, Bedoin and Honore 2000), which stipulates the same inferential divide between domain and kind level expectations. What is here called bizarre seems to correspond to what they call strange.

## Acceptance

The principles behind the acceptance or rejection of prodigies has been the focus of much previous research (Krauss 1933; Latte 1960; Luterbacher 1967; MacBain 1982; Rasmussen 2003; Rawson 1991; Rosenberger 1998; Warde-Fowler 1971; Wülker 1903). Unfortunately, it is one of the most obscure parts of the process. Except for two examples, we only have evidence of the prodigies that were accepted.

The key evidence is two prodigies that were not accepted. The passage runs as follows: "Two portents were not treated as public matters, the one because it took place in a privately owned spot: "Titus Marcius Figulus reported that a palm had sprung up in his catch-basin." The other because it had occurred in a non-Roman place: "at Fregellae, in the house of Lucius Atreus, a spear which he had bought for his son's service in the army was said to have blazed during the day for more than two hours in such a way that the fire consumed none of it."[21] From this passage previous research deduced two principles: a prodigy could not be accepted if it had occurred in a private (*privatus*) place, it had to be in a public (*publicus*) place and it could not be accepted if it occurred in a foreign (*peregrinus*) place, it had to be in a Roman (*romanus*) place.[22] These are not altogether unreasonable assumptions. The problem is that it does not accord well with the known accepted prodigies, since there are examples of prodigies occurring in both foreign and private places. Let us start with the private prodigies.

Until recently examples of accepted prodigies occurring on private ground have been completely ignored (Rasmussen 2003, 220; Rosenberger 1998, 29, n.52). We have, for example, a small number of prodigies that occur in private houses (Liv.41.16.6; Obs.51; Obs. 53). Another example is prodigies of hermaphrodites or monstrous births. They must likewise have occurred on private ground (MacBain 1982, 27). We can conclude, therefore, that the rule that prodigies had to occur in a public place is not a necessary rule.

The Romans did distinguish between foreign land (*ager peregrinus*) and Roman land (*ager Romanus*), but the Romans also operated with many other categories in between that are difficult to put a clear juridical term on. The individual relations between a city and Rome could be very different. Prodigies are reported from all these different categories of places.[23]

Attempts have been made to reconcile the discrepancy between the rule and the exceptions of known prodigies. Franz Luterbacher thought that the distinction was just not very rigid (Luterbacher 1967, 30). He has, though, been criticized for this since it is an *ad hoc* explanation. Elizabeth Rawson explained the discrepancy by stipulating that it came from the integration of local prodigy lists into the Roman ones after the areas had become Roman (Rawson 1991, 5–9). Unfortunately there is no evidence of such local collections. Bruce MacBain thinks that the distinction between public and private, and Roman and

---

21. Duo non suscepta prodigia sunt, alterum, quod in private loco factum esset, palmam enatam in inpluvio suo T. Marcius Figulus nuntiabat, alterum, quod in loco peregrino; Fregellis in domo L.Atrei hasta, quam filio militia emerat, interdiu plus duas horas arsisse, ita ut nihil eius ambureret ignis, dicebatur (Liv.43.13.6). These two prodigies are listed at the end of the other prodigies of the year. There are several puzzling features, most importantly that Livy or his source overlooks, as pointed out by (Rasmussen 2003: 219-223), that they are both actually private prodigies.

22. As demonstrated by Susanne William Rasmussen, this is still the most common view (Rasmussen 2003, 219–223)

23. Bruce MacBain has shown that 21% of the prodigies from outside of Rome come from foreign (*peregrinus*) land (MacBain 1982: 25). For a thorough treatment of the question see Szemler 1972, 34–36.

foreign had simply disappeared (MacBain 1982, 28). This does not, however, occur in Roman society in general. This solution therefore raises more questions than it answers: Why would the senate suddenly stop making such discriminations, which are absolutely central to Roman culture all the way through the republic and well into the principate (Fest. 284 L)? We can conclude that previous efforts have not been able to elucidate the basic principles behind acceptance of prodigies.

Since omens activate an inference of a counterintuitive agent, and since prodigies were often explicitly conceptualized as communications, it would be natural to assume that they followed principles from normal communication. One popular and well founded cognitive communication theory is the relevance theory of Dan Sperber and Deirdre Wilson (1995). According to Sperber and Wilson, humans do not communicate by encapsulating a message in a code, which is subsequently decoded by the listener. Rather, some sign is produced with the intention to inform of something. Technically this is described as a communicator producing a communicative stimulus. A communicative stimulus should be maximally relevant to what it is intended to inform. A communicative stimulus is interpreted as being the most relevant one the communicator could have chosen to communicate his informative intention to the interpreter.

In relation to the prodigies, the communicative stimulus is the prodigy and the communicator is the gods or Jupiter. Given that the informative intention of a prodigy is already known to be a warning to the Roman state, the most relevant communicative stimulus is one that involves the Roman state as directly as possible. The reason is that, if the gods wanted to communicate a warning to the Roman state, the most relevant way would be to place the sign (i.e. the prodigy) in as close a relation as possible to the Roman state.

Let me give an example from everyday communication. Consider for a moment that somebody wants to communicate a warning to you. The most relevant way would be to direct the warning as directly to you as possible, that is, either go as close as possible to you, or shout in your direction, or tell someone who knows you. Conversely if you hear someone shout "watch out" far away from you in a direction away from you, that is not the most relevant way to communicate a warning to you, and it is not very probable that the sign would be interpreted as a warning to you.

We should therefore expect that the stronger the connection of a prodigy to the Roman state, the more likely it was that it would be interpreted as a prodigy to the Roman state, as opposed to a private omen intended for someone else. The two previously suggested principles can be derived from this principle since public as opposed to private and Roman and as opposed to foreign land more directly involve the Roman state. We can therefore explain the two rejected prodigies by reference to only one rule and not two.

But as we saw above, previously suggested interpretations had problems explaining all the accepted prodigies, since some did not fit the predictions of the two principles: we found private prodigies among the accepted prodigies. Let us therefore see if the suggestion that the principle of relevance is more successful in explaining the acceptance of Roman prodigies.

To restate the hypothesis derived from the principle of relevance: the closer the prodigy is to the Roman state, the more probable is it that it will be interpreted as a prodigy to the Roman state. Closeness is, of course, a vague term but an all round rough measure of the degree of connection to the Roman state would be simple distance to Rome. Based on the assumption that prodigies were taken as communicative stimuli from a counterintuitive agent and the principle of optimal relevance, we should expect it to be more probable that a prodigy was accepted the closer it was to Rome. Fortunately, this hypothesis can be tested since in many cases we know the place, and therefore the distance to Rome. Consequently, we would expect the number of prodigies accepted to increase the closer we get to Rome. Mathematically that is a correlation between distance from the place of occurrence to Rome and number of prodigies.

The number of prodigies for each named location was summarized[24] and the beeline distance from this location to Rome was measured based on the map in *Putzger Historischer Weltatlas* (Putzger, Hansel and Leisering 1961). We could have taken the raw correlation between number of prodigies for each location and its distance to Rome but we are not interested in exact distance, and single observations from close by places would have skewed the data. If we had an observation of a single prodigy from 10 different places very close to Rome and only one kilometer apart, and a few from one place 500 kilometers from Rome, the correlation coefficient would appear mathematically to indicate a function linearly increasing with distance although the reverse is true. In order to avoid this, the observations were grouped in ranges of 25 kilometers. That would also have been more in accordance with the perceptions of the Romans: they would not have taken out a map and measured the precise distance, but rather have made a loose assessment of distance. In the context of ancient Roman transportation, 25 kilometers would have been a salient difference in distance. In consequence, a measure of distance based on ranges of 25 kilometers appears to be a better measure than exact distance. The number of prodigies in each 25 kilometer zone will then be summarized.

The distances for each observation were recoded into a variable designating the range. Thus the range 0-25 km was recoded as 1, 26–50 km as 2, and so forth. There were three outliers (more than 500 kilometers away). They were from Syracuse, Croton and Etna. They were excluded since closer inspection revealed that they were most likely omens. Their inclusion would, however, not change the conclusion. The number of prodigies for each range was summarized. A scatter plot with distance by range on the abscissa and the summarized number of prodigies for each range on the ordinate indicated a possible logarithmic function. A regression analysis for a linear as well as a logarithmic model was therefore made. The R square for the linear model was 0,53, which is significant ($p<0.001$), but the R square for the Logarithmic was 0,82, and an ANOVA revealed a significant result $F(1,14)= 67.15$ $p<0.001$. A scatter plot and the curve fit can be seen on Figure 7.6.

We can see a very clear relation between distance and the number of accepted prodigies. This is consistent with the hypothesis that prodigies were taken as communicative stimuli from a counterintuitive agent and the acceptance of them as pertaining to the Roman state at large was based on the basic communicative principle of relevance. There are some reservations though. First, it should be mentioned that the distribution is also consistent with other explanations: we would also expect that more prodigies would be reported to Rome the closer the location since people would come to Rome more frequently the closer they lived. The distribution would thus rather reflect the prodigies reported to the senate. This explanation would, however, also assume that the senate blindly accepted every prodigy. The only way to decide whether this or the alternative explanation proposed here is closer to historical reality would be to measure the accepted prodigies against the rejected. If very few were rejected the distribution would reflect the baseline of the reported prodigies. We know of two rejected prodigies, which indicate that there was a conscious selection. We do

---

24. The same list as in the previous section was used.

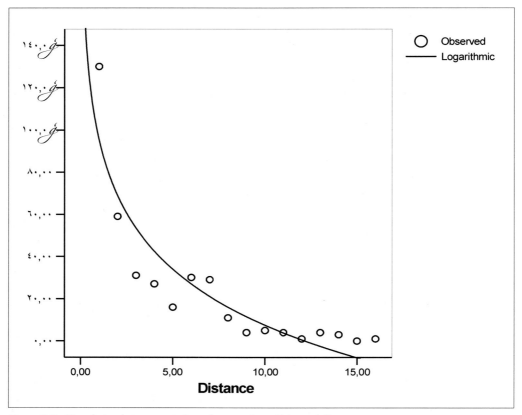

Figure 7.6   Correlation between number of accepted prodigies and distance.

not, however, know whether this was common or not. Were prodigies often or rarely rejected? One piece of evidence could maybe give us an indication. Livy mentions that earthquake prodigies should not be reported when one has already been accepted. This seems to indicate that the general willingness to report prodigies was great but that the number of accepted prodigies rarely exceed twenty as far as we can tell from the available sources. That would indicate a large number of rejected prodigy reports. All this is, of course, almost pure conjecture. I personally would find it peculiar if the senate indiscriminately accepted any prodigy, especially since we know that they sometimes called in witnesses and also actively rejected prodigies.

Another possible objection is that the distance is measured in beeline distance whereas the experienced distance through the roads would have been what was important. It would be a minor thesis of its own just to calculate the distances through the actual roads known and even that changed with time as new roads were constructed and one could sail or take another route. We are therefore left with this admittedly rough measure.

In conclusion, what can be gathered from the sources about the acceptance of Roman prodigies with all the possible imprecisions is consistent with the hypothesis that they were accepted according to the principle of relevance as stipulated in Sperber and Wilson's relevance theory. This interpretation is simpler than previous explanations that stipulated two principles, for both of which many exceptions could be found in the sources.

# Conclusion

With this essay I hope to have shown that cognitive theories can fruitfully contribute to historiographical research. Especially, the history of the long stretches, *longue durée*, seems to benefit from recent advances in our understanding of human cognition. With the example of the continuous report and acceptance of prodigies in the Roman republic, we were able to contribute a better understanding of certain aspects of prodigies. There are many aspects of Roman history that may benefit from new analyses informed by cognitive science. Old questions may be reconsidered and new questions may appear.

# References

Alles, G.D. 2006. "The So-Called Cognitive Optimum and the Cost of Religious Concepts." *Method and Theory in the Study of Religion* 18: 325–350.

Atran, S. 1990. *Cognitive Foundations of Natural History: Towards an Anthropology of Science*. Cambridge: Cambridge University Press.

Atran, S. and A. Norenzayan. 2004. "Religion's Evolutionary Landscape: Counterintuition, Commitment, Compassion, Communion." *Behavioral and Brain Sciences* 27: 713–730.

Barrett, J.L. and F.C. Keil. 1996. "Conceptualizing a Non-Natural Entity: Anthropomorphism in God Concepts." *Cognitive Psychology* 31: 219–247.

Barrett, J.L. and Nyhof, M.A. 2001. "Spreading Non-natural Concepts: The Role of Intuitive Conceptual Structures in Memory and Transmission of Cultural Materials." *The Journal of Cognition and Culture* 1: 69–100.

Beard, Mary, John A. North and S.R.F. Price. 1998. *Religions of Rome*. Cambridge: Cambridge University Press.

Beck, Roger. 2006. *The Religion of the Mithras Cult in the Roman Empire: Mysteries of the Unconquered Sun*. Oxford: Oxford University Press.

Bering, J.M. and B.D. Parker. 2006. "Children's Attributions of Intentions to an Invisible Agent." *Developmental Psychology* 42: 253–262.

Bloch, R. 1963. *Les prodiges dans l'antiquité classique: Grèce, Étrurie et Rome*. Paris: Presses universitaires de France.

Boyer, P. 1994. *The Naturalness of Religious Ideas*. Berkeley: University of California Press.

Boyer, P., N. Bedoin and S. Honore. 2000. "Relative Contributions of Kind and Domain-Level Concepts to Expectations Concerning Unfamiliar Exemplars: Developmental Change and Domain Differences." *Cognitive Development* 15: 457–479.

Boyer, P. and C. Ramble. 2001. "Cognitive Templates for Religious Concepts: Cross-Cultural Evidence for Recall of Counter-Intuitive Representations." *Cognitive Science* 25: 535–564.

Drews, R. 1988. "Pontiffs, Prodigies, and the Disappearance of the Annales Maximi." *Classical Philology* 83: 289–299.

Dumézil, G. 1970. *Archaic Roman Religion, with an Appendix on the Religion of the Etruscans*. Chicago, IL: University of Chicago Press.

Gladigow, B. 1979. "Konkrete Angst und offene Furcht: Am Beispiel des Prodigienwesens in Rom." In *Angst und Gewalt*, edited by H.V. Stitencron, 61–77. Düsseldorf: Impressum.

Gonce, L.O., M.A. Upal, D.J. Slone and R.D. Tweeney. 2006. "Role of Context in the Recall of Counterintuitive Concepts." *Journal of Cognition and Culture* 6: 521–547.

Gradel, I. 2002. *Emperor Worship and Roman Religion*. Oxford: Clarendon Press.

Hirschfeld, L.A. 1996. *Race in the Making: Cognition, Culture, and the Child's Construction of Human Kinds*. Cambridge, MA: MIT Press.

Keil, F.C. 1979. *Semantic and Conceptual Development: An Ontological Perspective*. Cambridge, MA: Harvard University Press.

Keil, F.C. 1989. *Concepts, Kinds, and Cognitive Development*, Cambridge, MA: MIT Press.

Krauss, F.B. 1930. *An Interpretation of Omens, Portents, and Prodigies Recorded by Livy, Tacitus, and Suetonius*. Philadelphia, PA: University of Pennsylvania.

Latte, K. 1960. *Römische Religionsgeschichte*. Munich: C.H. Beck.

Levene, D.S. 1993. *Religion in Livy*. Leiden: E.J. Brill.

Linderski 1995. *Roman Questions*. Stuttgart: Franz Steiner Verlag.

Lisdorf, A. 2004a. "At navigere i et farefuldt hav." *Religionsvidenskabeligt tidsskrift* 44: 27–41.

———. 2004b. "The Spread of Non-natural Concepts—Evidence from the Roman Prodigy Lists." *The Journal of Cognition and Culture* 4: 151–173.

———. 2005. "The Conflict over Cicero's House: An Analysis of the Ritual Element in 'De Domo Sua'." *Numen* 52: 445–464.

Luterbacher, F. 1967. *Der Prodigienglaube und Prodgienstil der Römer: Eine historisch-philologische Abhandlung*. Darmstadt: Wissenschaftliche Buchgesellschaft.

MacBain, Bruce. 1982. *Prodigy and Expiation: A Study in Religion and Politics in Republican Rome*. Bruxelles: Latomus Revue D'âEtudes Latines.

Martin, L.H. 2006. "The Roman Cult of Mithras: A Cognitive Perspective." *Religio. Revue pro religionistiku* 14: 131–146.

Norenzayan, A., S. Atran, J. Faulkner and M. Schaller. 2006. "Memory and Mystery: The Cultural Selection of Minimally Counterintuitive Narratives." *Cognitive Science* 30: 531–553.

Putzger, F.W., A. Hansel and W. Leisering. 1961. *Historischer Weltatlas Jubiläumsausgabe*. Bielefeld: Velhagen and Klasing.

Rasmussen, S.W. 2003. *Public Portents in Republican Rome*. Rome: L'Erma di Bretschneider.

Rawson, E. 1991. "Prodigy Lists and the Use of the Annales Maximi." In *Roman Culture and Society*, edited by E. Rawson, 1–15. Oxford: Clarendon Press.

Riess, E. 1995. "Omen." In *Paulys Realencyclopädie der classischen Altertumswissenschaft, NeueBbearbeitung*, vol. 18, 1, edited by W. Kroll and H. Wolff, 350–378. Stuttgart: Verlag J.B. Metzler.

Rosenberger, V. 1998. *Gezähmte Götter; Das Prodigienwesen der römischen Republik*. Stuttgart: Steiner.

Scheid, J. 2005. *Quand faire, c'est croire: Les rites sacrificiels des Romains*, Paris: Aubier.

Schmidt, P.L. 1968. "Iulius Obsequens und das Problem der Livius-Epitome: Ein Beitrag zur Geschichte der lateinischen Prodigien Litteratur." *Abhandlungen der geistes und sozialwissenschaftlichen Klasse, Jarhgang 1968*. Wiesbaden: Franz Steiner Verlag.

Sperber, D. and D. Wilson. 1995. *Relevance: Communication and Cognition*, 2nd ed. Oxford: Blackwell.

Sperber, D., D. Premack and A.J. Premack. 1995. *Causal Cognition: A Multidisciplinary Debate*. Oxford England: Clarendon Press.

Szemler, G.J. 1972. *The Priests of the Roman Republic: A Study of Interactions between Priesthoods and Magistracies*. Bruxelles: Latomus.

Warde-Fowler, W. 1971. *The Religious Experience of the Roman People: From the Earliest Times to the Age of Augustus*. New York: Cooper Square.

Whitehouse, H. and L.H. Martin. 2005. *Theorizing Religions Past: Archaeology, History and Cognition*. Walnut Creek, CA: Altamira.

Wülker, L. 1903. *Die geschichtliche Entwickelung des Prodigienwesens bei den Römern: Studien zur Geschichte und Überlieferung der Staatsprodigien*. Leipzig: Emil Glausch.

# What Might Cognitive Science Contribute to Our Understanding of the Roman Cult of Mithras?[1]

Aleš Chalupa

Mithraism seems to be an especially attractive target of various theories inspired by Cognitive Sciences. The attention of scholars usually concentrates on the analysis of Mithraic rituals, for example from the perspective of the "ritual form hypothesis" proposed by Robert N. McCauley and Thomas E. Lawson (2002), or the overall description of cult's sociopolitical and psychological features according to Harvey Whitehouse's "theory of the two divergent modes of religiosity" (2000, 2002, 2004).[2] The aim of this paper is rather different: to explore the possible contribution of these theories originating in the field of Cognitive Science of Religion to the elucidation of the vexed problem of historical origin of the Mysteries of Mithras.

## The Origin of Mithraism: From Franz Cumont until the Present

Mithraism appears in our historical sources, quite abruptly, in the last quarter of the first century CE,[3] which makes it the youngest representative of the so-called "Oriental mysteries." In the next three centuries, Mithraism spread to virtually all provinces of the Roman Empire, albeit in divergent degrees of profusion. The cult flourished especially during the second and third centuries CE and possibly reached its zenith during the reign of the Severan dynasty (Clauss 1992, 255–258), but it finally perished some time after Emperor Theodosius issued his edicts abolishing sacrifices to pagan gods. The last remnants of the cult probably disappeared in the first half of the fifth century CE, but the exact date is still

---

1. The preparation of this article was kindly supported by a grant from the Czech Science Foundation (GP401/09/P267).

2. See especially Beck (2004b) and Martin (2004, 2005, 2006a, 2006b). Martin (2007) tries to clarify the problem of the accurate transmission of the central Mithraic iconographic motif—the tauroctony—from the position of memetics.

3. About this early phase of the existence of Mithraism and the evidence coming down from this period see Merkelbach (1984, 147–149); Clauss (1990a, 31–32, 1992, 251–252, 2000, 21–22); Gordon (1994, 460–462, 467–468, 470); Beck (1998a, 118–119).

disputed.[4]

The historical origin of Mithraism remains mysterious in many respects. Mithraists themselves proclaimed Zarathuštra, the Persian prophet who gained some notoriety in the Graeco-Roman world, the mythical founder of their Mysteries.[5] Since no other competing version of the Mithraic foundation myth came down to us from antiquity, we can suppose that other inhabitants of the Graeco-Roman world either did not care or held the same opinion. The genesis of the cult was thus essentially connected with the Persian cultural context. Even though we can easily mark this claim as purely fictitious—we know many other examples of "foundation legends" of this kind—the situation seems to be more complicated. This "Persian" line of interpretation became intrinsically interwoven with the scientific research, because it played a major role at the beginnings of modern Mithraic studies.

Franz Cumont, the distinguished scholar of Hellenistic religions, scientifically grounded this unanimous opinion of the ancient world in his famous monograph completely devoted to the study of Mithraism, published at the very end the nineteenth century (Cumont 1896–1899).[6] In the view of the Belgian scholar, Mithraism was a product of cultural diffusion, an originally Persian religious cult—sometimes he even called it poetically "a branch torn from the ancient Mazdean trunk" (Cumont 1956, vi)—that spread beyond its natural borders due to convenient historical circumstances. To describe chronological phases of Mithraism and its constituents, Cumont used his famous and often cited "geological metaphor":

> An analysis of the constituent elements of Mithraism, like a cross-section of a geological formation, shows the stratifications of this composite mass in their regular order of deposition. The basal layer of this religion, its lower and primordial stratum, is the faith of ancient Iran, from which it took its origin. Above this Mazdean substratum was deposited in Babylon a thick sediment of Semitic doctrines, and afterwards the local beliefs of Asia Minor added to it their alluvial deposits. Finally, a luxuriant vegetation of Hellenic ideas

---

4. Some scholars maintain that Mithraism virtually ceased to exist even shortly before the time when the Theodosian Edicts were issued (cf. Turcan 1984, 222–223; Martin 1989, 12). Eberhard Sauer (1996, 2004), however, having analyzed coins discovered in some mithraea claims that Mithraic communities could still operate in some regions of the Roman Empire in the first half of the fifth century CE.

5. This opinion was clearly expressed by Porphyry in his treaty *On the Cave of the Nymphs* (ch. 6), in which he follows previous tradition (especially another Greek author Eubulos) possibly informed by authentic Mithraic sources:

   The Persians [i.e. Mithraists] too initiate candidates, giving a mystical account of the passage of souls down and out again and they call the place where this initiation happens a 'cave'. Zoroaster, as Eubulos tells us, was the first to dedicate a natural cave in nearby mountains of Persia, a cave surrounded by flowers and furnished with springs, in honor of Mithras, the maker and father of all. The cave was for him an image of the cosmos which Mithras created, its interior symmetrically arranged with symbols of the elements and regions of the cosmos. After Zoroaster it became the custom among others to perform ceremonies of initiation in caverns and caves, either natural or artificial. (English translation in Beard *et al.* 1998b, 90–91).

   Cf. also Origen, *Against Celsus* 6.22.

6. The appearance of this two-volume seminal book with the title *Textes et monuments figurés relatifs aux mystères de Mithra* was truly an epoch-making event in the modern study of Mithraism. The second volume (it was published before the first, in 1896) was a referential corpus diligently collecting all Mithraic archaeological monuments, epigraphic evidence and literary references known at that time. The first volume (published in 1899) was a first really scientific interpretative synthesis of Mithraism based exactly on this collection of evidence. The 'strong' Persian hypothesis propounded by this monograph and corroborated by carefully collected material evidence gave Cumont's interpretations an undisputed prevalence for a very long time. An abridged version of the first volume was later published separately and translated into many languages, including English (Cumont 1956).

burst forth from this fertile soil and partly concealed from view its true original nature.

(Cumont 1956, 30–31)

According to Cumont, the essential elements of Mithraism—the things that actually spread—were faith, doctrines, beliefs and ideas expressed predominantly in Mithras Myth, which he subsequently tried to reconstruct comprehensively (Cumont 1956, 130–140). This mythical narrative supposedly culminated in a central salvific act of Mithras—his sacrifice of a bull—that gave rise to the ubiquitous iconographic motif of the Mysteries: the tauroctony. This scenario of a cultural diffusion of Mithraic "theology" containing a visible doctrinal core enveloped and disguised in later "deposits" stayed in force until the 1970s of the twentieth century. A quick and probably definitive demise of this "strong Persian view" followed afterwards.

Richard Gordon (1975) forcefully attacked and persuasively disproved the validity of Cumont's central assumption that Western Mithraism could be meaningfully interpreted with references to Persian religious context and Persian religious texts. The point of contention did not bear so much on the question of possible presence of Persian elements in Mithraism,[7] but rather on the fact that the connection of this kind was very difficult to prove without the use of circular argumentation, where the conclusion verifies assumptions leading to its formulation (Gordon 1975, 220–221; cf. also Wikander 1951, 15–19). The following wave of criticism further accentuated other serious problems undermining the general plausibility of Cumont's scenario of Mithraic origins.[8]

Firstly, the mechanism of transmission proposed by Franz Cumont is largely unpersuasive. In his opinion, it was a Mithraic myth and comprehensive doctrine, two necessary components of Mithraic faith, which "infected" Roman soldiers stationed in the Eastern parts of the Roman Empire and thus facilitated the later spread of the Mysteries in the West. This scenario, however, has been seriously compromised. The medium of this proselytization, a so-called Zoroastrian pseuodoepigrapha (Bidez and Cumont 1938), are totally un-Mithraic in nature and what they express, moreover in a very unsystematic way, are Hellenistic views on Eastern cultures: they contain virtually no information about authentic Persian religious tradition (Beck 1991; cf. also Momigliano 1975, 141; de Jong 1997, 37), not to mention any clear-cut "theology." Moreover, everything we know about Western Mithraism seems to support the view that what was transmitted and what appealed most to the Romans was not predominantly Mithraic myth and textually integrated doctrine, but the Mithraic rituals and special bonds of community that this religion was capable of creating.

Also the importance of the Roman army, purportedly the major factor in transmission of Mithraism (Cumont 1956, 40–42; cf. also Widengren 1966, 253–254), should be seen in a proper perspective. It seems that the Roman army and its communication structures really played a crucial role in early phases of Mithraic transmission. Cumont's view, however, that the main medium of this propagation was Roman legions returning from Eastern campaigns, where they happened to be "infected" by Mithraism, is probably misleading or at least not completely satisfactory (cf. Daniels 1975, 272–274; Clauss 1992, 253–254; Liebeschuetz 1994, 208–209). Some military units evidently had already come into contact with Mithraism before their engagements in the East, directly in the Western part of

---

7. Richard Gordon never denied their possible presence in Mithraic ideology (1975, 218, 1978, 163–164) and he is still consistent with this opinion (1994, 471, 2001a).

8. See also other contributions in Hinnells 1975a, especially Colpe 1975, Hinnells 1975b and Bivar 1975. The first critical study uncompromisingly disputing some central assumptions of Cumont's interpretation of Mithraism, albeit unsuccessfully in an immediate perspective, was Wikander 1951.

the Roman Empire.[9]

Secondly, the well-attested form of Western Mithraism seems to be largely incompatible with the remnants of various Mithra cults that existed in Persia, Syria or Asia Minor regions (Colpe 1975, 399–404; cf. also Ries 1990; Boyce and Grenet 1991, 468–490). Some typically Mithraic structures, which mark this cult in the West, such as the mithraeum, tauroctony or peculiar system of seven initiatory grades, are relatively rarely attested in the East (cf. Roll 1977; Clauss 1992, 234–244) and when they do appear, they do not predate the oldest evidence of Western Mithraism.[10] Moreover, they are not indigenous: they demonstrably came from the Western parts of the Roman Empire, usually together with the Roman military forces. They seem to be fully evolved and completely standard, none of them can be seen as evidence of some proto-Mithraic phase (Roll 1977, 58–59; Beck 1984, 2014; Boyce and Grenet 1991, 488–489; Turcan 1993, 24–25).[11] All visual differences occasionally discernible on Eastern monuments can be ascribed to peculiarities of local iconographic style rather than to a different ideology more closely reflecting original Persian forms of Mithra's worship.

Thirdly, Cumont and his followers were unable to identify a historically attested community, where Mithraism could arise and from which it could later be transmitted. Their scenarios are very vague from this point of view. Lack of historical evidence is usually blamed (e.g. Cumont 1956, 15–16, 104–105), but the whole problem probably goes much deeper. Even the most sophisticated scenario of the discontinuous evolution of Mithraism from a hypothetical Persian predecessor introduced by Richard Gordon (2001a) does not try to specify at what time, where and inside which community Mithraic Mysteries could arise. Also the fact that we cannot discover any archaeological traces of this evolution—despite the fact that Mithraism is a cult so well attested in Western archaeological material—seems to be quite conspicuous and ominously eloquent. It is true that we can single out some iconographic motifs on some Western monuments that are very peculiar or rather unusual from the perspective of the Graeco-Roman religious tradition (Gordon 2001a, 293–295). On the other hand, they are well understandable from the point of view of various Persian religious traditions. Although we can possibly infer from these monuments that they are a product of genuine connections between western Mithraism and its Persian predecessor, we can never be completely certain that these peculiar features of Mithraic iconography did not arise spontaneously in the West (cf. Beck 2006a, 28–30), in the milieu of a religious cult which existed outside the mainstream of the Graeco-Roman religiosity.

9.   One of the oldest Mithraic dedications (*CIMRM* 1098; dated before about 90 CE), made for Mithras in Germania Superior by Gaius Lollius Crispus, a centurion of local auxiliary unit recruited from among Roman citizens (Schwertheim 1974, no. 59o; Huld-Zetsche 1986, 56), is especially significant in this regard.

10.   Mithraic monuments from Eastern provinces are usually late. So far, the only exception in this regard is a mithraeum discovered in the port city of Caesarea Maritima (Hopfe and Lease 1975; Bull 1978; Blakely *et al.* 1987; Gordon 2001b, 78–82). The dating of potsherds found there supports the view that this mithraeum had already existed some time around the year 80 CE (Blakely *et al.* 1987, 100), which makes it, paradoxically, the oldest reliably dated Mithraic temple we known of at the moment.

11.   In the near future, this conclusion could possibly be disproved by the definitive dating of a mithraeum discovered in the vicinity of the ancient city of Dolichos (modern Dülük in Turkey). This mithraeum (first Mithraic evidence from the ancient Commagene), situated in a natural cave, was provisionally dated, on the basis of a coin found there, to the period 25 BCE–25 CE (Schütte-Maischatz and Winter 2000, 99, 2001, 157). However, I agree with Roger Beck's reservation (2004a, 28–29) that this conclusion is rather premature and it would be prudent, before we get down to such a radical redescription of Mithraic origins, to wait for the definitive dating based on the final archaeological report.

These problems thwarting old Cumontian views and other theories about a Persian origin for Mithraism has recently led some scholars to a radical—sometimes probably too radical—redescription of the cult's history. According to this view, Mithraism is no longer a product of a long-term spontaneous evolution but a creation of a religious founder—not Zarathuštra in this case—but some individual, possibly of Eastern extraction, dwelling in Rome (Nilsson 1961, 675–676; Merkelbach 1984, 77; Clauss 1990a, 18, 2000, 7–8; Liebeschuetz 1994, 199; Mastrocinque 1998, 155–156). Persia and Asia Minor are no longer regarded as a cradle of Mithraism: they were replaced by Rome or nearby at the estuary of the Tiber River situated port town Ostia (Vermaseren 1981, 96–97; Merkelbach 1984, 75–77; Clauss 1990a, 17–18, 1992, 253–255, 2000, 7; Liebeschuetz 1994, 198–200). The importance of Persian elements in Mithraism is occasionally completely marginalized and practically reduced to their virtual nonexistence (most radically by Clauss 1990a, 17, 2000, 7–8).

But even these radical innovations still do not answer the most intriguing question of early Mithraic history: the fact of the apparently rapid and seemingly haphazard spread of the cult in the first phase of its existence (75–125 CE), to very distant provinces of the Roman Empire. Richard Gordon (1994, 467–468, 471) in his comprehensive review of the monograph written by Manfred Clauss (1992), the most influential proponent of a theory about the Roman origins of Mithraism, persuasively shows that, concerning the transmission of the Mysteries, the connection of Rome with the places where the oldest Mithraic monuments were discovered remains equally problematic as their connection with Asia Minor. Moreover, the form of Mithraism in this early period seems to be already fully developed and completely consistent with that attested in later phases of its existence, which can lead to a conclusion that the actual period when Mithraism came into being is not identical with the time of its appearance in archaeological material (cf. Volken 2004, 18–19).

The current consensus is probably close to the following: Mithras is undoubtedly a Persian deity; there could even be some authentic Persian motifs in Mithraism—and there probably are—but the Western variety of a cult is a product of the Graeco-Roman world and its formation (or rather invention) took place shortly before the time when the first Mithraic evidence appeared, in a region which is currently unidentified. However, the more clear outlines of this process are, because of the dearth of historical evidence, almost completely unknown to us.

## The Origin of Mithraism: Can Cognitive Sciences Be of Any Help?

The following conclusion seems to be inescapable: the historically oriented study of Mithraic beginnings has reached a kind of an impasse. In principle, two tentative strategies present themselves: either we patiently wait until new Mithraic evidence that decisively solves the question of the cult's genesis is discovered—which is rather passive, completely dependent on chance and not very likely in the end—or we inspect the existing evidence again, this time with some new theory or perspective in mind. At this point I would like to venture an idea that, maybe, some cognitively grounded theories of cultural transmission or religious ritual could provide us with some clues about, what we should look for and how to proceed with it.

But before we get down to this, yet another subject needs to be touched upon briefly. If the old Cumontian scenario of cultural diffusion is to be abandoned, the question arises how else we can conceive the problem of cultural communication or transmission of religious elements across time and space. One theory that seems to be especially rewarding is Dan Sperber's "epidemiology of representations" (1996, 24–27). We can consider Mithraism as a cultural system (or a religion, if we prefer this term), a body of public representations reflecting an inner set of mental representations. This set of representations is not "downloaded" or "copied" from one individual to another (or from one community to another), but it is communicated in the process of cultural selection. If a particular set of representations is found interesting and became widespread among members of a particular culture in a particular time, we can speak about a successful cultural phenomenon. To this horizontal dimension we can also add another one concerning a successful transmission of cultural phenomena across time (vertical dimension). Mithraism evidently succeeded in both of these tasks, albeit only for something more than three centuries.[12]

Providing that our investigation of Mithraic origins and early transmission is based on a Sperberian "epidemiology of representations," a knowledge of the cognitive processes undergirding differing modes of performativity, activating different memory systems and supporting different kinds of socio-religious structures will be of crucial importance (Martin 2005, 187–188). Therefore, we have to deal, albeit briefly, with the following three questions: 1) What was transmitted? 2) How it was transmitted? 3) What does it say about psychological and sociopolitical features of Mithraism?

## What Was Transmitted?

According to Franz Cumont, it was the narrative myth and propositionally expressed doctrine—"a genuine theology" (Cumont 1956, 105–106)—derived from Persian religious texts, with its liturgical superstructure. This doctrine allegedly found its most intimate expression in a Mithras myth whose critical sequences were depicted on the very rich Mithraic iconography, especially on the so-called "side scenes" that frame large number of the Mithraic tauroctonies especially those originating from the Rhinean and Danubian provinces. This figural art should also play a major role in the process of the religious education and indoctrination of Mithraic initiates.

This vision of doctrinal transmission via iconography and religious teaching is, however, problematic in many respects. The Mithraic iconography, especially the tauroctony with its "side scenes," should not be reduced, at least not completely, to some "picture Bible" (Turcan 1993, 72). To begin with, there is still an unanswered question of what exactly is depicted on the tauroctony and the other Mithraic iconographic motifs. The identification of animals, objects and persons appearing on the tauroctony either with particular constellations or stars,[13] together with a more careful analysis of Mithraic "side scenes" (Gordon 1980a),[14]

---

12. The question of why Mithraism finally disappeared lies outside the scope of the present article, the provisional answer, however, would probably be close to the statement that Mithraism either ceased to be an interesting religious alternative to those social groups from which it recruited its membership (Martin 1989, 12) or could not sustain growing pressure exerted by quickening pace of Christianization (Sauer 1996, 2004, 339–341; cf. also Chalupa 2005, 222–228).

13. The preliminary identification of these elements with their astral counterparts was already made in the nineteenth century by the German scholar K. B. Stark (1869, 19–20). His theory, however, fell into almost complete oblivion. The revival of this astral interpretation of the tauroctony and Mithraic ideology was instigated and facilitated by the demise of Cumontian consensus (for a short history of this scientific field see Beck 2004c). It is virtually certain that the tauroctony (on one level of its composition) reflects a particular region of the night sky (Beck 2004d). On the other hand, it would be an example of unjustifiable reductionism to claim that it is *only* a star map, because this motif certainly expresses other, non-astrological elements of Mithraic ideology as well (cf. Turcan 1981; Gordon 1988, 64–71; Martin 1994).

14. Richard Gordon (1980a, 219–220) holds the opinion that these side-scenes express especially broad mythological themes serving as "models" for Mithraic ritual activity.

persuasively undermined traditional Cumontian view that the tauroctony and other figural motifs are predominantly, if not only, sequences in a universal narrative myth (Beck 1984, 2081–2082, 2097–2098; Martin 1994, 217–219), ubiquitous in all Mithraic communities. According to some scholars (Beck 2004b, 88; Martin 2005, 196–198) that which was transmitted and what enabled the existence of relative uniformity of Mithraism across the Roman Empire, were common themes embedded in rituals and in the broader contextual background that Mithraists shared with their late antique contemporaries: prime examples would be the contemporary astrological context[15] or a popular reflection of the Platonic philosophical world-view.[16] For this relative stability of Mithraic representations there is no need to presuppose the existence of universal Mithraic doctrine systematically propagated by Mithraic "missionaries" or via Mithraic "sacred books" now lost. Cumont's lament (1956, 150) over a hypothetical canon of destroyed Mithraic sacred texts is in all probability nothing more than a futile sentiment, because these "books" have never existed (Burkert 1987, 70). That does not mean that Mithraists had no use for writing. They certainly had. But their literary production either fulfilled the cult's administrative purposes or provided Mithraists with mnemonic "devices" enabling smoother progress through sometimes apparently complicated initiatory rituals. The first type of these documents is conspicuously represented by the so-called *album* from Virunum (*AE* 1994, no. 1334; Piccottini 1994, cf. also Beck 1998b, 2006b), registering members of the local Mithraic community (together with information about two important moments in the history of this community). The second type could appear in the form of an Egyptian papyrus (these days kept in Berlin), which probably[17] contains a series of questions asked and answers required during initiation into one of the Mithraic grades (Brashear 1992). It would be absurd, though, to suppose that this dialog in some way incorporates a universal Mithraic "creed" binding for all communities scattered all over the Roman Empire. A private initiative of an unknown Mithraist provides probably a more persuasive explanation.

The consequences of this "de-doctrinalization" of Mithraism seem to be inescapable: more attention should be paid to Mithraism as a ritual system and also to social functions which Mithraism exercised and which certainly produced much of its appeal. Mithraism

15. This embeddedness of some Mithraic themes in contemporary astrological background (e.g. the tauroctony) could successfully prevent any undesirable "mutations." The tauroctony looked the way it looked because the heavens were like that, and if you knew that, your artistic license was practically limited. Luther Martin (2007) treats the tauroctony as a special case of Richard Dawkins's "self-normalizing" (or "error-correcting") meme (Dawkins 1999, xii): what gets "copied" and eventually transmitted is not the actual image of the tauroctony but implicit instructions how the tauroctony should be constructed. Nevertheless, some doubts whether such a concept of cultural transmission is practically applicable were raised by Dan Sperber (2000).

16. There are some indications based especially on Porphyry's treaty *On the Cave of the Nymphs* (ch. 6), but also on their comparison with our archaeological material, that Mithraic cosmology was Platonic in nature (cf. also Merkelbach 1984, 228–244 [even though some unwarranted and farfetched opinions of this German scholar are to be dismissed]). The crucial question, admittedly, is whether the information found in Porphyry is authentically Mithraic—that it reflects actual opinions of cult's initiates—or rather Porphyry's own Platonizing interpretations without any connection to real Mithraism whatsoever, as is consistently argued especially by Robert Turcan (1975, 1999). However, strong counterarguments expressed by Roger Beck (2000, 178–180, 2006a, 44–46), in my view, sufficiently undermine the validity of Turcan's claims.

17. For some critical discussion see Turcan 1993, 152–156. On the other hand, there is nothing in the text that would place it persuasively out of a Mithraic context.

seems to be a successful blend of two types of socio-religious institutions widespread in the late antiquity: a voluntary association (*collegium*) and mystery cult.

As a voluntary association Mithraism provided some very important social services.[18] It was an elective community of men[19] grouped together on the basis of pursuing common goals. Because a substantial part of Mithraists were young men torn from their own biological families—Roman soldiers and slaves, either privately owned or public ones who often worked in the imperial administration—membership in Mithraic communities could provide much desired security and compensate for the lack of social services in the unstable and often dangerous world in which they lived (Gordon 1972; Clauss 1990, 48–50, 1992, 275–279, 2000, 39–41; Liebeschuetz 1994; Volken 2004, 19–20). For example, now there is some evidence that Mithraists probably took care about burials of their deceased comrades, either in case they did not have their own families or wanted to be buried in the vicinity of a mithraeum to which they belonged.[20] The feeling of "fictive kinship" was induced and strengthened by common meal of all initiates,[21] which probably constituted a routine part of Mithraic religious activity and drew its inspiration from one very central act of Mithras legend: the feast of Mithras and Sun on the skin of the sacrificed bull. This conclusion about the centrality of a common meal can be supported by another conspicuous fact. Strictly speaking, from the architectural point of view,[22] a mithraeum is nothing more than a special kind of a *triclinium*—a dining room—where the place of honor was reserved for Mithras who was symbolically present on the tauroctony, usually positioned in the frontal niche of every mithraeum (Clauss 1990a, 122, 2000, 112–113). The Mithraic feast probably had a deeper sacramental significance as well, which could be reflected in a careful selection of chosen animals and consumed meals.[23] This ritual was probably frequently repeated[24] and in the intentions of McCauley and Lawson's "ritual form hypothesis" we can label it as a "special patient ritual."

In Mithraism, however, typologically very different rituals, which represented its mystery

---

18. About the taxonomy, functions and importance of voluntary associations *qua* elective religious communities in the Roman Empire see Ausbüttel 1982; Wilson 1996; Kloppenborg 1996; Bendlin 2002; Harland 2003. About Mithraism as a voluntary association see Beck 1996.

19. Women were not admitted into Mithraism (Chalupa 2005; Griffith 2006; *pace* David 2000). In all probability, their exclusion was not fortuitous, but had some deeper connection with certain features of Mithraic ideology (Gordon 1980b, esp. 57–64).

20. The information provided by the Mithraic *album* from Virunum seems to support this view, as well as the discovery of two cremation graves close to the walls of the mithraeum found in the German town of Wiesloch (Hensen 2001). This opinion was expressed already by Franz Cumont (1956, 171) and seems to be generally accepted (Clauss 2000, 139–140).

21. About Mithraic cult meals in their Graeco-Roman context, see Kane 1975. About fictive kinship groups in the ancient world, see Martin 1997.

22. A mithraeum was, of course, much more than a dining room. It seems to be reasonably certain that it was also constructed as an image of a cosmos (Porphyry, *On the Cave of the Nymphs* 6). For more elaborate explanation see Gordon 1976, 1988, 50–60; Beck 1994a, 2000, 154–167; 2006a, 102–152).

23. The analysis of animal skeletons found in refuse pits in the vicinity of a recently discovered mithraeum in Belgian town Tienen shows that all animals consumed during one very spectacular Mithraic feast (more than one hundred persons apparently took part in it) were of male sex (Martens 2004, 41). Because of quite a large number of animals killed (or sacrificed) this choice could not have been fortuitous and probably had some deeper significance connected with some features of Mithraic ideology.

24. Although we have no direct evidence about the frequency of Mithraic feasts, an interval at least once a month seems to be perfectly reasonable (cf. Beck 2004b, 97).

component, also existed. Mithraism can be regarded as a cult, whose visibility in a public context was most likely very low (Beard *et al.* 1998, 266).[25] Mithraea, small subterranean (or quasi-subterranean) places where initiates convened, were not open to the general public. The participation in the cult was dependent on previous initiation. Mithraism thus differs from other Graeco-Roman cults of "Oriental" deities by its consistently initiatory character (all members had to be initiated)[26] and also by its peculiar and very complex seven-grade initiatory system.[27] Concerning their structure, we know only very little about these initiatory rites. It seems, however, that they were physically strenuous and psychologically very exhaustive (Beck 2000, 146, n. 10; Martin 2006b, 134–137).[28] The nature of these rituals was apparently different from those represented by Mithraic feast. In the intentions of McCauley and Lawson's "ritual form hypothesis" they can be labeled as "special agent rituals," because through the initiator—this role was apparently taken over by Mithraic *Patres*, holders of the highest initiatory grade (Beck 2000, 149–150)—Mithras himself acted. An initiate's religious status was thus irreversibly changed.[29]

## How Was Mithraism Transmitted?

The dichotomy between two divergent structural models of Mithraism, voluntary association and mystery cult, is also reflected in the memory systems used during the process of codification and transmission of religious knowledge. The principal memory system used by Mithraists in this process was apparently semantic. Many Mithraic ritual activities took place frequently and their execution must have felt quite routine. Nonetheless, the "scripts" for these activities, gradually encoded in semantic memory, were evidently interspersed with a substantial number of episodic memories, usually connected with arduous initiatory rites (as far as we can trust some Mithraic imagery) that "spiced up" otherwise

25.  John Scheid (2001), however, tries to cast some doubts on this vision of Mithraism as a secret cult virtually unknown to the public. According to his view, at least in Rome or in Ostia, the general visibility of Mithraism was much more conspicuous than is usually admitted. Also Eberhardt Sauer (2005, 336; cf. also Liebeschuetz 1994, 212) independently expressed an opinion that Mithraism, especially in later phases, could have become increasingly more open to the public, because the cult was not able to finance its activity from the funds raised by initiates themselves and needed support of larger population.

26.  This was not a rule in case of other mystery cults, where the initiation can be regarded as a special service reserved for those more deeply interested and sufficiently rich (cf. Burkert 1987, 10–11).

27.  The assumption that all Mithraists underwent seven subsequent initiations, at least in theory, has been recently questioned by Manfred Clauss (1990b) and Robert Turcan (1999). Their arguments, however, leave me largely unpersuaded. For some arguments against Clauss's criticism, see Gordon 1994, 465–467.

28.  Our most important source of information about this aspect of Mithraic activities is the frescoes discovered in the Italian mithraeum of Santa Capua Vetere (Vermaseren 1971, 25–51 and tab. XXI–XXIII, XXV–XXVIII). This fact is also accentuated in some of our ancient literary sources (e.g. Ambrosiaster, *Commentary on the Old and New Testament* 113.11), even though their reliability can be in some cases seriously doubted. Also the theory about the ritual tattooing or branding of Mithraic initiates, expressed by Franz Cumont (1956, 157) on the basis of Tertullian (*The Prescription against Heretics* 40), is probably misleading (cf. Beskow 1979).

29.  This structural dichotomy is relatively important because it connects Mithraism with something Robert N. McCauley and Thomas E. Lawson (2002, 181–182) call a "balanced ritual system." According to them, "if balanced systems retain both *markedly* higher levels of sensory pageantry with their special agent rituals and conceptual schemes capable of controlling those rituals' interpretations, they *can* prove quite stable (2002, 182; italics original). We can suppose that Mithraism was quite successful in combining both these elements.

routine Mithraic activities (e.g., the common meal). Even though these highly emotional moments could occasionally trigger spontaneous exegetical reflections (cf. Whitehouse 2004, 113–115) on the part of individuals who participated in them, the meaning of Mithraic activities—or Mithraism *qua* religion—was provided by previously initiated members of the community, in part through verbal commentaries to the activities exercised.[30] This knowledge, however, cannot be seen solely as a product of some explicit Mithraic doctrine expressed verbally and learned by all Mithraists as a creed. It was also, to a large extent, a product of a rich symbolic system of great evocative power that was apprehended and realized by Mithraists during the ritual performance and interpretation of attention grabbing Mithraic imagery (Beck 2004b, 98; Gordon 1998, 234–236).

## What Does It Say About Psychological and Sociopolitical Features of Mithraism?

Mithraism was a complex religious phenomenon, where many divergent tendencies were interconnected: we can find in it many doctrinal and imagistic features (see Beck 2004b), and both "special agent" and "special patient" rituals (Martin 2004, 2005).[31] One thing is, however, reasonably certain: concerning its functional structure, Mithraism seems to be predominantly imagistic. It produced relatively small, self-sustained communities, where all initiates knew each other and underwent comparably same experiences.[32] Mithraism being a "secret" and relatively closed cult had no opportunity for public proselytization. Mithraic recruitment strategy had to be based on inter-personal relations that very likely resembled relations between patrons and clients: in other words, you had to be invited to become a Mithraist (Liebeschuetz 1994, 203–204; Aune 1998, 53; Volken 2004, 9; Beck 2006b, 193). This strategy, however, is in sharp incongruity (cf. Martin 2006b, 139–141) with the apparently rapid spread of Mithraism in the early phases of its existence.

There is only one possible solution to this paradox: what was so effectively spread was not Mithraism but Mithraic cells. In different words: the community, where Mithraism

---

30.  The ritual scene depicted on the so-called Mainz Mithraic Vessel (Huld-Zetsche 2004) can be meaningfully interpreted this way (Beck 2000, 153–154). Also the corrupted sentences, which we can partially decipher on the badly preserved frescoes in the Santa Prisca mithraeum in Rome (Vermaseren-Van Essen 1956, 187–239; Betz 1968) together with some literary testimonies (e.g. Firmicus Maternus, *On the Error of Pagan Religions* 19.1; Justin, *Apology* I.66) support the view that verbal commentaries played an important role in revealing Mithraic religious ideology to members being newly initiated into various Mithraic grades.

31.  Luther H. Martin (2005, 190) proposed that we should predominantly see Mithraism as a representative of the imagistic mode of religiosity. Even though I concede that there is a great amount of truth in his assessment, I am personally persuaded that some components of Mithraic religion could not be sustained and spread without the support of some doctrinal mechanisms. It is therefore better to see Mithraism as a successful blend of imagistic and doctrinal features, which supported each other and made Mithraism a very resilient and stable form of religiosity, even though the cult finally succumbed to the growing power of more universalistic Christianity.

32.  Relatively small dimensions of almost all Mithraic temples we know of effectively excluded participation of a large number of initiates. Some potential exceptions notwithstanding (cf. Martens 2004, 41–45), it is quite evident that only few Mithraists could dine together in one mithraeum simultaneously. In the moment when the number of initiates in one Mithraic cell exceeded acceptable level, the community split and a new cell with a new mithraeum was founded (Clauss 2000, 43). Although we have no irrefutable evidence, the names appearing on a Mithraic *album* from Virunum and also on another list of Mithraists from the same region (*AE* 1994, no. 1335; Piccottini 1994, 46, fig. 22) commemorating the building of a new Mithraic temple support this view (Piccottini 1994, 50). For a possible alternative explanation see Beck 2006b, 187–188.

existed in the early phase, or where it even originated, had to be highly mobile (Beck 1998, 118–119). This conclusion, if correct, has serious implications for the study of Mithraic origins. It shows that previous attempts to discover a geographically fixed locality, where Mithraism originated and from where it subsequently spread, is probably a famous "red herring": there was never such a place. Rather, our efforts should concentrate on the identification of a prospective community that had all the features necessary for the future successful propagation of the Mithraic Mysteries.

## The Search for a Prospective Community

As far as I know, only two theories about the origins of Mithraic cult and its early propagation which meet the aforementioned requirements have been proposed: the older one by a Swedish scholar Per Beskow in the late 1970s of the twentiety century, the other one relatively recently, in 1998, by Roger Beck.[33]

According to Per Beskow's theory (1978), Mithraism originated in the first century CE in the Bosporan kingdom (the region surrounding Crimean Peninsula) in the milieu of local religious guilds. These Bosporan *synodoi* and *thyasoi* had some remarkable characteristics that are in perfect accordance with many features of Mithraism: they were exclusively male; their members were recruited predominantly from the military ranks of local Bosporan aristocracy; they had a closed, esoteric character; the number of persons involved in one guild was limited to 15–20 individuals; they called each other *adelphoi* and stood under the leadership of a man with the title *Pater* (Beskow 1978, 15–16). Due to Roman military presence in this region, Mithraism could have possibly managed to "inoculate" some Roman soldiers who subsequently introduced their newly acquired cult to the Danubian provinces, from where Mithraism later spread to other places in the Roman world (Beskow 1978, 17–18, 1980, 13–14).

According to Roger Beck (1998, 2001), Mithraism was founded in the milieu of the Commagenian regal dynasty and its military and civil retainers, approximately during the third quarter of the first century CE and, therefore, sufficiently close in time to the appearance of the oldest cult's monuments and dedicatory inscriptions. Commagena is a region, where the existence of a syncretistic Hellenistic Mithra cult is attested (Waldmann 1973; Dörner 1975; Merkelbach 1984, 50–72),[34] and the dynasty was also connected, by family ties, with Tiberius Claudius Balbillus, the leading astrologer of the first century CE.[35] In the aftermath of civil war that broke out after the death of Emperor Nero (68/69 CE), the dynasty went into exile, moved to Rome and its members were granted Roman citizenship.

33. There is a third scenario as well, put forward by David Ulansey (1991). In his theory, closely connected with a quite amazing (and also highly implausible) astrological interpretation of the tauroctony, Ulansey, too, identifies a community where Mithraism supposedly arose, but this hypothetical group—Stoic philosophers from the Cilician city of Tarsos—is otherwise completely unattested and, if it really did exist, left no traces in our historiographical sources. Serious doubts about its existence can be thus expressed (cf. Beck 1994b, 38–39 and nn. 43–44; Clauss 2001).

34. See also web pages of International Nemrud Foundation <http//www.nemrud.nl/en/index.htm> (16.12.2007) with a quantity of useful information.

35. About his astrological 'style' and its similarity to some astrological elements found in Mithraism see Beck 2004e. Especially the so-called Lion monument from Nemrud Dagh (*CIMRM* 41; Beck 2006a, 227–239), depicting the conjunction of three planets and Moon in Leo on July 7, 65 BCE, seems to be analogically very similar to later custom of Mithraists to express astronomical situations iconographically (see very useful animation of this astronomical phenomenon on <http://www.nemrud.nl/en/zd_tekst1.asp> [16.12.2007], even though proposing a different date, July 14, 109 BCE).

Their dependants pursued military and civil careers.

If we compare both theories, the one proposed by Roger Beck seems to be more persuasive. First, it successfully connects two important traditions that played a major role in Mithraic "ideology": Persian religious tradition and Hellenistic astrology. Second, it shows how Mithraism burgeoning inside this community could be propagated in the Roman army and imperial administration, without causing any worries for the Roman authorities (Liebeschuetz 1994, 202–203; Clauss 2000, 24–25). Third, unlike the theory of Per Beskow, it operates with the cult spreading from the "inside"; the not entirely credible assumption about Roman legions being "infected" from the outside (by secret communities) can thus be avoided.

## Conclusion

Whether Roger Beck's theory is historically correct remains an open question. At the moment, there is no "hard" evidence that it is historically valid—that it describes how it was *really* done—and Roger Beck always claimed that what he has proposed was an ideal scenario, not a historical reconstruction (cf. Beck 1998a, 116–117). Cognitive science, of course, cannot compensate for the loss of historical evidence—much is lost, irretrievably so—but it can help us to assess whether this or that theory is, at least theoretically, possible, or, on the other hand, extremely improbable. And from this point of view, Roger Beck's scenario seems to include every necessary condition for being a successful and viable theory of Mithraic origins well grounded in our available historical data. His theory plausibly clarifies irregularities in the spread of early Mithraic communities, which would otherwise, seen from the perspective of traditional cultural diffusionism, remain mysterious. Roger Beck's scenario also credibly explains why Mithraism has exactly those features we know from the Western material and how they happened to be part of it. Cognitive science, thus, will not (and cannot) replace traditional historical methods, but it can, at least occasionally, supplement them and provide us with a very precious corrective device.

## References

### Abbreviations Used

*CIMRM* = Vermaseren, M.J. 1956–1960. *Corpus Inscriptionum et Monumentorum Religionis Mithriacae I-II*. Den Haag: Martinus Nijhoff.

*AE* = *L'Année épigraphique*

Aune, D.E. 1998. "Expansion and Recruitment among Hellenistic Religions: The Case of Mithraism." In *Recruitment, Conquest, and Conflict: Strategies in Judaism, Early Christianity, and the Greco-Roman World*, edited by P. Borgen, V.K. Robbins and D.B. Gowler, 39–56. Atlanta, GA: Scholar Press.

Ausbüttel, F.M. 1982. *Untersuchungen zu den Vereinen im Westen des Römischen Reiches*. Kallmünz: Lassleben.

Beard, M., J. North and S. Price. 1998a. *The Religions of Rome I: A History*. Cambridge: Cambridge University Press.

———. 1998b. *The Religions of Rome II: A Sourcebook*. Cambridge: Cambridge University Press.

Beck, R. 1984. "Mithraism Since Franz Cumont." *Aufstieg und Niedergang der römischen Welt*

II.17.4: 2002–2115.

———. 1991. "Thus Spake Not Zarathuštra: Zoroastrian Pseudoepigrapha of the Greco-Roman World." In *History of Zoroastrianism III: Zoroastrianism under Macedonian and Roman Rule,* edited by M. Boyce and P. Grenet, 491–565. Leiden: E.J.Brill.

———. 1994a. "Cosmic Models: Some Uses of Hellenistic Science in Roman Religion." *The Sciences in Greco-Roman Society,* edited by T.D. Barnes, *Apeiron* 27(4): 99–117.

———. 1994b. "In the Place of the Lion: Mithras in the Tauroctony." In *Studies in Mithraism*: edited by J. Hinnells, 29–50. Roma: L'Erma di Bretschneider.

———. 1996. "The Mysteries of Mithras." In *Voluntary Association in the Graeco-Roman World,* edited by J.S. Kloppenborg and S.G. Wilson, 176–185. London: Routledge.

———. 1998a. "The Mysteries of Mithras: A New Account of Their Genesis." *Journal of Roman Studies* 88: 115–128.

———. 1998b. "*Qui mortalitatis causa convenerunt*: The Meeting of Virunum Mithraists on June 26, A.D. 184." *Phoenix* 52: 335–344.

———. 2000. "Ritual, Myth, Doctrine, and Initiation in the Mysteries of Mithras: New Evidence from a Cult Vessel." *Journal of Roman Studies* 90: 145–180.

———. 2001. "New Thoughts on the Genesis of the Mysteries of Mithras." *Topoi* 11: 59–76.

———. 2004a. *Beck on Mithraism: Collected Works with New Essays.* Aldershot: Ashgate.

———. 2004b. "Four Men, Two Sticks and a Whip: Image and Doctrine in a Mithraic Ritual." In *Theorizing Religions Past: Archaeology, History and Cognition,* edited by H. Whitehouse and L.H. Martin, 87–103. Walnut Creek, CA: AltaMira Press.

———. 2004c. "The Rise and Fall of the Astral Identifications of the Tauroctonous Mithras." In R. Beck, *Beck on Mithraism: Collected Works with New Essays,* 235–249. Aldershot: Ashgate.

———. 2004d. "Astral Symbolism in the Tauroctony: A Statistical Demonstration of the Extreme Improbability of Unintended Coincidence in the Selection of Elements in the Composition." In R. Beck, *Beck on Mithraism: Collected Works with New Essays,* 251–265. Aldershot: Ashgate.

———. 2004e. "Whose Astrology? The Imprint of Ti. Claudius Balbillus on the Mithraic Mysteries." In R. Beck, *Beck on Mithraism: Collected Works with New Essays,* 323–329. Aldershot: Ashgate.

———. 2006a. *The Religion of the Mithras Cult in the Roman Empire: Mysteries of the Unconquered Sun.* Oxford: Oxford University Press.

———. 2006b. "On Becoming a Mithraists: New Evidence for the Propagation of the Mysteries." In *Religious Rivalries in the Early Roman Empire and the Rise of Christianity,* edited by L. Vaage, 175–194. Waterloo: Wilfried Laurier University Press.

Bendlin, A. 2002. "Gemeinschaft, Öffentlichkeit und Identität: Forschungsgeschichtliche Anmerkungen zu den Mustern solzialer Ordnung in Rom." In *Religiöse Vereine in der römischen Antike: Untersuchungen zu Organization, Ritual und Raumordnung,* edited by U. Egelhaaf-Gaiser and A. Schäfer, 9–40. Tübingen: J.C.B. Mohr (Paul Siebeck).

Beskow, P. 1978. "The Routes of Early Mithraism." In *Études Mithriaques,* edited by J. Duchesne-Guillemin, 7–18. Leiden: E. J. Brill.

———. 1979. "Branding in the Mysteries of Mithras." In *Mysteria Mithrae,* edited by U. Bianchi, 487–502. Leiden: E. J. Brill.

———. 1980. "The Portorium and the Mysteries of Mithras." *Journal of Mithraic Studies* 3: 1–18.

Betz, H.D. 1968. "The Mithras Inscriptions of Santa Prisca and the New Testament." *Novum Testamentum* 10: 62–80.

Bidez, J. and F. Cumont. 1938. *Les Mages hellénisés: Zoroastre, Osthanès et Hystaspe d'après la tradition greques*. Paris: Les Belles Lettres.

Bivar, A.D.H. 1975. "Mithra and Mesopotamia." In *Mithraic Studies II*, edited by J. Hinnells, 275–289. Manchester: Manchester University Press.

Blakely, J. A. *et al.* 1987. *The Joint Expedition to Caesarea Maritima, Excavation Reports. The Pottery and Dating of Vault 1: Horreum, Mithraeum and Later Uses* (vol. IV). Lewiston, NY: American School of Oriental Research.

Boyce, M. and Grenet, P. 1991. *History of Zoroastrianism III: Zoroastrianism under Macedonian and Roman Rule*. Leiden: E.J.Brill.

Brashear, W. M. 1992. *A Mithraic Catechism from Egypt <P. Berol. 21196>*. Vienna: Verlag Adolf Holzhausens Nfg.

Bull, R. J. 1978. "The Mithraeum at Caesarea Maritima." In *Études Mithriaques*, edited by J. Duchesne-Guillemin, 75–89. Leiden: E. J. Brill.

Burkert, W. 1987. *Ancient Mystery Cults*. Cambridge, MA: Harvard University Press.

Chalupa, A. 2005. "Hyenas or Lionesses? Mithraism and Women in the Religious World of the Late Antiquity." *Religio. Revue pro religionistiku* 13: 198–230.

Clauss, M. 1990a. *Mithras: Kult und Mysterien*. Munich: C. H. Beck.

———. 1990b. "Die Sieben Grades des Mithras-Kultes." *Zeitschift für Papyrologie und Epigraphik* 82, 183–194.

———. 1992. *Cultores Mithrae: Die Anhängershaft des Mithras-Kultes*. Stuttgart: Franz Steiner.

———. 2000. *The Roman Cult of Mithras: The God and his Mysteries*. Edinburgh: Edinburgh University Press.

———. 2001. "Mithras und die Präzession." *Klio* 83, 219–225.

Colpe, C. 1975. "Mithra-Verehrung, Mithras-Kult und die Existenz iranischer Mysterien." In *Mithraic Studies II*, edited by J. Hinnells, 378–405. Manchester: Manchester University Press.

Cumont, F. 1896. *Textes et monuments figurés relatifs aux mystères de Mithra II*. Bruxelles: H. Lamertin.

———. 1899. *Textes et monuments figurés relatifs aux mystères de Mithra I*. Bruxelles: H. Lamertin.

———. 1956. *The Mysteries of Mithra*, 2nd ed. New York: Dover Publication.

Daniels, C. M. 1975. "The Role of the Roman Army in the Spread and Practice of Mithraism." In *Mithraic Studies II*, edited by J. Hinnells, 249–274. Manchester: Manchester University Press.

David, Jonathan. 2000. "The Exclusion of Women in the Mithraic Mysteries: Ancient or Modern? *Numen* 47: 121–141.

Dawkins, R. 1999. "Forward." In *The Meme Machine*, edited by S. Blackmore, vii–xvii. Oxford: Oxford University Press.

Dörner, F. K. 1975. "Kommagene: Geschichte und Kultur einer Antike Landschaft." *Antike Welt* 6 (Sondernummer).

de Jong, A. 1997. *Traditions of the Magi: Zoroastrianism in Greek and Roman Literature*. Leiden: E. J. Brill.

Gordon, R. L. 1972. "Mithraism and Roman Society: Social Factors in the Explanation of Religious Change in the Roman Empire." *Religion* 2: 92–121.

———. 1975. "Franz Cumont and the Doctrines of Mithraism." In *Mithraic Studies I*, edited by J. Hinnells, 215–248. Manchester: Manchester University Press,.

———. 1976. "The Sacred Geography of a *Mithraeum*: The Example of Sette Sphere." *Journal of Mithraic Studies* 1: 119–165.

———. 1978. "The Date and Significance of CIMRM 593 (British Museum, Townley Collection)." *Journal of Mithraic Studies* 2: 148–174.

———. 1980a. "Panelled Complications." *Journal of Mithraic Studies* 3: 200–227.

———. 1980b. "Reality, Evocation and Boundary in the Mysteries of Mithras." *Journal of Mithraic Studies* 3: 19–99.

———. 1988. "Authority, Salvation and Mystery in the Mysteries of Mithras." In *Image and Mystery in the Roman World: Three Papers Given in Memory of Jocelyn Toynbee*, edited by J. Huskinson, M. Beard and J. Reynolds, 45–80. Cambridge: Alan Sutton.

———. 1994. "Who Worshipped Mithras?" *Journal of Roman Archaeology* 7: 459–474.

———. 1998. "Viewing Mithraic Art: The Altar from Burginatium (Kalkar), Germania Inferior." *Antigüedad: Religiones y Sociedades* 1: 227–258.

———. 2001a. "'Persei sub rupibus antri': Überlegungen zur Entstehung der Mithrasmysterien." In *Ptuj in römischen Reich. Mithraskult und seine Zeit: Akten des internationalen Symposion Ptuj, 11.–15. Okt. 1999*, edited by M. Gomer Vojkovič, 289–301. Ptuj: Pokrajinski Muzej Ptuj.

———. 2001b. "Trajets de Mithra en Syrie Romaine." *Topoi* 11: 77–136.

Griffith, A. B. 2006. "Completing the Picture: Women and the Female Principle in the Mithraic Cult." *Numen* 53: 48–77.

Harland, P.A. 2003. *Associations, Synagogues, and Congregations: Claiming a Place in Ancient Mediterranean Society*. Minneapolis: Fortress Press.

Hensen, A. 2001. "Der Tod des Mysten: Bestattungen vor Mithräen." In *Ptuj in römischen Reich. Mithraskult und seine Zeit: Akten des internationalen Symposion Ptuj, 11.–15. Okt. 1999*, edited by M. Gomer Vojkovič, 213–219. Ptuj: Pokrajinski Muzej Ptuj 2001.

Hinnells, J., ed. 1975a. *Mithraic Studies I–II*. Manchester: Manchester University Press.

———. 1975b. "Reflections on the Bull-slaying Scene." In *Mithraic Studies II*, edited by J. Hinnells, 290–312. Manchester: Manchester University Press.

Hopfe, L. M. and Lease, G. 1975. "The Caesarea Mithraeum: A Preliminary Report." *Biblical Archaeologist* 38: 1–10.

Huld-Zetsche, I. 1986. *Mithras in Nida-Heddernheim*. Franfurkt am Main: E. Henssler KG.

———. 2004. "Der Mainzer Krater mit den sieben Figuren." In *Roman Mithraism: The Evidence of the Small Finds*, edited by M. Martens and G. de Boe, 213–227. Brussels: Museum Het Toreke.

Kane, J. P. 1975. "The Mithraic Cult Meal in its Greek and Roman Environment." In *Mithraic Studies II*, edited by J. Hinnells, 313–351. Manchester. Manchester University Press.

Kloppenborg, J. S. 1996. "*Collegia* and *Thiasoi*: Issues in Function, Taxonomy and Membership." In *Voluntary Associations in the Graeco-Roman World*, edited by J.S. Kloppenborg and S.G. Wilson, 16–30. London: Routledge.

Liebeschuetz, J.H.W.G. 1994. "The Expansion of Mithraism Among the Religious Cults of the Second Century." In *Studies in Mithraism*, edited by J. Hinnells, 195–216. Roma: «L'Erma» di Bretschneider.

Martens, M. 2004. "The *Mithraeum* in Tienen (Belgium): Small Finds and What They Can Tell Us." In *Roman Mithraism: The Evidence of the Small Finds*, edited by M. Martens and G. de Boe, 25–26. Brussels: Museum Het Toreke.

Martin, L. H. 1989. "Roman Mithraism and Christianity." *Numen* 36: 2–15.

———. 1994. "Reflections on the Mithraic Tauroctony as a Cult Scene." In *Studies in Mithraism*, edited by J. Hinnells, 217–224. Roma: «L'Erma» di Bretschneider.

———. 1997. "Akin to the Gods or Simply One to Another? Comparison with Respect to Religions in Antiquity." In *Vergleichen und Verstehen in der Religionswissenschaft*, edited by H.-J.

Klimkeit, 147–159. Wiesbaden: Harrassowitz.

———. 2004. "Ritual Competence and Mithraic Ritual." In *Religion as a Human Capacity: A Festschrift in Honor of E. Thomas Lawson,* edited by T. Light and B.C. Wilson, 245–263. Leiden: E.J.Brill.

———. 2005. "Performativity, Discourse and Cognition: 'Demythologizing' the Roman Cult of Mithras." In *Rhetoric and Reality in Early Christianities*, edited by W. Braun, 187–217. Waterloo: Wilfried Laurier University Press.

———. 2006a. "Cognitive Science, Ritual, and the Hellenistic Mystery Religions." *Religion and Theology* 13: 383–395.

———. 2006b. "The Roman Cult of Mithras: A Cognitive Perspective." *Religio. Revue pro religion-istiku* 14: 131–146.

———. 2007. "Memes, Mithraism, and Transmission of the Mithraic Tauroctony." (conference paper, International Congress, Society of Biblical Literature, Vienna, July 22–26, 2007).

Mastrocinque A. 1998. *Studi sul mitraismo (il mitraismo e la magia).* Roma: Giorgio Bretscheider.

McCauley, R.N. and T.E. Lawson. 2002. *Bringing Ritual to Mind: Psychological Foundations of Cultural Forms.* Cambridge: Cambridge University Press.

Merkelbach, R. 1984. *Mithras.* Königstein/Ts.: Hein.

Momigliano, A. 1975. *Alien Wisdom: The Limits of Hellenisation.* Oxford: Oxford University Press.

Nilsson, M. P. 1961. *Geschichte der Griechischen Religion II,* 2nd ed. Munich: C. H. Beck.

Piccottini, G. 1994. *Mithrastempel in Virunum.* Klagenfurt: Verlag des Geschichtsvereines für Kärnten.

Ries, J. 1990. "Le culte de Mithra en Iran." *Aufstieg und Niedergang der römischen Welt* II.18.4: 2728–2775.

Roll, I. 1977. "The Mysteries of Mithras in the Roman Orient: The Problem of Origin." *Journal of Mithraic Studies* 2: 53–68.

Sauer, E. 1996. *The End of Paganism in the North-Western Provinces of the Roman Empire: The Example of the Mithras Cult.* Oxford: Tempus Reparatum.

———. 2004. "Not Just Small Change: Coins in Mithraea." In *Roman Mithraism: The Evidence of the Small Finds,* edited by M. Martens and G. De Boe, 327–353. Brussels: Museum Het Toreke.

Scheid, J. 2001. "Der Mithraskult im römischen Polytheismus." In *Ptuj in römischen Reich. Mithraskult und seine Zeit: Akten des internationalen Symposion Ptuj, 11.–15. Okt. 1999,* edited by M. Gomer Vojkovič, 99–103. Ptuj: Pokrajinski Muzej Ptuj.

Schütte-Maischatz, A. and E. Winter. 2000. "Kultstätten der Mithrasmysterien in Doliche." In *Gottkönige am Euphrat: Neue Ausgrabungen und Forschungen in Kommagene,* edited by J. Wagner, 93–99. Mainz: Philipp von Zabern.

———. 2001. "Die Mithräen von Doliche: Überlegungen zu den ersten Kultstätten der Mithras-Mysterien in der Kommagene." *Topoi* 11: 149–173.

Schwertheim, E. 1974. *Die Denkmäler orientalischer Gottheiten im Römischen Deutschland: Mit Ausnahme der ägyptischen Gottheiten.* Leiden: E. J. Brill.

Sperber, D. 1996. *Explaining Culture: A Naturalistic Approach.* Oxford: Blackwell.

———. 2000. "An Objection to the Memetic Approach to Culture." In *Darwinizing Culture: The Status of Memetics as a Science,* edited by R. Aunger, 163–173. Oxford: Oxford University Press.

Stark, K. B. 1869. "Die Mithrassteine von Dormagen." *Jahrbücher des Vereins von Altertumsfreunden im Rheinlande* 46: 1–25.

Turcan, R. 1975. *Mithras Platonicus: Recherches sur l'hellénisation philosophique de Mithra.* Leiden: E.J. Brill.

————. 1981. "Le Sacrifice mithriaque: innovation de sens et de modalités." In *Le Sacrifice dans l'antiquité* (Entretiens Fondation Hardt 17), edited by J. Rudhardt and O. Reverdin, 341–373. Vandœuvres–Genève: Fondation Hardt.

————. 1984. "Les motivation de l'intolérance chrétienne et la fin du Mithriacisme au IV<sup>e</sup> siècle ap. J-C." In *Actes du VII<sup>e</sup> Congrès de la Fédération Internationale des Associations d'Études Classiques II. Budapest, 3–8 septembre 1979*, edited by J. Harmatta, 209–226. Budapest: Akadémiai Kiadó.

————. 1993. *Mithra et le mithriacisme*, 2nd ed. Paris: Les belles lettres.

————. 1999. "Hiérarchie sacerdotal et astrologie dans les mystères de Mithra." In *La science des cieux: sages, mages et astrologues*. (Res Orientales 12), edited by R. Gyselen, 249–261. Leuven: Peeters Publishers.

Ulansey, D. 1991. *The Origins of the Mithraic Mysteries: Cosmology and Salvation in the Ancient World*, 2nd rev. ed. Oxford: Oxford University Press.

Vermaseren, M. J. 1971. *Mithriaca I. The Mithraeum at S. Maria Capua Vetere*. Leiden: E. J. Brill.

————. 1981. "Mithras in der Römerzeit." In *Die Orientalische Religionen im Römerreich*, edited by M.J. Vermaseren, 96–120. Leiden: E. J. Brill.

Vermaseren, M.J. and C.C. van Essen. 1965. *The Excavations in the Mithraeum of the Church of Santa Prisca*. Leiden: E.J. Brill.

Volken, M. 2004. "The Development of the Cult of Mithras in the Western Roman Provinces: A Socioarchaeological Perspective. *Electronic Journal of Mithraic Studies* 4. <http: //www.uhu. es/ejms/papers.htm> [24.8.2007].

Waldmann, H. 1973. *Die kommagenischen Kultreformen unter König Mithradates I. Kallinikos und seinem Sohn Antiochos I*. Leiden: E. J. Brill.

Whitehouse, H. 2000. *Argument and Icons: Divergent Modes of Religiosity*. Oxford: Oxford University Press.

————. 2002. "Modes of Religiosity: Towards a Cognitive Explanation of the Sociopolitical Dynamics of Religion." *Method and Theory in the Study of Religion* 14: 293–315.

————. 2004. *Modes of Religiosity: A Cognitive Theory of Religious Transmission*. Walnut Creek: AltaMira Press.

Widengren, G. 1966. "The Mithraic Mysteries in the Graeco-Roman World, With Special Regard to Their Iranian Background." In *La Persia e il mondo greco-romano*, Academia Nazionale dei Lincei, Anno 363, Quaderno 76, Roma, 433–456.

Wikander, S. 1951. "Études sur les mystères de Mithras." *Vetenskapsocieten i Lund: Årsbok 1950*. Lund: C.W.K. Gleerup, 5–46.

Wilson, S.G. 1996. "Voluntary Association: An Overview." In *Voluntary Associations in the Graeco-Roman World*, edited by J.S. Kloppenborg and S.G. Wilson, 1–15. London: Routledge.

# — 9 —

## Do the Multiple Initiations of Lucius in Apuleius' *Metamorphoses* Falsify the Ritual Form Hypothesis?

Douglas L. Gragg

In their 1990 book, *Rethinking Religion: Connecting Cognition and Culture*, E. Thomas Lawson and Robert N. McCauley introduced a "ritual competence theory," taking important cues from the linguistic competence theory of Noam Chomsky. Chomsky demonstrated, to the satisfaction of most linguists, that children do not acquire their native languages primarily through imitation or other forms of conscious effort (as an adult, for example, might learn a second language). Rather, he argued, normal humans come equipped with a cognitive mechanism—he called it, prosaically, a "language acquisition device"—that enables them, almost effortlessly, to *re-create* their native languages as they are exposed to them during a sensitive phase of development.[1]

One of the empirical observations upon which Chomsky built his argument was the fact that young children are able to distinguish well-formed and ill-formed sentences that they are hearing for the first time. He also noted that the human ability to distinguish such sentences does not even depend on whether the sentences are meaningful. For example, his famous sentence, "Colorless green ideas sleep furiously" (Chomsky 1957,15), is completely nonsensical, yet no one would deny that it is perfectly well-formed syntactically. Humans distinguish well-formed and ill-formed sentences in their native languages immediately (that is, instinctively), Chomsky argued, by means of a universal mental grammar.[2]

Lawson and McCauley argue that humans have analogous intuitions about well-formed and ill-formed action sequences.[3] These intuitions are based, they contend, on an "action-

---

1. See Chomsky (1957 and 1965). For a presentation of the theory that relates it to evolutionary theory and to recent findings in the cognitive sciences, see Pinker (1994).

2. Not everyone has accepted Chomsky's idea of universal grammar. The most interesting recent challenge is that of Dan Everett (2005). For a strongly critical response to Everett and his reply, see Nevins *et al.* (2007) and Everett (2007).

3. Lawson and McCauley were not the first to develop this analogy between cognition of language and cognition of action sequences. For example, semiotician Algirdas-Julien Greimas and colleagues developed a theory of "narrative grammar" and "semio-narrative competence," drawing explicitly on the work of Chomsky as well as that of anthropologist Claude Lévi-Strauss and folklorist Vladimir Propp (especially Greimas 1987; Greimas and Courtés 1982).

representation system" that is part of the standard cognitive equipment of anatomically modern humans, allowing them from an early age to distinguish "between agents and other entities and between actions and other events." An action, simply stated, involves an agent doing something. In some cases, the action involves an agent doing something to or for someone or something. In such cases, the target of the action can be called the "patient." Because ritual action shares this basic structure of every action, "the representation of religious rituals," McCauley and Lawson observe, "requires no special cognitive apparatus beyond the garden-variety cognitive machinery all normal human beings possess for the representation of agents and their actions."[4]

That is not to say that religious rituals, as forms of action, have no distinctive features. According to McCauley and Lawson, their *most* distinctive feature is the pivotal role that gods, ancestral spirits, or other such "superhuman" figures play in them. Depending on whether the superhuman figure is the actor or is acted upon, McCauley and Lawson distinguish between "special-agent" and "special-patient" rituals. This distinction forms the basis of what they call the "ritual form hypothesis" (McCauley and Lawson 2002, 6).

A classic example of a special-agent ritual is a rite of initiation, in which a superhuman figure acts to change the status of a religious postulant. The ritual form hypothesis predicts that a ritual of this sort will be performed infrequently—typically only once per individual postulant. Why, after all, would the powerful and effective action of a god need to be repeated? Because of its *gravitas*, such a ritual, the hypothesis predicts, will also likely involve significant expenditure of resources and be attended by a relatively high level of sensory pageantry. On the other hand, a special-patient ritual, such as an animal sacrifice, in which a worshipper offers something to a superhuman figure in exchange for favor or in gratitude for help already received, will likely be repeated, perhaps even frequently, and will likely involve a comparatively more modest level of expenditure and fanfare. In other words, the hypothesis suggests that, human cognition being as it is, ritual form, or "syntax," and intuitions about ritual frequency and propriety will correspond in predictable ways.

How might the validity of such an hypothesis be tested? One way would be to conduct controlled experiments, such as those designed by experimental psychologist Justin Barrett in collaboration with Tom Lawson (Barrett and Lawson 2001). Another way would be to search the large "databases" of ethnography and historiography to identify relevant cases that either confirm or falsify the hypothesis. My modest contribution here will be to consider briefly one relevant historical case.

In the second half of the second century of the Common Era, a well-to-do lawyer and small-time philosopher from Roman North Africa wrote a very fine novel. Apuleius—the only part of the author's name we know—called his book *Metamorphoses* (*Transformations*), though it later acquired an alternative title, *The Golden Ass*. It is the story of a young man from Corinth, named Lucius, whose inordinate curiosity about magic lands him in serious trouble. During an extended business trip in the region of Thessaly, he learns that the wife of his host is a sorceress, who is able to turn herself into a bird. Eager to experience this transformation for himself, he persuades the maid, who has become his lover, to fetch the necessary potion from the laboratory of her mistress. Unfortunately, the maid grabs the wrong vial, and Lucius is turned into an ass instead. The maid rushes off to get the antidote (he must eat some roses to return to human form), but, before she can return, a band

---

4.    These quotations are taken from McCauley and Lawson (2002, 11), in which they develop further their ritual competence theory and the "ritual form hypothesis" that is based on it.

of thieves breaks into the stable where he is hiding and whisks him away. The long series of disastrous (though often hilarious) misadventures that Lucius then suffers as a human trapped in the body of an ass makes up the bulk of the novel.

The relevance of the work to our purpose comes at the end. After almost a full year of shifting fortune at the mercy of one owner or another, Lucius gives his last owner the slip while they are visiting his own home town of Corinth. Escaping under the cover of darkness, he gallops the six miles to Cenchreae, a seaside town on the Aegean side of the isthmus, where, exhausted, he falls into a deep sleep on the beach. During the night, the goddess Isis appears to him in a dream, expressing her pity over his plight and offering him rescue if he will devote the rest of his life to her service. The goddess reveals how he is to eat roses from a garland offered by her priest during a processional in town the next day. Lucius follows her instructions and is restored to human form—to the great amazement of the crowds who witness the transformation. Lucius takes an apartment near the temple of Isis in Cenchreae and daily worships the goddess while he awaits her invitation to be initiated into her mysteries.

The initiation of Lucius, which is carried out in due course, is clearly what McCauley and Lawson would call a special-agent ritual, that is, one in which the superhuman figure plays the role of agent. This initiation, we are told, is something for which Lucius was "destined long ago" (*iam dudum destinatum*) by the goddess (11,19). It is something for which he must wait, a priest explains, until the date "is indicated by the nod of the goddess" (*deae nutu demonstrari*) since to perform the rite without her prior command is to act "sacrilegiously" (*sacrilegum*) (11: 21). The priest also interprets the meaning of the rite in terms of the action of the goddess. As "both the gates of the underworld and the guardianship of salvation are in the hands of the goddess," he says, the rite of initiation constitutes a kind of voluntary death from which she provides salvation (11: 21). When Lucius himself later describes the initiation—in the barest outline since he is not permitted to reveal any details—he says that he approached "the boundary of death" (*confinium mortis*) and came into the very presence of the gods (11: 23). He also says that he emerged from the rite "consecrated" (*sacratus*) and speaks of the festivities that followed as a celebration of his "birthday" (*natalem*) (11: 24).[5]

We noted earlier that the ritual form hypothesis predicts that special-agent rituals will typically involve significant expenditure of resources and be attended by a significant level of sensory pageantry. In the account of Lucius' initiation, we learn that he was, in fact, required to procure resources for the ritual at considerable expense (11: 23; cf. 11: 28 and 30). From hints in this story and from other evidence about the nature of initiation ritual in Graeco-Roman mystery cults,[6] we know that these rites also typically involved elaborate sensory stimulation.

We also noted earlier the prediction of the ritual form hypothesis that, because special-agent rituals are understood to entail powerful superhuman agency, they will be performed infrequently—generally only once per individual postulant. It comes, therefore, as a surprise (and a potential embarrassment for the hypothesis) that, after Lucius has moved from Cenchreae to Rome and spent a year in association with worshippers of Isis there, he is asked to undergo a *second* initiation—and then a *third*.[7]

---

5.     Translations of the Latin text published in Apuleius 1989 are my own unless otherwise indicated.

6.     See Gragg (2004, 76–77) and Gragg (2010).

7.     While it was not at all unusual in Graeco-Roman antiquity for an individual to be initiated into more

Of course, it is no good arguing that, because the story is fictional, this anomaly is irrelevant. If the hypothesis is valid, then the cognitive mechanisms that constrain human intuitions about ritual form "in the wild" should also constrain a novelist's intuitions about ritual form in imagination. What I will show in the remainder of this chapter is that these expected constraints are, in fact, represented quite strikingly in Apuleius' narrative about the second and third initiations of Lucius. On that basis, I will argue that, instead of falsifying the ritual form hypothesis, the story of the multiple initiations of Lucius actually provides strong confirmation of its validity.

A year after Lucius arrives in Rome and begins frequenting the temple of Isis located in the Campus Martius, the goddess appears to him in a dream, speaking to him of the need for a second initiation. Lucius' reaction is significant: "I wondered what she was up to, what further (rite) she could be proposing—and with good reason (*quidni?*), since it seemed to me that I had already (*iam dudum*) been fully initiated" (11: 26). Struggling with "conscientious misgivings"[8] (*religiosum scrupulum*) about this, he seeks the advice of his co-religionists and is assured that this second initiation should be considered not a repetition of the first but rather an initiation into the closely related cult of Osiris, the divine companion of Isis. This clarification resolves Lucius' "cloud of uncertainty" (*ambiguitatis caligo*) about the issue, and he submits to the ritual, this time having to sell most of his clothing to cover the cost (11: 27–28).

What is most striking about this account is that, even though the command to undergo a further initiation is given by the goddess herself, Lucius hesitates. The kind of misgivings Apuleius attributes to Lucius, when he is first faced with the idea of having to repeat his initiation, is precisely the kind the ritual form hypothesis leads us to expect. Lucius intuits that an initiation should not need to be repeated, and he surrenders his misgivings only when the apparent breach of ritual propriety is explained away with a religiously appropriate justification.

No sooner has Lucius completed this second initiation, however, than the gods (plural this time, perhaps meaning Isis and Osiris together) appear to him in his sleep with, as he puts it, "the unexpected and completely baffling commands" (*inopinatis et usquequaque mirificis imperiis*) that he undergo yet a third initiation. This time Lucius is not only perplexed but also suspicious:

> Uneasy (*sollicitus*)—with significant concern (*nec levi cura*) and utterly troubled (*oppido suspensus animi*)—I pondered anxiously why this new and unheard-of (*nova haec et inaudita*) proposal was being put forward by the gods. What element of the rite, already repeated once, could remain to be done? Undoubtedly, both priests handled my case incorrectly or incompletely (*perperam vel minus plene*). By Hercules, I was now even beginning to think twice about their honesty (*fide*) (11: 29).

Lucius goes on to describe himself as "worked up to the point of insanity" (*ad instar insaniae percitum*). The strength of the language Apuleius puts into the mouth of Lucius indicates the strength of his intuition that repeating the initiation would be inappropriate. He is "uneasy," "concerned," "troubled," "anxious," and "worked up." The idea strikes him as "unexpected," "baffling," "new," and "unheard-of." He can only assume that the priests had bungled the job previously so that his first two initiations were somehow defective.

Lucius receives a further bedtime revelation, however, assuring him that nothing is amiss.

than one cult, the idea of being initiated into the *same* cult more than once is quite surprising.

8.    This is the excellent rendering of E. J. Kenney (Apuleius 1998).

Rather than worry, the gods say, he should rejoice that they consider him worthy to experience three times what others, if they are fortunate, experience only once (11: 29). They explain that this third initiation is necessary because he had been required to leave behind the sacred clothing that he had received at his first initiation in Cenchreae. In order to receive a new set of vestments to wear on special occasions in Rome, he needed to repeat the ritual. Satisfied, oddly enough, by the gods' explanation, Lucius submits to initiation once more, spending lavishly again—more out of pious zeal, he says, than from a rational assessment of his assets (11: 30).

One must admit that the justification Apuleius has the gods provide for the third initiation seems rather contrived in comparison to the explanation given for the second one, and we wonder at Lucius' readiness to accept it. It made some sense that he undergo a second initiation in order to participate fully in the twin cult of Isis and Osiris at Rome, but the rationale given for the third one sounds almost trivial. It is important to note, however, that, like the previous rationale, this one is specifically *religious* in the sense that it appeals to a need that can only be satisfied ritually. What is even more important to note is that the relative *plausibility* of the justifications offered in the story for repeating initiation is not even particularly relevant to our consideration of the validity of the ritual form hypothesis. What is relevant is the fact that, in each case, a religiously appropriate justification for repetition is *considered necessary*, and it is this that makes the story a striking confirmation rather than a falsification of the ritual form hypothesis.

The argument can now be summarized succinctly. The ritual form hypothesis of McCauley and Lawson predicts that special-agent rituals, such as initiations, will involve relatively high levels of expenditure and sensory pageantry. The accounts of Lucius' initiations into the cults of Isis and Osiris in Apuleius' *Metamorphoses*, which describe lavish spending and dramatic rites, are consistent with these predictions. The ritual form hypothesis also predicts that special-agent rituals will be performed infrequently, typically only once per individual postulant. The fact that Lucius is initiated three times seems inconsistent with this prediction. Significantly, however, each time Lucius is commanded to undergo a further initiation, he expresses strong reservations about the appropriateness of doing so and concedes only after he has received a religiously appropriate justification. This behavior of Lucius testifies to the novelist's intuition, predicted by the ritual form hypothesis, that an initiation ritual should not normally be repeated. What at first appeared to be an historical counter-example provides, instead, strong support for the validity of the hypothesis.

## References

Apuleius. 1989. *Metamorphoses*. Edited and translated by J. Arthur Hanson in two volumes. Loeb Classical Library. Cambridge, MA: Harvard University Press.

Apuleius. 1998. *The Golden Ass, or Metamorphoses*. Translated with an introduction and notes by E. J. Kenney. New York: Penguin Books.

Barrett, Justin L., and E. Thomas Lawson. 2001. "Ritual Intuitions: Cognitive Contributions to Judgments of Ritual Efficacy," *Journal of Cognition and Culture* 1(2): 183–201. Reprinted in Slone 2006: 215–230.

Chomsky, Noam. 1957. *Syntactic Structures*. The Hague: Mouton Publishers.

———. 1965. *Aspects of the Theory of Syntax*. Cambridge: The MIT Press.

Everett, Daniel L. 2005. "Cultural Constraints on Grammar and Cognition in Pirahã," *Cultural Anthropology* 46(4): 621–646.

———. 2007. "Cultural Constraints on Grammar in Pirahã: A Reply to Nevins, Pesetsky, and Rodrigues." Manuscript available at http: //ling.auf.net/lingBuzz/000427.

Gragg, Douglas L. 2004. "Old and New in Roman Religion: A Cognitive Account." In *Theorizing Religions Past: Archaeology, History, and Cognition*, edited by Harvey Whitehouse and Luther H. Martin, 69–86. Walnut Creek, CA: AltaMira Press.

———. 2010. "Parables, Cognitive Shock, and Spontaneous Exegetical Reflection." In *Religious Narrative, Cognition, and Culture: Image and Word in the Mind of Narrative*, edited by Armin W. Geertz and Jeppe Sinding Jensen, 209–217. London: Equinox.

Greimas, Algirdas-Julien. 1987. *On Meaning: Selected Writings in Semiotic Theory*. Translated by Paul J. Perron and Frank H. Collins. Minneapolis: University of Minnesota Press.

Greimas, Algirdas-Julien, and Joseph Courtés. 1982. *Semiotics and Language: An Analytical Dictionary*. Translated by Larry Crist *et al.* Bloomington: Indiana University Press.

Lawson, E. Thomas, and Robert N. McCauley. 1990. *Rethinking Religion: Connecting Cognition and Culture*. Cambridge: Cambridge University Press.

McCauley, Robert N., and E. Thomas Lawson. 2002. *Bringing Ritual to Mind: Psychological Foundations of Cultural Forms*. Cambridge: Cambridge University Press.

Nevins, Andrew Ira, David Pesetsky, and Cilene Rodrigues. 2007. "Pirahã Exceptionality: A Reassessment." Manuscript available at http: //ling.auf.net/lingBuzz/000411.

Pinker, Steven. 1994. *The Language Instinct: How the Mind Creates Language*. New York: HarperCollins.

Slone, D. Jason, ed. 2006. *Religion and Cognition: A Reader*. London: Equinox.

## — 10 —

## Religion Explained?
## Lucian of Samosata and the Cognitive Science of Religion

Ulrich Berner

### Introduction: Cognitive Theories—Old and New

About 15 years ago, Stewart Guthrie reintroduced the concept of "anthropomorphism" as designating the essential feature of religion (Guthrie 1993, 177–204). The title of his book—*Faces in the Clouds*—indicated already the central tenet of his theory of religion, claiming that "religion consists of seeing the world as humanlike" (Guthrie 1993, 4). Over the following years, Pascal Boyer has developed an even more comprehensive cognitive theory, focussing on the "projections of intuitive belief-desire psychology onto non-intentional objects" (Boyer 1996, 92). He provided lists of supernatural concepts, including examples that illustrate the anthropomorphizing tendency. Among other entities he mentions "statues that listen" and "gods who have meals and fall in love" (Boyer 1996, 83; cf. 2002b, 68). Both of these examples may be inspired by memories of classical Greek religion – who does not think of the famous statue of Zeus at Olympia, or the Homerian gods on mount Olympus having meals and falling in love? Thus it does not seem unreasonable to bring materials from ancient Greek religion to a discussion of recent cognitive approaches to the study of religion. With regard to the critical attitude, often underlying cognitive theories of religion it may be of particular interest to focus on Lucian of Samosata, an author of the second century C.E., who is known for his sceptical or even critical attitude towards religion. Before going into details, however, it is necessary to reflect on the concept of "anthropomorphism" and recall that it is not at all a new concept in the study of religion. Everyone will remember the old theory of animism discussed among the ancestors of Religious Studies in the nineteenth century, particularly by Edward B. Tylor, who is mentioned by Pascal Boyer, although not very often and not in a very detailed way (Boyer 1994, 405; 2002a, 17).

When Tylor in 1866 published an article on "The Religion of Savages", he chose an example that he considered to be illustrative for the animistic way of thinking. Drawing upon one of the children's magazines, he reproduced a story "a certain preacher or teacher"

131

had told to a class of school children as "a useful practical lesson"—the story of a broom-stick that felt neglected (Tylor 1866, 71). Tylor did not identify with the tendency of his source, which had been ridiculing superstition and propagating an enlightened kind of religion. He was more inclined to defend the animistic view of the world as being a quite meaningful operation of the human mind, certainly not something to be despised as non-sense (Tylor 1866, 86). Tylor's example—a broomstick that feels neglected—is similar to one of the examples given by Justin Barrett, adapted from one of Boyer's articles: "a hammer that feels neglected", given as an example of what is called in terms of the new cognitive theories, the principle of violating the expectations of intuitive psychology, one of the "Intuitive-knowledge-domain violations" (Barrett 2006, 91; cf. Boyer 2003, 100–103).

The new theories focussing on anthropomorphism as the essential feature of religion, it seems, are closely related to the old theories of animism. The difference lies, perhaps, with the controversy about the intuitive or counterintuitive basis for animistic beliefs. In any case, Guthrie seems to be very much in line with Tylor, interpreting anthropomorphism as attributing humanity to the world. Also it should be noticed that the new tendency to explain religion in Darwinian terms of evolutionary psychology is not totally new, since Tylor was deeply influenced by Darwinism, even corresponding with Darwin himself. Nearly a century ago, Jane Harrison highlighted this connection in an article on the influence of Darwinism on the study of religions, stating at the very beginning, that the title of her paper "might well have been 'The Creation by Darwinism of the Scientific Study of Religions'" (Harrison 1915, 143).

Thus it seems reasonable to view the new cognitive approach to the study of religion from an historical perspective, as going back at least to the emergence of the science of religion in the nineteenth century, closely related to the emergence of Darwinism, and to agnosticism as a modern version of scepticism, the creed of Darwin himself (Darwin 1989, 124f). And it may be of special interest to trace this history as far as possible, following the tradition of scepticism back to antiquity where it originated as an independent and critical reflection upon traditional religious beliefs and rituals.

Lucian's work provides a good starting point, since he is known as a sceptic and critic of all the contemporary religious traditions, including Christianity—his work was put on the *index librorum prohibitorum* of the Catholic church in 1590, while it was appreciated in the era of European enlightenment (cf. Nesselrath 2001a, 30). Lucian seemingly aimed at making religious myths and rituals look ridiculous, while also polemicizing the various schools of philosophy, appreciating only scepticism and, to some extent, Epicureanism, as the school that was widely considered as being anti-religious (cf. Nesselrath 2001b). One of the most interesting texts in this respect is Lucian's "*Philopseudes*" ("The Lovers of Lies"), including among other miraculous stories the famous tale about "The sorcerer's apprentice" (cf. Ribbat 2001).

## "The Lovers of Lies, or the Unbeliever"—Lucian on Superstition and Religion

### *Lucian's examples*

In a fictitious conversation with a friend, Lucian gives a report about a discussion between a group of people, who believe in magical techniques of healing and other miraculous events, and a sceptic—obviously the alter ego of the author himself. The title already indicates the author's tendency: from his point of view, all these believers are to be regarded as lovers of lies.

When asking what kind of lies these people believe in, the modern reader will recognize a lot of examples known from recent texts in the cognitive science of religion, as, for instance, stories about inanimate objects turning into living beings, or visual appearances of gods and demons. So Lucian describes the belief in supernatural intentional agents and the fascination of counter-intuitive concepts—all of them known so well from the cognitive science of religion, as, for instance, from the list of "Intuitive-knowledge-domain violations" given by Pascal Boyer and Justin Barrett. One of Boyer's favourite examples, it will be remembered, is "statues as intentional actors" (Boyer 1999, 881).

Lucian provides two examples of this kind. One of the "lovers of lies" tells a story about a statue, representing the Corinthian general Pellichus, that was seen moving around at night:

> "As soon as night comes," he said, "he gets down from the pedestal on which he stands and goes all about the house; we all encounter him, sometimes singing, and he has never harmed anybody. One has but to turn aside, and he passes without molesting in any way those who saw him. Upon my word, he often takes baths and disports himself all night, so that the water can be heard splashing." (Lucian 19)

All the hearers, but Lucian himself, believe in the truth of this story about the moving statue. To imagine a statue that takes a bath may, perhaps, be called a strongly counter-intuitive concept. This exaggeration, however, is in line with Lucian's tendency to ridicule counter-intuitive assumptions. In any case, the sceptic, representing Lucian's tendency, remains unconvinced. His comment is:

> "Well, Eucrates," I said, "as long as bronze is bronze and the work a product of Demetrius of Alopece, who makes men, not gods, I shall never be afraid of the statue of Pellichus..."
>
> (Lucian 20)

This sceptical position, however, does not prevail in the discussion. On the contrary, another story of a moving statue is told: a bronze Hipppocrates who was also seen walking around and interacting with living persons (Lucian 21).

Lucian, the sceptic, does not believe in such a violation of ontological categories and he does not use counter-intuitive concepts. What strikes him, however, is the fact that some people do believe in such weird things, and he comes close to modern adherents of scepticism, as, for instance, Michael Shermer (1997), when he raises the question:

> Can you tell me, Philocles, what in the world it is that makes many men so fond of lying that they delight in telling preposterous tales themselves and listen with especial attention to those who spin yarns of that sort? (Lucian 1)

## Lucian's questions

Lucian keeps reflecting upon the question of why people believe in stories like these, about walking statues or post-mortal existence of souls, even adult and educated people. He relates the disappointing experience with a Pythagorean philosopher who joined the group and participated in the discussion, and, instead of opposing the superstitious people on scientific grounds, supported their beliefs by providing further examples of miraculous events (Lucian 29–32). The sceptic, near the end of the discussion states his opinion that at least the youth should not be exposed to hearing such stories:

> You ought to be easy with them and not accustom them to hear things like this which will abide with them and annoy them their lives long and will make them afraid of every sound by filling them with all sorts of superstition. (Lucian 37)

133

Lucian comes closest to modern cognitivists when he observes that these stories about supernatural intentional agents have an innate tendency to stick in one's memory:

> I should be glad if I could anywhere buy at a high price a dose of forgetfulness, so that the memory of what I heard may not stay with me and work me some harm (Lucian 39).

Thus Lucian has observed already what modern cognitivists call the "attention-grabbing power" of counter-intuitive concepts (cf. Boyer 1996, 95). In addition, Lucian has used a metaphor that fits nicely into modern critical reflections on cognition and religion: he compares the spread of superstitious beliefs to the infectious disease that is caused by the bite of a mad dog—an equivalent for the modern metaphor of the "viruses of the mind" (cf. Dawkins 2004).

Lucian is again very much in line with modern scientists and critics of religion like Richard Dawkins, when he expresses his conviction that "we have a powerful antidote to such poisons in truth and in sound reason brought to bear everywhere. As long as we make use of this, none of these empty, foolish lies will disturb our peace." (Lucian 40).

Although Lucian was very much aware of the attention-grabbing potential of counter-intuitive concepts, he could not, of course, explain it in terms of a Darwinian worldview. As he could not yet refer to evolutionary psychology, he could not but couch his questions in polemical terms as why people love lies. One could say that Lucian's questions have been answered by the cognitive science of religion. In any case, it is quite clear that he himself did not share the beliefs of many of his contemporaries and that he regarded these beliefs as superstition (*deisidaimonia*), not as religion (*eusebeia*), making use of a distinction already used by Theophrast and Plutarch.

### Lucian's intentions

The question arises whether or not the sceptic's criticism of superstitious beliefs implies a critical attitude towards religion on the whole, comparable to a modern scientific approach of studying religion as a natural phenomenon (cf. Dennett 2006, 34). However, one should not forget that sceptical philosophers did not hesitate to participate in religious rituals, as, for instance, Pyrrhon who is said to have been elected high priest in his community (Diogenes Laertios IX, 64). Also the possibility has to be taken into consideration that Lucian is in line with those philosophers who criticized anthropomorphic ideas of the gods just in order to replace these misleading ideas by more appropriate ones, as, for instance, Xenophanes, who emphasized that the one true god is totally different from human conceptions:

> One god, greatest among gods and men,
> In no way similar to mortal men in body or in thought.
>
> (Diels/Kranz 21B23. Translation: Waterfield 2000, 26)

So the question remains: was Lucian criticizing superstition only, or superstition and religion alike, or, to put it in different terms: is Lucian a religious person, though in a different sense, or is he an irreligious person? A point of departure for discussing this question is one section in this text, the "The Lovers of Lies, or the Unbeliever." The sceptic does not believe in miraculous healing, as, for instance, the power of certain incantations to drive off fevers. Therefore, he comes under suspicion to be a total unbeliever, an atheist:

> "It seems to me," said Deinomachus , "that when you talk like that you do not believe in the gods, either, since you do not think that cures can be effected through holy names."
>
> (Lucian 10)

The sceptic's defensive answer is:

> "Don't say that, my dear sir!" I replied. "Even though the gods exist, there is nothing to prevent that sort of thing from being false just the same. For my part, I revere the gods and I see their cures and all the good that they do by restoring the sick to health with drugs and doctoring." (Lucian 10)

Lucian, it seems, tries to make clear that it is possible to worship the gods differently—not in a superstitious way but in a way that is consistent with scientific evidence. Since Lucian is neither a theologian nor a philosopher in a strict sense, he can't be expected to develop his own religious view in a systematic way. Also it should be taken into consideration that as an author he may be trying to convey different messages to different groups among his readers: believers and unbelievers among his readers may be equally satisfied when hearing ridiculous stories about the gods of mythology—one group taking it as criticism of mythology only, that not disprove a deeper spiritual conception of the gods or God; the other group taking it as the rejection of any belief in gods. Lucian's own individual religiosity is very difficult to grasp, if at all.

However, the decisive question remains: should Lucian be regarded as an outsider to religion, an irreligious person? Lucian, it seems, does not believe in gods as supernatural intentional agents who violate ontological categories in a counter-intuitive way. According to the understanding of religion widely presupposed in cognitive theories, Lucian would have to be regarded as an irreligious person. However, this would mean taking over the view of the believers who are presented by Lucian as superstitious people, as "lovers of lies". And there is no reason to take over such a definition into the science of religion, neglecting the other, more sophisticated understanding of religion carefully indicated by Lucian as another possibility: religion without superstition, revering the gods without believing in miraculous healing and other stories about the counter-intuitive behaviour of supernatural intentional agents.

## Explaining Religion or Superstition?

### *Distinguishing between religious concepts and ways of religious conceptualization*

Saying that cognitive theories explain superstition only, not religion, may sound misleading, since there is no uncontroversial definition of either of these terms. It seems reasonable, however, to distinguish between concepts and ways of conceptualization, and, correspondingly, between the task of understanding the content of religious concepts and the task of explaining the mechanism of religious conceptualizations. Religious beliefs consist of both of these components: concepts for interpreting the world and ways of conceptualization for communicating the religious concepts of the world. Lucian's work can serve as a starting point for illustrating this distinction.

In his "*dialogi deorum*", Lucian portrays Zeus as a tyrant, greedy for power and acting without any moral responsibility (cf. Berdozzo 2008). Lucian's way of presenting Zeus in these dialogues seems to aim at making the audience laugh about the god—it is obvious that Lucian himself does not believe in the existence of such a supernatural intentional agent. However, his description of Zeus could be the metaphorical expression of a deeply pessimistic view of the world, interpreting it as being governed by brutal force alone, without any relationship to justice. This basic religious concept—a "blik" in terms of Hare's philosophy of religion (1978; cf. Berner 1997, 158f)—can be conceptualized in different ways: in ab-

135

stract or in anthropomorphic terms, either by denying the existence of gods or by describing the gods as greedy for power and unjust, the religious concept remaining the same.

So the basic question religious people are concerned with, is not "are there supernatural intentional agents?" but rather: "are the events in the world connected in a morally consistent way?" The more optimistic view of the world that there might be such a morally consistent connection can be conceptualized in anthropomorphic as well as in abstract terms, with or without assuming the existence of a supernatural intentional agent. The best known example of a non-anthropomorphic conceptualization is the law of karma in classical Buddhism, postulating a morally consistent connection between human deeds and their consequences. This Buddhist conception is logically equivalent to an anthropomorphic conceptualization that postulates the existence of a powerful god who judges human deeds in a morally consistent way. Both these views, the theistic and the non-theistic one, share the same religious concept, the difference lying with the way of conceptualization.

Another example from Hellenistic literature may be useful to illustrate the possibility of different religious concepts within the same framework of conceptualization. Chariton of Aphrodisias, an author of the first century CE, in his novel *Callirhoe* relates the story of a couple that suffers a lot of misfortunes, until in the end, after a long time of uncertainty, happiness is regained. And it is Callirhoe who suffered most, although she had been an extremely faithful worshiper of Aphrodite, who is regarded as the supreme divine power. The central religious problem the author touches upon does not concern the existence of the goddess Aphrodite but rather her personality: whether or not the goddess is reliable and consistent in her behaviour towards faithful adherents. Losing faith, in this case does not mean questioning the existence of the goddess but questioning her reliability. In quite a number of prayers to Aphrodite, inserted into the novel, the author exposes this problem, presenting the view of the human actor as oscillating between accusation and adoration (Chariton 3,10.6; 8,4.10; cf. Berner 2005, 98f)—indicating different religious concepts within the same framework of conceptualization. The same religious problem could well be shifted into a different ontological framework, by abandoning the anthropomorphic conceptualization of *Tyche*, the goddess of Fortune (Chariton 8,1.2), and discussing in abstract terms which kind of fate people can expect if they act reliably and faithfully themselves.

Based on these examples from antiquity, it seems possible to define different kinds of conflicts between religious conceptions: conflicting conceptualizations of a shared concept, and conflicting concepts within a shared framework of conceptualization. This distinction may be illustrated by some examples from later periods of European religious history.

## Conflicts of Religious Conceptualizations

The famous trial of Galileo in the seventeenth century may serve as an example of a conflict of conceptualizations without a conflict of religious concepts. As he tried to make clear again and again, for instance, in his letter to the Grand Duchess Christina, Galileo did not want to question the authority of the Bible as the sacred writings, the primary purpose of which is "the service of God and the salvation of souls" (Galileo 1615,182). He did not challenge the concept of God as giving laws for humans leading to eternal life, made accessible in the Bible and the sacraments of the church. Galileo was quite sure, however, that "Nature, on the other hand, is inexorable and immutable", and "never transgresses the laws imposed upon her" (Galileo 1615, 182). So he could not avoid challenging the ontological framework of conceptualizing God as a supernatural agent who would intervene in human affairs by breaking the laws of nature. Some theologians among Galileo's contemporaries, as, for instance, the Jesuit Didacus Astunica and the Carmelite monk Antonio Foscarini, followed his argument and did not see any problem with adjusting the conceptualization of God to the new cosmology, as long as the concept of God remained the same. However, at that time, only a minority of theologians were able and willing to make this distinction.

Another example might be the "controversy about atheism" at the University of Jena in 1798/99, when the German philosopher Johann Gottlieb Fichte was accused of being an atheist, since he had published and defended an article, written by the school teacher Friedrich Karl Forberg, which was understood as having denied the existence of God. Fichte tried in vain to convince his opponents that he was not abandoning the concept of God, but only breaking with the old way of conceptualizing the idea of God as "a special substance" (Fichte 1999, 107). According to Fichte, what is central to religion is not belief in the existence of a supernatural being, but belief in a moral law governing the world:

> Es liegt kein Grund in der Vernunft, aus jener moralischen Weltordnung herauszugehen und vermittelst eines Schlusses vom Begründeten auf den Grund noch ein besonderes Wesen, als die Ursache desselben, anzunehmen;… (Fichte 1798, 19)

Fichte was very sure that he did not deviate from the Christian tradition and its concept of God. So he did not hesitate to return the accusation of atheism to his opponents (Fichte 1999, 108f; cf. Berner 1994, 772). This controversy on atheism, leading to the dismissal of the philosopher from his university, was about different conceptualizations of a shared religious concept.

## Conflicts of Religious Concepts

A totally different case is the controversy between John Calvin and his opponent Sebastian Castellio, concerning the question of whether or not it was right to burn Michael Servet who had been condemned for heresy (Castellio 1554; cf. Berner 2004, 26–29). Calvin and Castellio did not disagree over the ontological framework of conceptualization, since they were adherents to the same reformed version of Christianity in the age of Reformation. What was controversial was rather the concept of God as the basis for the norms of Christian behaviour: Calvin's concept of God emphasized his austerity, as shown by the stern figure of Moses, excluding tolerance towards notorious heretics and even demanding to kill them. Castellio's concept of God, on the contrary, emphasized his gentleness, as shown by the mild figure of Jesus, demanding tolerance towards heretics and excluding the right to kill them.

Another example might be the controversy about witch-trials in the seventeenth century, between the Jesuit Friedrich Spee, the defender of witches, and his Jesuit opponents, who were advocating the torture and burning of witches ( Spee 1631; cf. Berner 2007a, 68). In line with the Jesuit Adam Tanner, his precursor as a critic of the witch-trial procedures, Spee did not challenge the ontological framework of conceptualizing the evil forces. So he did not openly deny the existence of supernatural intentional agents ultimately at work. What was under discussion was not the question of whether or not the devil exists, but the question of whether or not God demands that his followers apply all means of violence to exterminate the followers of the devil. The conflicting positions in this controversy about witch-trials were ultimately derived from different religious concepts within a shared framework of conceptualization.

137

# Summary

The cognitive approaches contribute considerably to the study of religion by explaining, with reference to evolutionary psychology, a mechanism of religious conceptualization—the anthropomorphizing tendency that has been dominant for a long time in history as invariant to cultural varieties. However, the study of religion must not neglect the hermeneutical task of understanding the content of the various religious concepts themselves—apart from the way of conceptualization. The explanatory task, it may be added, cannot be restricted to cognitive theories. It has to include sociological theories, too, since the dynamics of religious history, as, for instance, the trial of Galileo, or the rise and decline of witch-trials in early modern Europe, could not be explained by focusing on mechanisms of cognition only (cf. Berner 2007b, 175f).

What modern cognitivists describe as religious beliefs, Lucian has regarded as superstitious beliefs. There is no good reason, however, to limit the concept of religion to these beliefs in supernatural intentional agents and other counter-intuitive assumptions, excluding Lucian's own view as irreligious. Lucian's scepticism could well be considered as a special kind of religion that is conceptualized in a different way. In history there may have always been individuals like Lucian, conceptualizing their religious concepts of the world in an alternative way, not by anthropomorphizing, or at least being aware of the problems of anthropomorphism, as, for instance, Dio Chrysostom, an author of the first and second century C.E. With regard to the famous statue of Zeus at Olympia, Chrysostom raised the critical question whether the human shape is "appropriate to a god" (*Olympic discourse* 52). In defense of anthropomorphic statues, he answered this question by contending that humans "in their perplexity" seek to "indicate that which is invisible und unportrayable by means of something portrayable and visible, using the function of a symbol and doing so better than certain barbarians, who are said to represent the divine by animals…" (*Olympic discourse* 59; cf. Klauck 2000, 192–213).

These critical religious minds, rejecting anthropomorphism or at least reflecting upon its limits and functions, probably have always been in the minority (cf. Guthrie 1993, 183–185). However, this minority will, perhaps, grow and prevail in the future, if the evolution of the human mind, which the cognitive theories of religion refer to, goes on for a long time.

# References

## *Editions and Translations*

[Castellio, Sebastian]. 1554. Châteillon, Sébastien. *De haereticis an sint persequendi et omnino quomodo sit cum eis agendum, …* Reproduction en facsimilé de l'édition de 1554. Genève: Droz 1954.

Chariton. Callirhoe. 1995 Edited and Translated by G.P. Goold. The Loeb Classical Library. Cambridge, MA: Harvard University Press.

Dio Chrysostom. 1977. *The Twelfth or Olympic Discourse: On Man's First Conception of God.* In Dio Chrysostom. With an English Translation by J.W. Cohoon. Five Volumes, vol. II. The Loeb Classical Library. Cambridge, MA: Harvard University Press.

Dion von Prusa. 2000. *Olympische Rede oder über die erste Erkenntnis Gottes.* Eingeleitet, übersetzt und interpretiert von Hans-Josef Klauck. Mit einem archäologischen Beitrag von Balbina Bäbler. (SAPERE Band II). Darmstadt: Wissenschaftliche Buchgesellschaft.

Fichte, Johann Gottlieb. 1991 [1798]. "Über den Grund unseres Glaubens an eine göttliche Weltr-egierung" In *Appellation an das Publikum. Dokumente zum Atheismusstreit Jena 1798/99,* edited by Werner Röhr, 11–22. Leipzig: Reclam.

———. 1991 [1799]. "J.G. Fichtes, des philosophischen Doktors und ordentlichen Professors zu Jena, Appellation an das Publikum über die durch ein Kurfürstlich Sächsisches Konfiska-tionsreskript ihm beigemessenen atheistischen Äußerungen." In *Appellation an das Publi-kum,* edited by Werner Röhr, 84–126. Leipzig: Reclam.

Galilei, Galileo. 1957 [1615]. "Letter to the Grand Duchess Christina (1615)." In *Discoveries and Opinions of Galileo.* Translated with an Introduction and notes by Stillman Drake, 175–216. New York: Doubleday.

Lucian of Samosata. 1969. "The Lover of Lies, or the Doubter (Philopseudes sive Incredulus)." In *Lucian in Eight Volumes,* vol. 3, with an English Translation by A.M. Harmon. The Loeb Classical Library. Cambridge MA.: Harvard University Press.

———. 2001. *Die Lügenfreunde oder der Ungläubige.* Eingeleitet, übersetzt und mit interpre-tierenden Essays versehen von Martin Ebner, Holger Gzella, Heinz-Günther Nesselrath, Ernst Ribbat, (SAPERE vol. 3). Darmstadt: Wissenschaftliche Buchgesellschaft.

Spee, Friedrich. 1631. *Cautio criminalis, seu de processibus contra sagas liber. Ad magistratus Ger-maniae hoc tempore necessarius,..auctore incerto theologo orthod.* Rinthelii (Reprint Rinteln: Bösendahl 1971).

## *Literature*

Barrett, Justin. 2006. "Exploring the Natural Foundations of Religion." In *Religion and Cognition: A Reader,* edited by D. Jason Slone, 86–98. London: Equinox.

Berdozzo, Fabio. 2008. "Die Figur des Zeus in Lukians Dialogi Deorum." In *Religion und Kritik in der Antike,* edited by Ulrich Berner and Ilinca Tanaseanu-Döbler. Münster: LIT Verlag.

Berner, Ulrich. 1994. "Religion und Atheismus." In *The Notion of "Religion" in Comparative Rese-arch,* edited by Ugo Bianchi, 769–776. Rome: "L'erma" di Bretschneider.

———. 1997. "Religionswissenschaft und Religionsphilosophie." *Zeitschrift für Religionswissen-schaft* 5: 149-178.

———. 2004. "Kreuzzug und Ketzerbekämpfung: Das Alte Testament in der theologischen Argu-mentation des Mittelalters und der Reformationszeit." In *Impuls oder Hindernis?Mit dem Alten Testament in multireligiöser Gesellschaft,* edited by Joachim Kügler, 17–30. Münster: LIT Verlag.

———. 2005. "Das Gebet aus der Sicht der analytischen Religionsphilosophie." In *Opfer und Ge-bet in den Religionen,* edited by Ulrich Berner, Christoph Bochinger, and Rainer Flasche, 87–104. Gütersloh: Gütersloher Verlagshaus.

———. 2007a. "Synkretismus—Begegnung der Religionen." In *Kultur und Religion in der Begeg-nung mit dem Fremden,* edited by Joachim G. Piepke, 47–74. Nettetal: Steyler Verlag.

———. 2007b. "Aufklärung als Ursprung und Aufgabe der Religionswissenschaft." In *Watchtow-er Religionswissenschaft: Standortbestimmungen im wissenschaftlichen Feld,* edited by Anne Koch, 161–180. Marburg: diagonal-Verlag.

Boyer, Pascal. 1994. "Cognitive Constraints on Cultural Representations: Natural Ontologies and Religious Ideas." In *Mapping the Mind: Domain Specificity in Cognition and Culture,* edited by L. A.Hirschfeld and S. A.Gelman, 391–411. Cambridge: Cambridge University Press.

———. 1996. "What Makes Anthropomorphism Natural: Intuitive Ontology and Cultural Repre-sentations." *Journal of the Royal Anthropological Institute* (N.S.) 2: 83–97.

———. 1999. "Cognitive Tracks of Cultural Inheritance: How Evolved Intuitive Ontology Governs Cultural Transmission." *American Anthropologist* 100(4): 876–889.

⸻. 2002a. *Religion Explained. The Human Instincts that Fashion Gods, Spirits and Ancestors.* London: Vintage.

⸻. 2002b. "Why do Gods and Spirits Matter at All?" In *Current Approaches in the Cognitive Science of Religion*, edited by Ilkka Pyysiäinen and Veikko Antonen, 68–92. London: Continuum.

⸻. 2003. "Evolution of the Modern Mind and the Origins of Culture: Religious Concepts as a Limiting Cas." In *Evolution and the Human Mind: Modularity, Language and Meta-Cognition,* edited by Peter Carruthers and Andrew Chamberlain, 93–112. Cambridge: Cambridge University Press.

Darwin, Charles. 1989. *The Autobiography of Charles Darwin.* Edited by Nora Barlow. Vol. 29 of The Works of Charles Darwin, edited by Charles H. Barrett and R.B. Freeman. London: William Pickering.

Dawkins, Richard. 2004. "Viruses of the Mind." In *A Devil's Chaplain. Selected Essays*, edited by Latha Menon, 151–172. London: Phoenix.

Dennett, Daniel. 2006. *Breaking the Spell. Religion as a Natural Phenomenon.* New York: Viking.

Guthrie, Stewart. 1993. *Faces in the Clouds: A New Theory of Religion.* New York: Oxford University Press.

Hare, Richard M. 1978. "Theology and Falsification. By Antony Flew, R.M. Hare and Basil Mitchell." In *The Philosophy of Religion*, edited by Basil Mitchell, 13–22. Oxford: Oxford University Press

Harrison, Jane. 1915. "The Influence of Darwinism on the Study of Religions." In *Alpha and Omega*, edited by Jane Harrison, 143–178. London: Sidgwick and Jackson.

Klauck, Hans-Josef. 2000. "Zu religionsphilosophischen und theologischen Aspekten der Rede." In Dion von Prusa, *Olympische Rede, oder, Über die erste Erkenntnis Gottes*, edited by H.-J. Klauck and Balbina Bäbler, 186–216. Darmstadt: Wissenschaftliche Buchgellschaft.

Nesselrath, Heinz-Günther. 2001a. "Lukian: Leben und Werk." In Lucian, *Die Lügenfreunde oder der Ungläubige*, edited by Martin Ebner, 11–31. Darmstadt: Wissenschaftliche Buchgesellschaft.

⸻. 2001b. "Lukian und die antike Philosophie." In Lucian, *Die Lügenfreunde oder der Ungläubige,* edited by Martin Ebner, 135–152. Darmstadt: Wissenschaftliche Buchgesellschaft.

⸻. 2001c. "Lukian und die Magie." In Lucian, *Die Lügenfreunde oder der Ungläubige*, edited by Martin Ebner, 153–162. Darmstadt: Wissenschaftliche Buchgesellschaft.

Ribbat, Ernst. 2001. "'Die ich rief, die Geister…' Zur späten Wirkung einer Zaubergeschichte Lukians." In Lucian, *Die Lügenfreunde oder der Ungläubige*, edited by Martin Ebner, 183–193. Darmstadt: Wissenschaftliche Buchgesellschaft.

Shermer, Michael. 1997. *Why People Believe Weird Things: Pseudoscience, Superstition, and Other Confusions of Our Time.* New York: W.H. Freeman and Company.

Tylor, Edward B. 1866. "The Religion of Savages." *The Fortnightly Review* 6: 71–86.

Waterfield, Robin. 2000. *The First Philosophers: The Presocratics and Sophists.* Translated with Commentary by Robin Waterfield. Oxford: Oxford University Press.

# — 11 —

## Explaining Magic: Earliest Christianity as a Test Case

István Czachesz

### Introduction

In this article, I will propose a new cognitive explanation of magic and apply it to early Christian evidence from the first and second centuries AD. I will argue that magic emerges and survives due to three factors. (1) Subconscious learning mechanisms create false links between our actions and events in our environment. (2) Miracle stories that are transmitted for a variety of reasons give support to magical belief and performance (and vice versa). (3) A set of explanatory techniques make such false connections plausible. The article elaborates on the results of a former study on magic in the canonical and in apocryphal Acts of the Apostles (Czachesz 2007d).

There have been some former attempts in the cognitive science of religion to explain magic. The most comprehensive among them is Jesper Sørensen's recent monograph on magic (2007; cf. Sørensen 2002). Sørensen (2007, 9–30) offers an overview of earlier so-cial-scientific theories of magic and then uses G. Fauconnier and M. Turner's theory of cognitive blending (2002) to examine how people reason about rituals. He distinguishes two types of magic (2007, 95–139). In "transformative magical action," *essential qualities* are transferred from elements belonging to one domain to elements belonging to another domain (e.g. the bread becomes the body of Christ). In "manipulative magical action," magical practices change the state of affairs inside a domain by manipulating elements in another domain (e.g. sunset is delayed by placing a stone on a tree). Here the *relation between elements* is changed, whereas essential qualities remain the same. With the help of blending theory, Sørensen explains how people establish a link between two domains (spaces), relying on either part-whole structures or conventional and perceptual likeness. In his *Magic, Miracles and Religion* (2004, 90–112), Ilkka Pyysiäinen argues that sympathetic magic is based on essentialist thinking: magical effects are mediated by imperceptible essences. Both authors also ask about the relation of magic to religion. Pyysiäinen argues (2004, 96–97) that magic is about effects in known reality, while in religion natural actions effect supernatural reality. According to him, magic and religion support each other: on one hand, magic is easier to falsify (its results are visible), and therefore it needs the support of religious explanations; on the other hand, magic supports religion by offering individual motivation. For Sørensen (2007, 186–191), magic is embedded in most religious rituals and is one of the major forces that cause religious innovation.

It is not our task to offer here a detailed discussion of these former explanations. We have to note, however, that Frazer's ideas of sympathetic magic (1911, 11–48) have influenced both authors (as Sørensen acknowledges, 2007, 95–96). The use of blending theory certainly enables us to give a formal account of the kind of analogical reasoning that already Tylor and Frazer uncovered in magic as well as to make new predictions, such as about the centrality of elements used in magic and its connection to the efficacy of magic or the role of ritual agents and their ascribed magical agency (Sørensen 2007, 128–133). Yet the question arises whether analogical reasoning provides a sufficient explanation for magic. In many cases analogies (mappings across domains) seem to constitute retrospective interpretations of magic rather than its underlying mechanisms. For example, healing blindness with saliva and mud (Gospel of Mark 8: 23; Gospel of John 9: 6; Tacitus, *Historiae* 4.81) does not obviously involve analogical reasoning. With reference to other sources (Book of Tobit 2: 10; Acts of the Apostles 9: 18), however, we can stipulate that people in antiquity imagined blindness as the formation of "scales" on the surface of the eyes, which one could then attempt to "remove" by the above-mentioned method. As with cognitive blending theory in general, it is often difficult to anchor the "blends" in empirical evidence, and the creativity of the interpreter (rather than formal rules) plays an important role in establishing the "mental spaces" involved in the blend. Moreover, there are a variety of ways to use connections with superhuman agents to bring about changes in both visible and invisible realities through prayers, offerings, and sacrifices. Although analogy may appear in such cases, as well (e.g. as analogy between particular goals and the things being offered or sacrificed), this is not at all necessary.

The explanation put forward in this article proceeds from more elementary, subconscious, pre-cognitive forms of learning. Whereas in Sørensen's theory of magic theories of ritual and magical agency need to be established before one can start to explain magic, in my explanation these levels will be added to an underlying, elementary pattern of magical behavior. In this context we have to mention Stuart A. Vyse's work on magic (1997), which uses B.F. Skinner's work on superstitious conditioning in animals and related human experiments. Whereas Vyse has identified, in my view, the proper starting point for an explanation of magic, the book actually does not move beyond "superstition" and fails to explain how magic differs from it. In this article I will use Skinner's insights as well as subsequent experimental work on his concept of superstitious conditioning, and show how this line of research can be combined with other evidence to provide a new explanation of magic.

## Magic and Religion

Whether "magic" and "religion" need to be handled as two different entities is an important question and the way we answer this question has far-reaching implications for explaining magic. If there is no difference between the two, then "magic" and "religion" are merely two labels that refer to the same cultural phenomenon and putting forward an explanation of magic is not different from explaining religion in its totality.

The much-debated dichotomy of "religion" and "magic" has been first proposed by representatives of the intellectualist school of religion studies, Edward B. Tylor (1871) and James G. Frazer (1911). Although the views of Tylor and Frazer were different in many respects, both of them associated "magic" with an earlier, primitive stage of human thought, and religion with a later, more developed stage. Once established by these scholars, the dichotomy of religion and magic has underlain the work of generations of theorists in religious studies, such as W. Wundt, G. van der Leeuw, É. Durkheim, M. Mauss, M. Weber, and W.J. Goode – although the exact meaning of the terms has changed from time to time (Versnel 1991; Braarvig 1999; Stevens 1996; Pyysiäinen 2004, 90–112; Middleton 2005). In subsequent theorizing about religion, however, the distinction between magic and religion has become a suspicious principle. For example, Claude Lévi-Strauss (1966, 220–228) argued that it serves to mark off (assumedly inferior) outsiders from ones' own (assumedly superior) culture. The Zande people (living in south-Western Sudan and accurately studied by E. E. Evans-Pritchard) claim, for example, that surrounding people are more involved in magic than themselves, even as Westerners similarly call other cultures superstitious. The condemnation of the distinction made between religion and magic has become especially widespread under the influence of postmodernism. According to this view, "magic" is an ethnocentric and pejorative term, a Western projection about non-Westerners, an invention of the Victorian middle-class for the purpose of self-definition against colonial subjects and domestic peasants, and a tool that serves for social discrimination (Kuklick 1991; Smith 1995; Kapferer 1997; Braarvig 1999, 21–27; Fowler 2005).

More recently, however, scholars have warned that the colonial and ethnocentric misuse of the term "magic" does not necessarily mean it is altogether useless as a category for the study of culture (Thomassen 1997; Braarvig 1999; Bremmer 2008, 347–352; Pyysiänen, 2004, 96). Thus, the distinction between religion and magic might serve to express the different attitudes, goals, and social positions of their performers (Braarvig 1999, 51–53), the direction of supernatural causation, or the motivational and contextual sides of "magico-religious" practice (Pyysiänen, 2004, 96–112). A look at the origins of the word in classical Greek culture might also help us to judge more adequately about the analytical potential of the term "magic." As Jan Bremmer argues (2008, 235–247), in the fifth and fourth centuries BC the term *magos* (magician) was a term of abuse in Greek tragedy, rhetoric, and earlier philosophy, whereas it was neutral or positive with the historians and Aristotelian philosophy. According to Herodotus, the Persian Magi were specialists in interpreting dreams (Herodotus 1.107–108, 120, 128; 7.19) and celestial events (7.37), they offered libations (7.43), and performed sacrifices (7.113–114, 191). As Bremmer remarks (2008, 235–247), the classical Greek association of magic with the Persians, among whom Magos was a frequent proper name, also provides interesting insights about the role of magic in the creation of "the other." Whereas the Persians were representing "the other" in Athenian rhetoric, on account of their despotism, slavishness, luxury and cruelty, which were the exact opposite of Greek virtues, at the same time the Greeks were highly impressed by them and imitated them in many spheres of life. To these observations we can add a piece of evidence from the New Testament that reveals positive attitude toward Magi. In the infancy narrative of the Gospel of Matthew, we read about three Magi (*magoi*) who came from the East to Jerusalem to find and adore (*proskynein*) the newborn king of the Jews (Gospel of Matthew 2: 1–2). When they saw that the star they were following had stopped over the place where Jesus was born, they "rejoiced with very great joy" (verse 10, *echarêsan charan megalên sfodra*). As Ulrich Luz rightly observed (1992, 118), this scene suggested for contemporary readers a positive image of the Magi and their astrological wisdom. In the eyes of Matthew and his readers, the Magi did not need to convert from any godless practice but from the very beginning they were doing the right thing.

143

In the canonical and apocryphal Acts of the Apostles, "magicians" are employed as stock adversaries of the apostles. Two magicians are featured in the canonical Book of Acts: Simon and Bariesus (or Elymas). In Acts 8: 9, Simon is introduced as a practitioner of magic (*mageuôn*) in the city of Samaria (rebuilt as *Sebastê* under Herod the Great). Not only is he advertising himself as "something great" but also the people give him the title "the power of god that is called great" (v. 10: *hê dynamis tou theou hê kaloumenê megalê*). The text explains that people were attracted to Simon because he "amazed them with his magic (v. 11: *hai magieai*)." When he sees "the great signs and miracles" (v. 13: *sêmeia kai dynameis*) performed by Philip, Simon is taken by the same kind of amazement (*ekstasis*) as were his followers before; he believes and receives the baptism. There are four important conclusions regarding magic that we can draw from this passage. First, Simon is not condemned for his practice. Whereas this silence cannot be interpreted as a positive attitude, the neutral presentation of Simon's art in this episode is certainly different from the reaction given on his activity in the *Acts of Peter* 9, where he is called "most wicked" (*improvissimus*) and a "troubler" (*sollicitator*) and "deceiver" (*seductor*) of "simple souls" (Czachesz 1998 and 2007a, 85–123). We can add that the conflict in the subsequent episode (Book of Acts 8: 17–24) is not about Simon's magic as rather his offering money so that he can give people the Holy Spirit by the laying on of hands. Second, the parallels between Simon's and Philip's impact on the people (especially the latter's impact on Simon himself) suggests a great deal of phenomenological similarity between the appearances of the two wonderworkers. There is no effort in the text to deny such a parallel, but in fact it is strengthened by the repetitive structure of the narrative. Third, Philip wins the people of the city for himself because he outperforms Simon. This is a case of "magical competition" of the sort that is first attested in biblical literature in 1 Kings 18 (Elijah and the Baal priests) and will take place in the *Acts of Peter* between Peter and Simon. Fourth, despite the phenomenological similarity, the terminology is clearly creating an image of Simon as "the other": his deeds are "magic" (*magai*), whereas Philip performs "signs and miracles" (*sêmeia kai dynameis*).

A more militant attitude toward magical practice in Acts starts with Paul's missionary journeys. When Paul, Barnabas, and John Mark arrive at Paphus on Cyprus, they are confronted with the Jewish magician Bar-Jesus or Elymas (Book of Acts 13: 6–12). This time the conflict is narrated in very much the same way as the competition of Peter and Simon in the *Acts of Peter*. The proconsul is interested in Paul's message, but Elymas tries to turn him away. Paul responses to the challenge, calls him "full of deceit (*dolos*) and villainy (*rhadiourgia*)," "son of devil," "enemy of all righteousness," and finally strikes him with temporary blindness. When he sees the outcome of the competition, the proconsul becomes a believer. Three observations have to be made in connection with this episode. First, although he subsequently qualifies the activity of Bar-Jesus as *dolos* and *rhadiourgia*, the reason of Paul's demonstration of power is not Bar-Jesus' practice as rather his attempt to turn away the proconsul from the missionaries. Second, Paul's move of calling temporary blindness on Bar-Jesus is an act of magic itself, by which he outperforms the magician and convinces the proconsul. Third, the apostle is reported to have acted "filled with the Holy Spirit." In this context the Holy Spirit appears as a so-called *parhedros* (lit. one that sits nearby), a figure of a supernatural assistant who collaborates with the magician (see below). This attitude to magic is different from the coercive approach when the magician tries to persuade the divinity to assist him in reaching his own ends. The magician often calls the supernatural assistant "lord" or "ruler" and himself "servant."

Another spectacular confrontation with magic occurs in Book of Acts 19: 11–20. While

Paul was in Ephesus, God did extraordinary miracles through him: "when the handkerchiefs and aprons that had touched his skin were brought to the sick, their diseases left them and the evil spirits came out of them." However, when the seven sons of the Jewish high-priest Sceva tried to exorcise a man invoking the name of Jesus, the demons turned against them, so that they must flee out of the house naked and wounded. People all over Ephesus heard about this, Jesus' name was praised, and many of them who practiced superstition (*perierga praxantoi*) collected their books and burnt them publicly. Similarly as in the other two conflicts with magicians in the Book of Acts, *magic* is confronted with *magic*. In terms of the above-mentioned ancient theory, we can conclude that the coercive approach of the priest's sons failed when they tried to invoke Paul's *parhedros*. After comparing the healings and exorcisms caused by "Paul's laundry" in this episode with the powers communicated by Peter's shadow (Book of Acts 5: 15) and the hem of Jesus' garment (Gospel of Luke 8: 44), Klauck (2000, 98) admits that "these phenomena are externally very similar," but suggests that there was a difference in the "system of convictions involved." It would be illusory, however, to hypothesize that Paul and his followers had a radically different world-view from that of their adversaries. References to the assumed "allergy" of Jews against all sorts of magic on account of the Old Testament (e.g. Luz 1992, 118) are equally anachronistic and misleading (cf. Jeffers 1996). The very fact that Paul's adversaries in these episodes are themselves Jews excludes such an interpretation. In spite of Biblical prohibitions, magic was not only tolerated but actively practiced in the Qumran community (García Martínez 2002, 33). It was not only Christians who used the label "magician" for their adversaries. Their enemies, both Jews and pagans, have condemned Jesus as a magician (Origen, *Against Celsus* 1. 28, 38, 47; *Tractate Sanhedrin* [Babylonian Talmud] 107b; Arnobius, *Adversus nationes* 1.43; cf. Kollmann 1996). Rather than choosing from religion and magic, the question was which approach to magic and which particular *parhedros* people in a particular culture or group thought to be more powerful than others.

For the same reasons, the accounts of magic in the Book of Acts cannot be interpreted as pejorative descriptions of other peoples' practices, which we have earlier seen in contemporary Western and African contexts. Attributing to this writing a distinction between religion and magic is even further from the truth. The practices of John, Paul, Peter, and Philip are phenomenologically not different from the practices of their adversaries. Even early Christian writings admit that the apostles were identified in their cultural milieu as magicians (*Acts of Paul* 15; *Acts of Andrew*, Epitomy 12 and 18; *Acts of Thomas* 20). The key to the interpretation of magic in the Book of Acts seems to be the theory of coercion and *parhedros*: magical practices that are performed in other ways than using the assistance of the Holy Spirit as *parhedros* must be condemned. If we accept this solution, it is not a sheer coincidence any longer that the Book of Acts, the New Testament writing that pays the most attention to the Holy Spirit, also contains the most references to the Christian and non-Christian use of magic.

In conclusion, a dichotomy of magic and religion is not supported by the evidence from religious antiquity and earliest Christianity. In antiquity it was possible to use the term "magic" to describe one's own practices, the activities of other people in one's culture, or the practices of other cultures; but the use of "magic" in opposition with "religion" can be excluded. Such a use was also impossible, because hardly any shared concept of "religion" existed. To take just a few obvious examples, most religions of Greco-Roman Antiquity were first of all cults, which could be described in terms of their rites and institutions. The interpretation of mythology, together with the discussion of the great issues of life, lay outside the realm of religion. Judaism was a complex national, cultural and ethnic phenomenon, and had the tendency to involve the entirety of life, rather than being limited to certain cultic events. Christianity attempted to coordinate mythology, rituals, social life, philosophical thought, and ethics. More than other religions of the period, it was divided from the beginning by fierce philosophical debates. In conclusion, there existed a more or less clear, shared concept of magic, without an equally clear and shared concept of religion. The first steps toward establishing the dichotomy of religion (that is, Christianity) and magic was taken by Augustine, but this is beyond the scope of this essay (cf. Graf 2002). At the same time, identifying magic with religion would be an equally big mistake: the variety of forms of religion that we have just illustrated cannot be subsumed under the category of magic.

## Defining Magic

In the foregoing section we have seen that neither a sheer dichotomy of "magic" and "religion," nor a complete identification of them describe their relation adequately. When people in antiquity used the term "magic" to mark boundaries between cultural practices, this was not necessarily because they saw the practices of "magicians" essentially different from their own practices (or practices ascribed to their own religious heroes). In this context, we could say that "magic" denotes the manipulation of visible reality with the help of superhuman agents. This can occur either within or outside of an institutional, religious setting. This preliminary (and narrow) definition raises the following two questions: (1) Does magic always make use of superhuman agents? (2) Is the manipulation of *invisible* realities to be excluded from magic?

According to Sørensen (2007, 164), a number of psychological factors facilitate and strengthen the representation of "certain event-states as the result of 'magical' actions by super-human agents." Sørensen, who applies Lawson and McCauley's ritual form hypothesis to magical rituals, suggests that "the performance of magical rituals has as a prerequisite … the ascription of magical agency to some element found in the ritual" (2007, 97). Whereas we will also use agency as an explanatory factor of the success of magic, the involvement of superhuman agency in every form of magic is far from obvious. For example, the use of spells to stop bleeding is attested since Homer (*Odyssey* xix. 457–458) and many of such spells contain no reference to supernatural agents (Graf 2005, 291–292). We can only speculate whether the spells were pronounced in the framework of rituals in a way that presupposed the involvement of supernatural agency. I suggest that including supernatural agency in a definition of magic is not the best strategy for two reasons. First, as our examples show, magic can be performed without reference to superhuman agents. Healing can be attributed to natural and/or human causes. This may involve some sort of agency, but it makes no sense to extend "magical agency" to just any kind of human of natural agent. Second, in ancient culture (as in any pre-scientific worldview) we have to presuppose the involvement of supernatural agents such as demons or ancestors in all domains of life. In this sense any action taken by ancient people was connected with supernatural agency. Although we can stamp this as a "magical worldview," but this is hardly helpful in explaining magic as a particular domain and in extending such a theory to contemporary magic.

The other question is if the manipulation of invisible reality—or supernatural reality, as Pyysiäinen (2004, 96–97) calls it—needs to be excluded from the definition of magic. It does not seem to have any advantage from the explanatory point of view to put sacrifice that secures the support of the gods, for example, into a different category (religion) than the healing of a patient by exorcism (magic). On one hand, most contact with the gods, even if it manipulates the supernatural world in the first instance, does intend to influence the state of affairs in visible reality, as well. Manipulations that purportedly influence visible reality, on the other hand, often attempt in fact to bring about changes in supernatural reality, such as expelling a demon from a patient. Is baptism first of all about invisible, supernatural qualities, such as washing away sin—as Pyysiäinen (2004, 97) argues? Maybe it is in elite theological discourse (where most probably integration into the Church as *communio sanctorum* is the major concern), but certainly not in the heads of the parents and the congregation, where baptism is more about fulfilling social expectations and securing the future of the child by integrating her into the religious and larger community, as well as gaining God's protection and support for her. I do not want to deny that there may exist purely supernatural concerns behind ritual acts. Such rituals do not qualify as magic in my categorization.

I suggest that we call "magic" the illusory manipulation of visible or invisible realities: magic assumedly changes the state of affairs in visible or invisible reality, whereas in actuality it does not. This is in a sense a strongly *etic* approach, inasmuch as a particular behavior qualifies as magic not because of what its performer believes about it, but rather on account of what the modern investigator believes about it from the point of view of modern science. It also abandons criteria related to the form of magic: a spell, the manipulation of objects, a prayer, an offering, or a sacrifice can be equally proper means of magic.

This (broad) definition has various advantages over the previous (narrow) one (see above). First, we do not have to decide what is visible and invisible—or in Pyysiäinen's (2004, 96–97) terminology, "known" and "supernatural"—reality. Deciding that question would imply very complex discussions about what counts as "visible" or "*not* supernatural." Second, we do not have to know beforehand the explanations people give to their actions, such as the involvement of supernatural or magical agency. Third, the definition gives up even mild forms of cultural relativism: magic is not defined from the point of view of different cultures but solely from the point of view of empirical truth as established by modern science (and a modern scientific worldview). The choice of such an approach is not meant as a value judgment about other cultural perspectives. It is a move that follows logically from the decision of the cognitive science of religion to anchor the study of religion in scientific methods and principles rather than in interpretative ones—or at least to shift the emphasis in that direction.

Since our understanding of magic does not include a reference to the underlying beliefs and the procedures employed, instances of contemporary alternative medicine may also fall under the rubric of magic, even though they might operate with pills or complicated technology. Our definition excludes, on the other hand, cases where procedures *do work*, even if they are based on wrong theories (in terms of modern science) about the reality to be changed and the mechanisms underlying the procedure. If the patient is actually cured due to a placebo effect, we talk about a case of folk- or alternative medicine rather than magic. In such cases there are underlying causal mechanisms that science can potentially discover and explain. Medical anthropology makes an important difference between healing and cure. The latter means the removal of a disease or injury in the modern sense, whereas healing means the restoration of the well-being of the patient, particularly in social and psychological terms. John Pilch (2000) has argued that many early Christian miracle stories (e.g. about Jesus) may refer to actual *healings* in the latter sense, which is also the

147

goal of much folk medicine. It is not the task of this article to explore such alternatives, but the way magic is combined with other medical procedures in ancient sources suggests it was (at least many times) intended to actually cure the patient (e.g. Plato, *Republic* 426b and *Charmides* 155e–156e; Pliny, *Natural History* 24–32; Pseudo-Hippocrates, *On Regimen in Health* 4; Furley 1993; Leven 2004; van der Eijk 2004).

Another group of manipulations is clearly directed at realities that by their nature exclude the possibility of any empirical control. Even in such cases, as I have mentioned above in connection with baptism, explicit, theologically correct accounts of the manipulations might differ from people's implicit or private interpretations and expectations. However, in cases where procedures secure one's favorable lot in life after death or people receive invisible cosmic energies, or are released from Purgatory, science has no means to check their efficiency. Although such beliefs might be labeled as "magical" from the perspective of a scientific *worldview*, they are religious actions without a magical component in terms of our definition.

## Magical Behavior is Rooted in Superstitious Conditioning

In the 1940s, Harvard psychologist Burrhus Frederic Skinner, known as the father of "behaviorism", placed a hungry pigeon in a cage equipped with an automatic feeder (Skinner 1948; Morse and Skinner 1957; cf. Vyse 1997, 59–97; Wulff 1997, 129–39). A clock was set to give the bird access to the food for five seconds in regular intervals. Instead of just waiting passively for the next appearance of the food, most of the birds started to perform various kinds of repetitive behaviors: one was turning counter-clockwise two or three times between two feedings, another was thrusting its head into one of the upper corners, a third was moving its head as if tossing an invisible bar, two displayed a pendulum motion of the head and body, yet another bird made pecking and brushing movements toward the floor. Skinner called this behavior "superstitious conditioning." He suggested that "superstitious conditioning" developed because the birds happened to execute some movement just as the food appeared, and as a result they repeated it. If the subsequent presentation of food occurred before a not too long interval, the response was strengthened further. Skinner observed that fifteen seconds was a particularly favorable interval of feeding for the development of the response. Skinner suggested that the behavior he observed with pigeons is analogous to the mechanism of some human superstitions, such as rituals performed to change one's luck with cards or movements of the arm after a bowler released the ball.

Skinner's suggestions about human analogies inspired further experimentation. In the late 1980s, Gregory A. Wagner and Edward K. Morris (1987) designed a mechanical clown, Bobo, that dispensed a marble from its mouth at regular intervals. They promised preschool children they would receive a toy (that they actually received anyway) if they collect enough marbles in an eight-minute session. The session was repeated once a day for six days. Children developed responses similar to those of Skinner's pigeons: they grimaced before Bobo, touched its face, wriggled, smiled at him, or kissed his nose. Koichi Ono (1987) experimented with twenty Japanese university students. The students were asked to take a seat in a booth that was equipped with a counter, a signal lamp (with three colors), and three levers. They were not required to do anything specific but were told they may earn scores on the counter if they do something. Scores appeared on the counter either at regular or random intervals, but without any consistence with the light signals and anything students did. Three of the twenty students developed "superstitious behavior": one student pulled a lever several times and then held it, consistently repeating this pattern for 30 minutes; another student developed a different pattern of pulling the levers; the third student performed a complex sequence of movements that gradually changed during the session." The most spectacular was the behavior of a female student.

> About 5 min into the session, a point delivery occurred after she had stopped pulling the lever temporarily and had put her right hand on the lever frame. This behavior was followed by a point delivery, after which she climbed on the table and put her right hand to the counter. Just as she did so, another point was delivered. Thereafter she began to touch many things in turn, such as the signal light, the screen, a nail on the screen, and the wall. About 10 min later, a point was delivered just as she jumped to the floor, and touching was replaced by jumping. After five jumps, a point was delivered when she jumped and touched the ceiling with her slipper in her hand. Jumping to touch the ceiling continued repeatedly and was followed by points until she stopped about 25 min into the session, perhaps because of fatigue. (Ono 1987, 265)

The behavioral patterns observed in these experiments are acquired by the elementary learning mechanism of "operant conditioning," a phenomenon exhaustively studied by Skinner. In operant conditioning, the animal learns about the relationship of a stimulus and the animal's own behavior (Skinner 1938, 19–21; Schwartz *et al.* 2002, 131–245). For example, Skinner placed a hungry rat in a small box containing a lever. When the rat pressed the lever, a food pellet appeared. The rat slowly learned that food could be obtained by pressing the lever, and pressed it more and more often. In terms of the law of reinforcement, the probability of the rat's response (pulling the lever) increases if it is followed by a positive reinforcer (presentation of food). The previously mentioned experiments differed from this basic setting inasmuch as the subjects' action did not influence the presentation of the reinforcer. It is interesting to examine which reinforcement schedules result in the strongest conditioning (Ferster and Skinner 1957; Schwartz *et al.* 2002, 217–224). One might expect that this to be continuous or monotonous, invariable reinforcement. In fact, the opposite is true: continuous reinforcement leads to the lowest rate of responding, whereas the "variable ratio schedule" leads to the fastest rates of responding. Variable ratio means that every nth (e.g. fifth or tenth) response is rewarded on the average, but the gap between two rewards can be very short or very large. In real life, the latter type of rewarding schedule is found in fishing and gambling, for example, which might be an important factor in people getting so easily addicted to these activities (cf. Eysenck 2004, 267).

The spontaneous development of ritualized behavior as a response to positive reinforcement that is independent of the response suggests that operant conditioning is the source of magical behavior. Notice that the emergence of "magical" activities in the experiments did not rely either on an explanatory mechanism—be it implicit (such as analogical reasoning or agency) or explicit (such as ghost beliefs or theological doctrines)—or on long-term memory and cultural transmission (such as counterintuitive ideas and miracle stories). Whereas it is difficult to compare the results of different experiments with each other because of the different methods and setups employed in them, it is remarkable that six of Skinner's eight pigeons developed "superstitious" behavior (and such demonstrations have become classroom routine) and seventy-five percent of preschoolers did so in Wagner and Morris' experiment, but only three of the twenty Japanese students behaved in that way in the score collecting game. The explanation for this difference might be that (everything else being equal) the ability and willingness to use explicit reasoning based on natural causation in connection with a task (which we can expect of university students in the given setting) seems to diminish the chance of developing a "magical" response.

Further we can ask if there is a connection between the development of magical behavior and the "reinforcement schedule" of the conditioning. In particular, the unexpected success of variable reinforcement schedules (such as found in gambling and fishing) raises the question of whether a similar effect is at work in magic. Whereas experiments on "superstitious conditioning" manipulated reinforcement intervals and applied random reinforcement, no experimentation has been dedicated to the problem of variable schedules under such circumstances, to my knowledge. There are at least some hints, however, that certain reinforcement schedules may particularly support the development of magical behavior. We will approach this problem from the perspective of probability in reinforcement schedules.

In 1960, the French-American mathematician Benoît Mandelbrot introduced the word "fractal." A fractal is a recursive geometrical structure: it is a shape that can be subdivided into parts, each of which is a reduced-size copy of the whole, such as the famous "Sierpinski triangle." In other words, fractals are based on self-similarity. Such geometrical shapes are widespread in nature; one only has to examine the structure of a snowflake through a magnifying glass. Fractals fascinate us and have been widely used in architecture, for example in gothic cathedrals, long before Mandelbrot came up with the notion (cf. Csermely 2006, 231–237). Following a similar pattern, we can create fractal-like structures in other domains, as well. For example, scholars have found that both the pitch and the volume of Bach's music display fractal-like self-similarity (Voss and Clarke 1975, 1978; Hsü and Hsü 1991; Shi 1996).

Now let us see how fractal-like structures appear in reinforcement schedules. Tossing coins is a simple form of gambling. Mathematician Daniel Bernoulli (1700–1782) analyzed a game where the player wins one ducat if a tossed coin lands "heads," two ducats if it lands "heads" for a second time, four if it lands "heads" for a third time, with the payoff doubling as long as the coin keeps landing "heads" (Bernoulli 1738 [1954]; cf. Dehling 1997). It can be easily realized that whereas the reward keeps doubling, the chance of winning the doubled reward is half the chance of winning the original amount. In other words, the chance for different payoffs follows a so-called "power-law" distribution (in which the independent variable is raised to a constant power, with some simplification). As a consequence, the probability distribution of the expected return is scale-free (such as the fractals seen above) and has no typical value. The game is also known as the "St. Petersburg paradox," because the bank should ask an infinite price for participation in it, but no sensible player would pay even a moderately high price for it. Recently it has been suggested that other forms of gambling and exciting games in general also involve such regularities (Csermely 2006, 25–31). In fact, scholars have demonstrated that the distribution of dividends in various horse races follows such a rule (Park and Domany 2001; Ichinomiya 2006).

In sum, gambling may be addictive not only because it has a variable reinforcement schedule, but also because this variability, at least in some forms of gambling, follows a fractal-like (power-law) distribution. If operant conditioning is a relevant factor for the development of magical practices, and variable schedules following a power-law distribution strengthen this effect, some especially widespread forms of magic may be good candidates to demonstrate this relation. Let us take rainmaking as an example.

Rainmaking is a universally known form of magic that is performed even in developed countries (Bownas 2004; Dunnigan 2005; Boudon 2006). In Greco-Roman antiquity, the official and private practice of rainmaking is attested since archaic times and continues beyond the Christianization of the Empire (Graf 2005, 298). According to Tertullian (ca. 160–ca. 220), Christians were able to obtain rain through prayer (*Apology* 5). Rainfall obviously follows a variable schedule; therefore, we may think about rain dances as responses to a variable reinforcer. A closer look at this schedule also reveals that it has a fractal-like (power-law) distribution: both the time intervals and the amount of rainfall are distributed in such a way (Peters and Christensen 2002). A rainmaking ritual that is accidentally followed by rain may motivate the repeated use of the ritual, launching a chain of ritual responses to the variable (and fractal-like) reinforcement schedule of rainfall. The plausibility of "making rain" with a ritual is somewhere between the "efficiency" of magical cures for headache and the elicitation of earthquakes that ruin prisons, examples frequently occurring in ancient magic. But even the latter form of magic, which is surprisingly important in both Christian sources and the Greek Magical Papyri, has some relation with power-law distribution: the frequency and magnitude of earthquakes are also described by power-laws. Experimental work on conditioning examines short-term effects in individuals. Additional theoretical and experimental work is needed in order to reveal the possible effects of long-term reinforcement schedules, such as the distribution of rainfall or earthquake.

## Miracle Stories Generate Belief in Magic

Miracle is one of the most widespread genres of early Christian literature. Miracles make up the bulk of the Gospels, two of them starting with Jesus' miraculous birth and all four of them (in their present form, at least) ending with his resurrection. The apostles perform numerous miracles in the Book of Acts. Miracles fill the pages of the Apocryphal Acts of the Apostles, apocryphal gospels, and the Acts of the Martyrs. The tradition goes on unbroken in hagiography and continues in present day (evangelical) preaching and the Roman Catholic cult of the saints.

In general, miracle stories in early Christian literature pay little if any attention to how miracles were performed. The story of Eutychus contains one of the few hints we have. When the apostle Paul was teaching in the city of Troas, a young man called Eutychus was overcome by sleep, fell out of a window of the third floor, and was picked up dead. "But Paul went down, and bending over him took him in his arms, and said: 'Do not be alarmed, for his life is in him' " (Book of Acts 20: 9–10). The healing power of Peter's shadow and of pieces of clothes that touched Paul's body provide some further technical references. We have already discussed the latter episode (Book of Acts 19: 11–12); in the former narrative (Book of Acts 5: 15–16) we read that people "carried out the sick into the streets, and laid them on cots and mats, in order that Peter's shadow might fall on some of them as he came by. A great number of people would also gather from the towns around Jerusalem, bringing the sick and those tormented by unclean spirits, and they were all cured." In the *Acts of Peter* 26 we read that Simon Magus bowed three times over the head of a young man before he raised him. In another passage that we discussed above, Jesus mixed saliva with sand to cure a blind man (Gospel of John 9: 6–7).

In spite of the inclusion of some technical details, these accounts were obviously written with the purpose of demonstrating the power of Jesus' apostles and not as recipes that believers could imitate. We do not read, for example, about new converts accomplishing such deeds. These miracle stories do not necessarily imply any actual magical performance. The circulation of such narratives, together with the fact that even today's readers understand and appreciate them, demonstrates that both ancient and contemporary readers have cognitive structures which enable them to process stories about magical acts and find them interesting. This also implies that for the circulation and successful transmission of these narratives it is not necessary that the practices described in them were ever actually performed. To mention an analogy, widespread narratives about speaking animals in the Apocryphal Acts of the Apostles (Matthews 1999; Czachesz 2008) do not necessarily mean that such speaking animals have ever been seen or ever existed.

In my studies about the use of grotesque imagery in early Christian literature (Czachesz 2007a; 2009, 2011) I have argued that many of the fantastic details in early Christian texts (and probably in other religious traditions) can be explained with reference to two archaic cognitive mechanisms of our minds. First, grotesque images tamper with cross-cultural ontological expectations, either by creating things that violate such expectations or by describing transformations of things (metamorphoses) in ways that violate such expectations. Second, grotesque images trigger involuntary imitation and activate archaic alarm systems in the brain that produce fear and disgust. I will show that these two mechanisms are also responsible for the success of miracle stories. Both mechanisms that underlie the popularity of miracle stories are deeply rooted in evolutionary history. Our minds, as evolutionary psychologists have argued (e.g. Barkow *et al.* 1992), did not develop to think about just anything in the world, but primarily to secure our survival in an ancestral environment in face of a particular set of challenges. Therefore, we are predisposed to pay attention to certain aspects of the world around us (e.g., predators, prey, human faces, depth), and react in particular ways to that information (e.g., fighting, fleeing, cooperating, mating). The human mind is not a blank slate when we are born but it is rather a well-adapted organ, which we can use to solve specific tasks in the world. Whereas the influence of the environment on child development is certainly important, it can be argued that the most archaic structures of the mind will nevertheless emerge in a wide range of cultural and environmental conditions.

In a series of experiments conducted in the 1970s, Frank C. Keil (1979, 46–62) has demonstrated that humans share a number of ontological categories that make sense of their environment. Keil (1989, 196) argued that ontological categories represent "the most fundamental conceptual cuts one can make in the world, such as those between animals and plants, artifacts and animals, and the like." His experiments have also shown that "at the ontological level there are clusters of properties that unambiguously and uniquely belong to all members of a given category at that level. All animals are alive, have offspring, and grow in ways that only animals do" (Keil 1989, 214). In other words, people have particular expectations toward things belonging to a particular category. Psychologists have not yet reached a final agreement regarding the set of basic ontological categories, but the following list is widely supported: HUMAN, ANIMAL, PLANT, ARTIFACT, and (natural) OBJECT (Keil 1979, 48; Atran 1989, 7–16 and 2002, 98; Boyer 1994b, 400–401, 2001, 90).

One of the core hypotheses of the cognitive science of religion is Pascal Boyer's theory of "minimal counterintuitiveness," which suggests that religious ideas violate intuitive expectations about ordinary events and states, inasmuch as they "combine certain schematic assumptions provided by intuitive ontologies, with nonschematic ones provided by explicit cultural transmission" (Boyer 1994a, 48, 121, and passim). Or, as he more recently summarized his theory, "religious concepts generally include explicit violations of expectations associated with domain concepts," that is, they violate the attributes that already children intuitively associate with ontological categories (Boyer and Ramble 2001, 538). The idea of a ghost that can go through walls, for example, is based on the ontological category of human beings, but violates our expectations about intuitive physics that should otherwise apply to humans. Concepts that contain such violations, Boyer suggests, "are more salient than other types of cultural information, thereby leading to enhanced acquisition, representation, and communication."

For the purposes of this article, it is important briefly to survey the experimental work related to Boyer's theory. The first experiments, conducted by Justin Barrett and Melanie Nyhof (2001) as well as by Charles Ramble and Boyer himself (2001), seemed to confirm that minimally counterintuitive ideas are remembered better than ordinary, bizarre, or maximally counterintuitive ones. Bizarre items (Barrett and Nyhof 2001) included a highly unusual feature that violates no category-level assumption: for example, for a living thing to weigh 5000 kilograms is strange, but not excluded by ontological expectations about living things. Maximally counterintuitive things (Boyer and Ramble 2001) combine multiple violations of ontological categories: "only remembering what did not happen" already violates expectations for objects with a psychology (such as humans or animals), but this feature was added to an object without psychological processes (such as a piece of furniture). Other experiments (Atran 2001, 100–107; Norenzayan and Atran 2004; Gonce *et al.* 2006; Upal *et al.* 2007), however, have yielded two important observations that seem to call for a revision of the original theory. First, it turned out that the overall advantage of minimally counterintuitive ideas in transmission is caused by contextual effects, primarily by narrative frames such as the ones used in both above-mentioned experiments. Second, the experiments have shown that in the long run (after a week) minimally counterintuitive ideas do enjoy an advantage, independently of contextual effects. That is, their memory decays less than the memory of ordinary or maximally counterintuitive objects. A fresh look at Barrett and Nyhof's results (2001, 85–87, 89–90) reveals that also in their experiment the memory of counterintuitive ideas decayed less; they paid no attention to this factor probably because of the absolute advantage of such concepts in both immediate and delayed recall in the experiment.

The original purpose of developing the notion of minimally counterintuitive ideas has been to explain widespread beliefs in ancestors, sprits, and gods (Boyer 2001, 58–106; Pyysiäinen 2003, 9–23). But the theory (as understood in light of the growing body of experimental data) has a broader implication: texts, especially ones (initially) transmitted orally, tend to develop minimally counterintuitive features. Along those lines one can explain, for example, the dominance of particular types of narratives about the death and resurrection of Jesus (Czachesz 2007b). Consider the following two hypothetical alternatives to the episode of Paul and Eutychus. (1) "The boy fell out of the window and broke his leg. Paul hurried downstairs, lifted him up, and laid him on a bed. He took a piece of wood and cloths and secured the broken leg by splints." (2) "The boy fell out of the window and died. Paul did not go down but prayed to God. The boy came back to life, turned into an owl and flew back to the third floor. From that day he could remember everything he heard." In terms of what we know about memory and counterintuitiveness, my prediction is that the first narrative would fare quite well in short-term recall, but would decay quickly thereafter. The second version, in contrast, contains too many counterintuitive details (rising from the dead, turning into an animal, remembering everything), and would not be faithfully encoded in memory. A single counterintuitve detail, Paul raising the dead boy (violating the ontological expectation that dead bodies do not revive), is necessary but also enough so that the episode would be advantaged in long-term (and due to context effects, perhaps even in short-term) recall and therefore transmitted with more success than the other two.

A minimally counterintuitive element can be identified in many other biblical and apocryphal miracle narratives. We mention only a few examples. According to the *Arabic Infancy Gospel* 36, Jesus in his childhood modeled animals from clay and then made them behave (run, fly, eat) like real animals. The apostle Peter brings a smoked tunny fish back to life in *Acts of Peter* 13 (cf. Herodotus 9.120.1). In addition to Paul's example mentioned above, Jesus, the apostles, and Simon Magus raise dead people on several occasions (e.g. Gospel of Luke 7: 11–17; Gospel of John 11: 38–44; *Acts of Peter* 28). Healing from a distance is also counterintuitive, because people are not supposed to act on anything without being physically present (at least this seems to follow from expectations about physicality; Spelke 1990; Spelke and Kinzler 2007; Barrett 2008). Such a violation of intuitive expectations occurs when Paul's pieces of clothes are taken to the sick and heals them or the sick are put under Peter's shadow. Jesus (in the Gospel of John 4: 46–54) also heals from a distance. The absence of stories about raising a dead person from a distance supports this interpretation. For example, when Jesus is underway to Bethany and learns his friend Lazarus has died, he finishes his journey, comes to the tomb, and only then he raises Lazarus (Gospel of John 11: 38–44). A combination of acting from a distance *and* raising someone from the dead would be excessively counterintuitive and therefore not advantaged in the transmission. Notice that the cognitive processing of such narratives does not require an explicit theory of the causal mechanisms that bring about healing. Ancients might have had quite different theories about such operations than do modern Westerners. Also the substantial differences between the medical views of ancient elites (as recorded in the works of Hippocrates and Galen, for example) and of the non-elite and mostly illiterate majority cannot be stressed enough (Pilch 2000, 103). The very occurrence of minimally counterintuitive elements makes these narratives successful in ancient as well as modern cultural environments, regardless of the variety of explanations that people would provide for them if asked.

Not all attention-grabbing details are necessarily counterintuitive. The healing of a lame person is certainly spectacular (Gospel of Mark 2: 1–11), but there is nothing about it that contradicts our expectations related to cross-cultural ontological categories. Also healing a blind person by applying saliva to the eyes (Gospel of Mark 8: 22–26; Gospel of John 9: 6–7) is remarkable but not counterintuitive. Saliva does contain healing substances and we intuitively make use of it when we put a wounded finger into our mouth. There is a tendency, especially in the Gospel of John, to make "normal" instances of folk medicine more impressive by emphasizing some extraordinary circumstances: the man healed in Gospel of John 9 was born blind and the one healed at the pool of Bethsaida had been crippled for thirty-eight years (5: 1–20).

Some miracle stories also trigger involuntary imitation and activate archaic alarm systems in the brain that produce fear and disgust. Let us have a quick look at how these cognitive mechanisms work. Children imitate facial expressions and other bodily movements at a very early age, indeed, right after birth (Meltzoff 2002; Hurley and Chater 2005). Imitation enables us to engage in joint action and sophisticated cooperation (Brass and Heyes 2005; Uddin *et al.* 2007). We can also use imitation when we do not actually carry out the imitated actions. On the analogy of the mirror neurons in monkeys, it has been found, that also in humans the observation of actions performed by others activates cortical motor representation—that is, brain areas are activated that are responsible for the movement of different parts of the body (Gallese *et al.* 2004). There are similar findings about emotion:

the same brain parts that are involved in the feel of disgust and pain are also activated when we empathize with such emotions (Keysers *et al.* 2004; Singer *et al.* 2004). Not only do we not actually have to carry out actions or be exposed to pain in order to empathize with them, but also a limited amount of information is sufficient to activate the relevant brain areas and elicit empathy (Gallese *et al.* 2004).

I suggest that various details of the healing miracles in early Christian texts act on our involuntary system of imitation and empathy. We read about people who are seriously ill and desperately seek healing (e.g. Gospel of Mark 2: 1–12). Parents seek help for their sick or already dead children (e.g. Gospel of Mark 1: 21–43). These effects are further amplified by the presentation of extreme (e.g. lameness, blindness), repulsive (e.g. "leprosy"), or spectacular (e.g. "demoniacs") symptoms and diseases. Many of the stories and vivid details are likely to elicit fear and disgust. These are two basic emotions that have deep (if not the deepest) evolutionary roots (Ward 2006: 315). Fear is responsible for detecting threat and occurs rapidly and without conscious awareness: for example, people suffering from phobias react to the images of snakes or spiders even when they see them without noticing it (that is, subliminally). Disgust is thought to be originally responsible for avoiding contamination and disease by eating, but its usage has extended with time. In sum, many healing miracles include details about conditions and symptoms that are likely to produce empathy and trigger basic emotional systems. Further, it is logical to assume that after such starting conditions, healing stories evoke more positive feelings when problems are miraculously solved in the end. I suggest that these effects direct attention to healing miracles and generate a set of emotional memories (Eichenbaum 2002: 261–281) about them, which increases their memorability. This hypothesis is further supported by the recent experimental finding that emotionally arousing details in stories enhance the memorability of the gist and details (both central and peripheral) of the narrative (Laney et al. 2004).

We can conclude that miracle stories spread for reasons that are independent from both the actual practice of magic and explanations connected to magic and miracle. This does not mean, however, that magic is completely independent from miracle. Repeated exposure to miracle stories obviously familiarizes listeners with magical concepts and provides them with narrative patterns and other means to make sense of them. Such stories may be embedded into social and institutional contexts (ancestral tradition, mythology) that enhance their credibility and significance. In this way, miracle stories provide cultural interpretation and positive feedback to the superstitious behavioral patterns that develop from a completely different background.

## Adding an Explanatory Framework to Magic

What kind of evidence do we have about actual magical practice among early Christians? Already from a very early period, as early as 53 or 54 CE, we can gain evidence of magical activity among Christian believers from Paul's first epistle to the Corinthians (Köster 1980, 554; Wolff 1996, 13):

> To each is given the manifestation of the Spirit for the common good. To one is given through the Spirit the utterance of wisdom, […] to another gifts of healing by the one Spirit, to another the working of miracles, to another prophecy, to another the discernment of spirits, to another various kinds of tongues, to another the interpretation of tongues." (1 Corinthians 12: 7–10)

In this passage, Paul writes about magical specialists: healers, miracle workers, and exorcists, who are in the company of teachers, prophets, and other Church officials. This is a very interesting source also because the epistle predates extant texts about the miracles of Jesus and the apostles. What was the relation between magical practice and miracle stories in earliest Christianity? One can argue that tradition about Jesus and the apostles could have circulated in oral transmission before Paul's time—but such a hypothesis is impossible to test because of the lack of evidence. It is also possible, however, that it was magical practice that inspired the miracle stories about Jesus and the apostles. Christianity could have incorporated already existing magical lore. Magical specialists who converted to Christianity could be among the healers and miracle workers mentioned in 1 Corinthians.

This example suggests that the relation of magic and miracle might be less linear than we have outlined above. It seems rather a dialectical relationship, in which miracle stories generate belief in magic, and magical practice creates an interest for miracle stories. It might be also useful to make a distinction between individual magical practice, on one hand, and the social and historical development of traditions, on the other. At the personal level, miracle stories (and superstitious cultural traditions) can confirm spontaneously developed superstitious behaviors. At a historical level, magic can be institutionalized and use miracle stories as a justification of existing practices: believers imitate Jesus and the apostles.

The so-called long ending of the Gospel of Mark suggests that not only specialists, but all believers could perform magic: "these signs will accompany those who believe: by using my name they will cast out demons; they will speak in new tongues; they will pick up snakes in their hands, and if they drink any deadly thing, it will not hurt them; they will lay their hands on the sick, and they will recover" (Gospel of Mark 16: 17–18). This passage can be likely dated to the first half of the second century (Metzger 1971, 125; Kelhoffer 2000, 234–244). It would have been meaningless to add such a sentence to the Gospel unless there was an actual interest in at least some of the practices on the list. This passage therefore provides indirect evidence that at least some second century Christians were performing some kind of magic. If you believe, you can do it yourself.

Can we also say something about the actual form of early Christian magic? The question is not easy to answer because it is difficult to establish criteria to separate Christian and non-Christian magic. The only case when it is possible to make such a distinction with certainty is the mention of a holy name in a text, such as the name of Christ or Mary. Examples of Christian magic from the early second century onward are numerous and we restrict ourselves to a few examples. The famous Gold Lamella from the second century was used to cure headache: "Turn away, O Jesus, the Grim-Faced One, and on behalf of your maidservant, her headache, to (the) glory of your name, IAÔ ADÔNAI SABAÔTH I I I <...> OURIÊL <...> OURIÊL GABRIÊL" (Kotansky 2002, 37–46; cf. PGM XVIIIa.1–4). The following two texts describe how to evoke earthquake and rescue people from prison:

> I praise [you, I glorify] you, I invoke you today [God, who is alive] for ever and ever, who is coming upon [the clouds] of heaven, for the sake of the whole human race, Yao [Sabaoth] <...>, [Adon]ai Eloi <...>. I am Mary, I am Mariham, I am the mother of the life of the whole world, I am Mary. Let the rock [split], let the darkness split before me, [let] the earth split, let the iron dissolve <...>. (London Oriental Manuscript 6796[2], 9–25; Meyer 2002; 2003; cf. idem 2006).
>
> Copy the power [of a figure drawn on the manuscript] on sherds [?] of a new jar. Throw them to him. They will force him out onto the street, by the will of God. Offering: mastic, alouth, koush. (Heidelberg Coptic text 686, 14.251; Meyer and Smith 1999, 339)

These two examples are especially intriguing because in the Acts of the Apostles, the apostles together, then Peter alone, and finally Paul and Silas are miraculously delivered from prison (see above). These texts bring us back to the concept of the *parhedros*, a supernatural assistant who collaborates with the magician (Graf 1997, 107–115; Scibilia 2002). To acquire a *parhedros* one has to undergo specific initiatory rituals. The *parhedros* can assume one of four different forms: it might be (temporarily) materialized in human shape; assimilated to a deity, e.g. "Eros as assistant"; identified with an object, such as an iron lamella inscribed with Homeric verses; or represented by a demon. According to one of the Greek Magical Papyri, the *parhedros* might be used for the following purposes: to bring on dreams, to couple women and men, to kill enemies, to open closed doors and free people in chains, to stop attacks of demons and wild animals, to break the teeth of snakes, to put dogs to sleep (PGM I. 96–130). The *parhedros* can also bring forth water, wine, bread and other food (but no fish and pork). The Holy Spirit often appears as a *parhedros* assisting magic, such as in Paul's description of magical activities in the Corinthian congregation or in the miracle stories of the Book of Acts. A similar function is often fulfilled by "God's name" or "Jesus' name." Early Christian sources mention various instances of magic that we can identify with ones that could be typically achieved with the help of *parhedroi*, such as delivery from prison, exorcism, killing enemies (Book of Acts 5: 1–11), as well as magical manipulations of wine and food. As we have noticed, miraculous rescue from prison is mentioned particularly frequently in Christian sources; this motif is widely attested in ancient literature (Euripides, *Bacchae* 447–448; Ovid, *Metamorphoses* 3.699–700; Josephus, *Jewish Antiquities* 18.29). The general idea that we can gather from many examples of early Christian magic is that Christians were superior to their competitors in their methods of using supernatural assistance as well as the *parhedroi* who assisted them were superior to those of their competitors. The relation between magic and its explanation was complex: on one hand, explanations supported the practice of magic; on the other hand, the theological content was piggybacked onto the success of miracle stories and magical practices.

At first sight it might seem that this ancient theoretical framework into which the episodes were inserted is in diametrical opposition to the world-views of the modern readers and should be a reason to dismiss the narratives as superstition. Many modern Westerners reject the supernatural as an explanatory framework. On this account, ancient stories of magic might be entertaining episodes but lack referentiality to the actual state of affairs. Alternatively, they are expressions of psychological contents and not of external realities. Other modern Westerners, particularly theologians, might hold a consistently monotheistic view of the world. In this framework, the supernatural is acceptable as long as there is one God, but also, according to them, demons belong to the superstitions of the past. On this account, the underlying mechanism of the stories is that God controls natural and psychological forces.

Whereas contemporary Western thought prefers such alternative theories about magic in early Christian texts, we have good reasons to believe that the traditional conceptual framework did not lose its explanatory power. How can we explain that? Among members of the cross-culturally shared ontological categories, animals and humans are thought about as self-propelling, intentional agents: they perceive what is going on around them, react to those events, have goals and form plans (Leslie 1994; 1996). The needs of both social life and predation might have contributed to the development of mental modules which focus on agents in the environment (Barton 2000). In our evolutionary past, the dangers of not detecting an agent were much more serious than mistakenly detecting one that was not there. Consequently, intentional agency provides one of the most fundamental explanatory frameworks to make sense of the world around us (cf. Dennett 1971; 1983; 1987). According to Stewart Guthrie, Justin Barrett, and other representatives of the cognitive science of religion, humans' oversensitive reaction to the (potential) presence of agency in the environment has substantially contributed to the emergence of belief in gods and spirits (Guthrie 1993; Barrett 1996 and 2000; Pyysiäinen 2009; cf. Burkert 1996). Although modern Westerners are educated to reason about their environment in terms of mechanistic causality, they are able to do so only if they have ample time and resources. It is likely that our first hand reactions are based on intentional agency as much as the reactions of our ancestors were. Although we do not think about sickness as caused by demons, we still speak about it as something that attacks, tortures, and finally leaves us....

In an experiment conducted by Emily Pronin, Daniel M. Wegner, and their collaborators, participants were instructed to perform a "voodoo ritual" with a doll (Pronin *et al.* 2006, 220–223). They were introduced to a confederate who behaved either offensively or neutrally, and who later played the role of the "victim" of magic. Then participants were asked to generate "vivid and concentrate thoughts" about the victim (who was in the neighboring room) and prick the doll in particular ways. Finally, the victim came back and reported having a slight headache. It turned out that participants who had ill thoughts about their victims (because of the victims' offensive behavior) were likely to think that they caused the victims' headache, whereas participants meeting neutral victims were less likely to think so. In sum, university students, especially ones who were motivated to have evil thoughts about their victims, were easily made to believe they could curse victims by performing magic. What can we conclude from this experiment for our discussion of magic? We have suggested that intuitive reasoning about agency supplies a cross-cultural explanatory framework for processing stories of magic. The experiment of Pronin and others shows that modern Westerners, who have no explicit beliefs about demons, are able to use such reasoning in connection with their own behavior: ill thoughts combined with magical manipulation can damage other people's health.

What the experiment did not examine was the influence of information that participants received about the potential effects of voodoo: all participants equally received such information. Would participants in the experiment have come to the same conclusion if they had not been told about the potential effects of voodoo? Since the experimenters did not pay attention to this factor (familiarity with voodoo was not tested and everybody received the same introduction), we can only speculate about the role of previous knowledge. It is likely, however, that without introduction to the possible effects of voodoo the feeling of magic would have been less significant.

Are superstitious conditioning, miracle stories, and the intuition of agency enough to keep magical practice going? In the voodoo experiment, success was guaranteed. The same is true of the stories in the canonical and apocryphal Acts: the success rate of magic is one hundred percent. But how does real-life magic deal with the less favorable chances? In the case of healing (rather than causing) headache there was certainly much probability that the headache ceased after some time. Even harder diseases might be healed and give the impression of successful magic—but what about delivery from chains and imprisonment? Among the explanatory techniques underlying magic we will mention two that increase the "success rate" of magic by manipulating available evidence (cf. Gilovich 1991).

"Confirmation bias" means a tendency to seek evidence that is consistent with one's hypothesis and to avoid seeking falsificatory evidence (Eysenck and Keane 2005, 470–480). In

Peter Wason's classical experiment (1960 and 1968), subjects had to discover a simple relational rule between three numbers (2–4–6) by generating other sets of three numbers which the experimenter checked against the rule. It was discovered that subjects insisted on an initial hypothesis and chose only sets of numbers that matched it. Subsequent experimental work has supported Wason's findings. Recently Martin Jones and Robert Sugden (2001) have shown that information which is interpreted as confirming a hypothesis increases subjects' confidence in the truth of the hypothesis, even if that information has no value in terms of formal logic. Finally, experiments have shown how confirmation bias works in a social context: supporters have seen more fouls with players of the opponent team than with their own players (Eysenck 2004, 328). In sum, information that may be seen as confirming one's hypothesis (or prejudice) is sought for and interpreted as such, whereas information falsifying it is avoided and ignored. It is easy to see that this universal cognitive attitude plays an important role in collecting "evidence" for the effectiveness of magic.

Not only are people biased toward confirming evidence, but they are also extremely good at downplaying counterevidence. Magical practices are not vulnerable to unsuccessful performances, because there is a wealth of explanatory strategies for dealing with such situations. As Boyer pointed out, "rituals can never fail, but people can fail to perform them correctly" (Boyer 1994, 208). Anthropologist E.E. Evans-Pritchard has recorded a number of ready-made explanations among the Zande that can be used to account for the failure of an oracle: "(1) the wrong variety of poison having been gathered, (2) breach of a taboo, (3) witchcraft, (4) anger of the owners of the forest where the creeper grows, (5) age of the poison, (6) anger of the ghosts, (7) sorcery, (8) use" (Evans-Pritchard 1937, 330). In other words, the efficiency of magic is protected by the irrefutable circular reasoning that magic succeeds only when all necessary conditions are fulfilled, and we know that all conditions have been fulfilled only if the magic succeeds.

## Magic Explained

The new cognitive explanation of magic is based on the interplay of three components: superstitious conditioning, miracle stories, and explanatory methods. We have argued that magic is based on subconscious learning that generates superstitious behavior, as well as on a subconscious selective process that favors miracle stories, which further reinforce such behavior. We can summarize our findings as follows. (1) By operant conditioning we learn to "manipulate" reinforcers in the environment that are independent of our actions. "Superstitious" behavior develops regardless of any explanatory framework. Not only is the learning procedure subconscious, but also superstitious behavior itself may remain completely unnoticed. This is characteristic of other kinds of conditioned behavior, as well: for example, students can condition a lecturer to move in certain ways by reinforcing his actions by nodding (Vyse 1997, 75–76). As a result, we execute ineffective manipulations routinely, without being aware of them. (2) Miracle stories are memorable and interesting because they manipulate cross-cultural ontological categories (especially by favoring minimally counterintuitive details) and elicit empathy and emotions. These cognitive factors make them successful regardless of whether we practice magic or believe in it. But the vitality of such accounts also makes them important sources of inspiration and justification for magical practices. In turn, people's own superstitious behavior might cause such stories to be more attractive. (3) Various kinds of implicit and explicit explanations are attached to magical manipulations. In addition to analogical reasoning, which has been thoroughly studied in previous research, we have examined explanations based on agency in antiquity as well as in a contemporary experiment. Other cognitive factors include particular techniques to collect "evidence" about the effectiveness of magic. We have argued that magic is not based on such explanatory techniques and they can differ from one type of magic to the other. They are, however, essential for the integration of magic into individual and shared systems of belief.

# References

Atran, S. 1989. "Basic Conceptual Domains." *Mind and Language* 4: 7–16.

———. 2002. *In Gods We Trust: The Evolutionary Landscape of Religion*. New York: Oxford University Press.

Barkow, J.H. *et al.* eds. 1992. *The Adapted Mind: Evolutionary Psychology and the Generation of Culture*. New York: Oxford University Press.

Barrett J.L. 1996. "Anthropomorphism, Intentional Agents, and Conceptualizing God." dissertation, Ithaca, NY: Cornell University.

———. 2000. "Exploring the Natural Foundations of Religion." *Trends in Cognitive Sciences* 4: 29–34.

———. 2008. "Coding and Quantifying Counterintuitiveness: Theoretical and Methodological Reflections." *Method & Theory in the Study of Religion* 20: 308–338.

Barrett J.L. and M.A. Nyhof. 2001. "Spreading Non-natural Concepts: The Role of Intuitive Conceptual Structures in Memory and Transmission of Cultural Materials." *Journal of Cognition and Culture* 1: 69–100.

Barton, R.A. 2000. "Primate Brain Evolution. Cognitive Demands of Foraging or of Social Life?" In *On the Move: How and Why Animals Travel in Groups?*, edited by S. Boinski, 204–237. Chicago, IL: University of Chicago Press.

Bernoulli, D. 1738. "Specimen theoriae novae de mensura sortis." *Commentarii Academiae scientiarum imperialis Petropolitanae* 5: 175–192.

———. 1954. "Exposition of a New Theory on the Measurement of Risk." trans. Louise Sommer, *Econometrica* 22: 23–26.

Boudon, R. 2006. "Homo Sociologicus: Neither a Rational nor an Irrational Idiot." *Papers: Revista de sociologia* 80: 149–169.

Boyer, P. 1994a. *The Naturalness of Religious Ideas: A Cognitive Theory of Religion*. Berkley, CA: University of California Press.

———. 1994b. "Cognitive Constraints on Cultural Representations." In *Mapping the Mind: Domain Specificity in Cognition and Culture*, edited by L.A. Hirschfeld and S.A. Gelman, 91–411. Cambridge: Cambridge University Press.

———. 2001. *Religion Explained: The Human Instincts that Fashion Gods, Spirits and Ancestors*. New York: Basic Books.

Boyer, P. and C. Ramble. 2001. "Cognitive Templates for Religious Concepts: Cross-cultural Evidence for Recall of Counter-intuitive Representations." *Cognitive Science* 25: 535–564.

Bownas, G. 2004. *Japanese Rainmaking and other Folk Practices*. London: Routledge.

Braarvig, J. 1999. "Magic: Reconsidering the Grand Dichotomy." In *The World of Ancient Magic: Papers from the First International Samson Eitrem Seminar at the Norwegian Institute at Athens, 4–8 May 1997*, edited by D.R. Jordan, H. Montgomery and E. Thomassen, 21–54. Bergen: Norwegian Institute at Athens.

Brass, M. and C. Heyes. 2005. "Imitation: Is Cognitive Neuroscience Solving the Correspondence

Problem?" *Trends in Cognitive Sciences* 9: 489–495.

Bremmer, Jan N. 2008. *Greek Religion and Culture, the Bible, and the Ancient Near East.* Leiden: Brill.

Burkert, W. 1996. *Creation of the Sacred: Tracks of Biology in Early Religions.* Cambridge, MA: Harvard University Press.

Csermely, P. 2006. *Weak Links: Stabilizers of Complex Systems from Proteins to Social Networks.* Berlin: Springer.

Czachesz, I. 1998. "Who is Deviant? Entering the Story-World of the *Acts of Peter.*" In *The Apocryphal Acts of Peter: Magic, Miracles and Gnosticism,* edited by J.N. Bremmer, 85–96. Leuven: Peeters.

———. 2007a. *The Grotesque Body in Early Christian Literature: Hell, Scatology, and Metamorphosis,* Habilitationsschrift. Heidelberg: Theologische Fakultät der Ruprecht-Karls Universität Heidelberg.

———. 2007b. "Early Christian Views on Jesus' Resurrection: Toward a Cognitive Psychological Approach." *Nederlands Theologisch Tijdschrift* 61: 47–59.

———. 2007c. *Commission Narratives: A Comparative Study of the Canonical and Apocryphal Acts.* Leuven: Peeters.

———. 2007d. "Magic and Mind: Toward a Cognitive Theory of Magic, with Special Attention to the Canonical and Apocryphal Acts of the Apostles." In *Neues Testament und Magie: Verhältnisbestimmungen.* Special issue of *Annali di Storia dell'Esegesi,* edited by T. Nicklas and Th. J. Kraus, 295–321.

———. 2008. "Speaking Asses in the Acts of Thomas." In *Balaam and His Speaking Ass,* edited by G.H. van Kooten and G.M. van Ruiten, 275–285. Leiden: Brill.

———. 2009. "Metamorphosis and Mind: Cognitive Explorations of the Grotesque in Early Christian Literature." In *Metamorphoses: Resurrection, Body and Transformative Practices in Early Christianity,* edited by T. Karlsen Seim and J. Økland, 207–230. Berlin: DeGruyter.

———. 2011. *The Grotesque Body in Early Christian Literature: Hell, Scatology, and Metamorphosis.* London: Equinox, in press.

Decety, J. 2007. "A Social Cognitive Neuroscience Model of Human Empathy." In *Social Neuroscience: Integrating Biological and Psychological Explanations of Social Behavior,* edited by E. Harmon-Jones and P. Winkielman, 246–270. New York: Guilford.

Dehling, H.G. 1997. "Daniel Bernoulli and the St. Petersburg Paradox." *Nieuw archief voor wiskunde,* Vierde Serie 15: 223–227.

Dennett, D. 1971. "Intentional Systems." *Journal of Philosophy* 68: 87–106.

———.1983. "Intentional Systems in Cognitive Ethology: The 'Panglossian Paradigm' Defended." *Behavioral and Brain Sciences* 6: 343–390.

———. 1987. *The Intentional Stance.* Cambridge, MA: MIT Press.

Dunnigan, A. 2005. "Rain." In *Encyclopedia of Religion,* vol. 11, edited by Lindsay Jones, 7602–7605. Detroit, MI: Thomson Gale.

Eichenbaum, H. 2002. *The Cognitive Neuroscience of Memory: An Introduction.* Oxford: Oxford University Press.

Eijk, P. J. van der. 2004. "Divination, Prognosis and Prophylaxis: The Hippocratic Work 'On Dreams' (*De victu* 4) and Its Near Eastern Background." In *Magic and Rationality in Ancient Near Easter and Graeco-Roman Medicine,* edited by H.F.J. Horstmanshoff and M. Stol, 187–218. Leiden: Brill,

Evans-Pritchard, E.E. 1937. *Witchcraft, Oracles and Magic among the Azande.* Oxford: Clarendon Press.

Eysenck, M. W. 2004. *Psychology: An International Perspective.* Hove: Psychology Press.

————. and M.T. Keane. 2005. *Cognitive Psychology. A Student's Handbook.* Hove: Psychology Press.

Fauconnier, G. and M. Turner. 2002. *The Way We Think: Conceptual Blending and the Mind's Hidden Complexities.* New York: Basic Books.

Ferster, C.B. and B.F. Skinner. 1957. *Schedules of Reinforcement.* New York: Appleton-Century-Crofts.

Fowler, R.I. 2005. "The Concept of Magic." In *Thesaurus cultus et rituum antiquorum*, vol 3, edited by J. Ch. Balty *et al.*, 283–286. Basel: Fondation pour le Lexicon Iconographicum Mythologiae Classicae and Los Angeles: Getty Publications.

Frazer, Sir J.G. 1911. *The Golden Bough: A Study in Magic and Religion.* Part One, vol. 1. London: MacMillan.

Furley, W. D. 1993. "Besprechung und Behandlung: Zur Form und Funktion von *EPÔIDAI* in der griechischen Zaubermedizin." In *Philanthropia kai eusebeia: Festschrift für Albrecht Dihle zum 70. Geburtstag*, edited by G.W. Most *et al.*, 80–104. Göttingen: Vandenhoeck and Ruprecht

Gallese, V. *et al.* 2004. "A Unifying View of the Basis of Social Cognition." *Trends in Cognitive Sciences* 8: 396–403.

García Martínez, F. 2002. "Magic in the Dead Sea Scrolls." In *The Metamorphosis of Magic from Late Antiquity to the Early Modern Period*, edited by J.N. Bremmer and J.R. Veenstra, 13–33. Leuven: Peeters.

Gilovich, T. 1991. *How We Know What Isn't So: The Fallibility of Human Reason in Everyday Life.* New York: The Free Press.

Gonce, L.O. *et al.* 2006. "Role of Context in the Recall of Counterintuitive Concepts." *Journal of Cognition and Culture* 6: 521–547.

Graf, F. 1997. *Magic in the Ancient World.* Trans. F. Philip. Cambridge, MA: Harvard University Press.

————. 2002. "Augustine and Magic." In *The Metamorphosis of Magic from Late Antiquity to the Early Modern Period*, edited by J.N. Bremmer and J.R. Veenstra, 87–103. Leuven: Peeters.

————. 2005. "Wetterriten." In *Thesaurus cultus et rituum antiquorum (ThesCRA), Vol. 3, Divination, prayer, veneration, hikesia, asylia, oath, malediction, profanation, magic, rituals, (addendum to vol. II) consecration*, edited by V. Lambrinoudakis and J.Ch. Balty, 298–299, Los Angeles, CA: J. Paul Getty Museum.

Guthrie, S.E. 1993. *Faces in the Clouds. A New Theory of Religion.* Oxford: Oxford University Press.

Hsü K. and A. Hsü. 1991. "Self-similarity of the '1/f Noise' Called Music." *Proceedings of National Academy of Sciences USA*, 88: 3507–3509.

Hurley, S. and N. Chater. 2005. "Introduction: The Importance of Imitation." In *Perspectives on Imitation: From Neuroscience to Social Science*, vol 1, edited by S. Hurley and N. Chater, 1–52. Cambridge, MA.: M.I.T. Press.

Ichinomiya, T. 2006. "Power-law Distribution in Japanese Racetrack Betting." *Physica A: Statistical Mechanics and its Applications* 368: 207–213.

Jeffers, A. 1996. *Magic and Divination in Ancient Palestine and Syria.* Leiden: Brill.

Jones M. and R. Sugden. 2001. "Positive Confirmation Bias in the Acquisition of Information." *Theory and Decision* 50: 59–99.

Kapferer, B. 1997. *The Feast of the Sorcerer: Practices of Consciousness and Power.* Chicago, IL: University of Chicago Press.

Keil, F.C. 1979. *Semantic and Conceptual Development: An Ontological Perspective.* Cambridge, MA: Harvard University Press.

———. 1989. *Concepts, Kinds, and Cognitive Development*. Cambridge, MA: M.I.T. Press.

Kelhoffer, J.A. 2000. *Miracle and Mission: The Authentication of Missionaries and their Message in the Longer Ending of Mark*. Tübingen: Mohr Siebeck.

Keysers, C. *et al.* 2004. "A Touching Sight: SII/PV Activation During the Observation and Experience of Touch." *Neuron* 42: 335–346.

Klauck, H.-J. 2000 (1996). *Magic and Paganism in Early Christianity: The World of the Acts of the Apostles*. Trans. B. McNeil. Edinburgh: T & T Clark.

Kollmann, B. 1996. *Jesus und die Christen als Wundertäter: Studien zu Magie, Medizin und Schamanismus in Antike und Christentum*. Göttingen: Vandenhoeck and Ruprecht.

Kotansky, R. 2002. "An Early Christian Gold Lamella for Headache." In *Magic and Ritual in the Ancient World*, edited by P. Mirecki and M. Meyer, 37–46. Leiden: Brill.

Köster, H. 1980. *Einführung in das Neue Testament im Rahmen der Religionsgeschichte und Kulturgeschichte der hellenistischen und römischen Zeit*. Berlin: DeGruyter.

Kuklick, H. 1991. *The Savage Within: The Social History of British Anthropology, 1885–1945*. Cambridge: Cambridge University Press.

Laney, C. *et al.* 2004. "Memory for thematically arousing events." *Memory and Cognition* 32: 1149–1159.

Leslie, A. 1994. "ToMM, ToBy, and Agency. Core Architecture and Domain Specificity." In *Mapping the Mind*, edited by L. Hirschfeld and S. Gelman, 119–148. Cambridge: Cambridge University Press.

———. 1996. "A Theory of Agency." In *Causal Cognition*, edited by D. Sperber *et al.*, 121–141. Oxford: Clarendon Press.

Leven, K.-H. 2004. " 'At Times these Ancient Facts Seem to Lie Before Me Like a Patient on a Hospital Bed'—Retrospective Diagnosis and Ancient Medical History." In *Magic and Rationality in Ancient Near Eastern and Graeco-Roman Medicine*, edited by H.F.J. Horstmanshoff and M. Stol, 369–386. Leiden: Brill.

Lévi-Strauss, C. 1966. *The Savage Mind*. Chicago, IL: Chicago University Press.

Luz, U. 1992. *Das Evangelium nach Matthäus*, 3rd. ed, vol 1. Zürich: Benziger Verlag and Neukirchen-Vluyn: Neukirchener Verlag.

Matthews, Ch. R. 1999. "Articulate Animals: A Multivalent Motif in the Apocryphal Acts of the Apostles." In *The Apocryphal Acts of the Apostles*, edited by F. Bovon *et al.*, 205–232. Cambridge, MA.: Harvard University Press.

Meltzoff, A. N. 2002. "Elements of a Developmental Theory of Imitation." In *The Imitative Mind: Development, Evolution, and Brain Bases*, edited by A.N. Meltzoff and W. Prinz, 19–41. Cambridge: Cambridge University Press.

Metzger, B.M. 1971. *A Textual Commentary of the Greek New Testament*. Stuttgart: United Bible Societies.

Meyer, M. 1996. *The Magical Book of Mary and the Angels (P. Heid. Inv. Kopt. 685)*. Heidelberg: Winter.

———. 2002. "The Prayer of Mary Who Dissolves Chains in Coptic Magic and Religion." In: P. Mirecki and M. Meyer, eds., *Magic and Ritual in the Ancient World*, 407–415. Leiden: Brill.

———. 2003. "The Prayer of Mary in the Magical Book of Mary and the Angels." In *Prayer, Magic, and the Stars in the Ancient and Late Antique World*, edited by S. Noegel *et al.* 57–67. University Park: The Pennsylvania State University Press.

Meyer, M. and R. Smith, eds. 1999. *Ancient Christian Magic: Coptic Texts of Ritual Power*. Princeton, NJ: Princeton University Press.

Middleton, J. 2005. "Theories of Magic." In *Encyclopedia of Religion* 8, edited by Lindsay Jones, 5562–5569. Detroit: Thomson Gale.

Morse, W.H. and B.F. Skinner. 1957. "A Second Type of Superstition in the Pigeon." *American Journal of Psychology* 70: 308–311.

Norenzayan, A. and S. Atran. 2004. "Cognitive and Emotional Processes in the Cultural Transmission of Natural and Nonnatural Beliefs." In *The Psychological Foundations of Culture,* edited by M. Schaller and C.S. Crandall, 149–169. Mahwah, NJ: Lawrence Erlbaum Associates.

Ono, K. 1987. "Superstitious Behavior in Humans." *Journal of the Experimental Analysis of Behavior* 47: 261–271.

Park K. and E. Domany. 2001. "Power-Law Distribution of Dividends in Horse Races." *Europhysics Letters* 53: 419–425.

Pearson, J. 2002, *Belief Beyond Boundaries: Wicca, Celtic Spirituality and the New Age.* Aldershot and Milton Keynes: Ashgate.

Peters, O. and K. Christensen. 2002. "Rain: Relaxations in the Sky." *Physical Review* E 66: 036120.

Pilch, J.J. 2000. *Healing in the New Testament: Insights from Medical and Mediterranean Anthropology.* Minneapolis, MN: Fortress Press.

Pronin, E. *et al.* 2006. "Everyday Magical Powers. The Role of Apparent Mental Causation in the Overestimation of Personal Influence." *Journal of Personality and Social Psychology* 91: 218–231.

Pyysiäinen, I. 2003. *How Religion Works. Toward a New Cognitive Science of Religion.* Leiden: Brill.

———. 2004. *Magic, Miracles, and Religion. A Scientist's Perspective.* Walnut Creek, CA: AltaMira Press.

———. 2009. *Supernatural Agents: Cognitive Science of Supernatural Agency.* Oxford: Oxford University Press.

Scibilia, A. 2002. "Supernatural Assistance in the Greek Magical Papyri: The Figure of the *Parhedros.*" In *The Metamorphosis of Magic from Late Antiquity to the Early Modern Period*, edited by J.N. Bremmer and J.R. Veenstra, 71–86. Leuven: Peeters.

Schwartz, B. *et al.* 2002. *Psychology of Learning and Behavior,* 5th ed. New York: Norton.

Shi, Y. 1996. "Correlations of Pitches in Music." *Fractals* 4: 547–553.

Singer, T. *et al.* 2004. "Empathy for Pain Involves the Affective But Not the Sensory Components of Pain." *Science* 303: 1157–1162.

Skinner, B.F. 1938. *The Behavior of Organisms.* New York: Appleton-Century-Crofts.

———. 1948. "'Superstition' in the Pigeon." *Journal of Experimental Psychology* 38: 168–172.

Smith, J.Z. 1995. "Trading Places." In: M. Meyer and P. Mirecki, eds., *Ancient Magic and Ritual Power*, 13–27. Leiden: Brill.

Sørensen, J. 2002. "'The Morphology and Function of Magic' Revisited." In *Current Approaches in the Cognitive Science of Religion*, edited by I. Pyysiäinen and V. Anttonen, 177–202. London: Continuum,

———. 2007. *A Cognitive Theory of Magic.* Walnut Creek, CA: AltaMira.

Spelke, E.S. 1990. "Principles of Object Perception." *Cognitive Science* 14: 49–56.

Spelke, E.S. and K.D. Kinzler. 2007. "Core knowledge." *Developmental Science* 11: 89–96.

Stevens, P. 1996. "Magic." In *Encyclopedia of Cultural Anthropology* 3, edited by D. Levinson and M. Ember, 721–726. New York: Holt.

Stewart, P.J. and A. Strathern. 2004. *Witchcraft, Sorcery, Rumors, and Gossip.* Cambridge, Cambridge University Press.

Thomassen, E. 1997. "Is Magic a Subclass of Ritual?" In *The World of Ancient Magic: Papers from* the First International Samson Eitrem Seminar at the Norwegian Institute at Athens, 4–8 May 1997, edited by D.R. Jordan, H. Montgomery and E. Thomassen, 55–66 Bergen: Norwegian Institute at Athens.

Tylor, E.B. 1871. *Primitive Culture: Researches into the Development of Mythology, Philosophy, Religion, Art, and Custom.* London: John Murray.

Uddin, L .Q. *et al.* 2007. "The Self and Social Cognition: The Role of Cortical Midline Structures and Mirror Neurons." *Trends in Cognitive Sciences* 11: 153–157.

Upal, M.A. *et al.* 2007. "Contextualizing Counterintuitiveness: How Context Affects Comprehension and Memorability of Counterintuitive Concepts." *Cognitive Science* 31: 415–439.

Versnel, H.S. 1991. "Some Reflections on the Relationship Magic-Religion." *Numen* 38: 177–197.

Voss R.F. and J. Clarke. 1975. "1/f Noise in Music and Speech." *Nature* 258: 317–318.

———. 1978. "1/f Noise in Music. Music from 1/f Noise." *Journal of Acoustical Society of America* 63: 258–263.

Vyse, S.A. 1997. *Believing in Magic: The Psychology of Superstition.* Oxford: Oxford University Press.

Wagner G.A. and E.K. Morris. 1987. "'Superstitious' Behavior in Children." *The Psychological Record* 37: 471–488.

Ward, J. 2006. *The Student's Guide to Cognitive Neuroscience.* Hove: Psychology Press.

Wason, P. 1960. "On the Failure to Eliminate Hypotheses in a Conceptual Task." *Quarterly Journal of Experimental Psychology* 12: 129–140.

———. 1968. "Reasoning about a Rule." *Quarterly Journal of Experimental Psychology* 20: 237–281.

Wolff, C. 1996. *Der erste Brief des Paulus an die Korinther.* Berlin: Evangelische Verlagsanstalt.

Wulff, D.M. 1997. *Psychology of Religion: Classic and Contemporary*, 2nd ed. New York: J. Wiley and Sons, 1997.

# — 12 —

# Beneath the Surface of History?

## Donald Wiebe

*Enthusiastic evolutionists do at times forget about vertical integration, they do at times overgen-eralize from data from a single society, and they do at times create stories about past adaptive advantage that serve only to account for current results than to generate new hypotheses: In short, they do, at times, need and benefit from criticism.*

(Jerome Barkow, *Missing the Revolution* 2006, 41)

## The Problem of Historical Explanation

My concern in this essay parallels that raised by Alan Bullock in his response to the "New History" of Fernand Braudel and the *Annales* school in France. For Bullock, the metaphor of different levels of history that suggested the historian could escape the messiness of the contingency and subjectivity involved in accounting for individual events, and the persons engaged in them, is seriously flawed; that the metaphor confuses historical understanding with the generalizing perspective the social scientists bring to their attempts to understand contemporary society. Bullock queries whether *"getting beneath the surface of history"* is an over-simplified and over-rationalized version of history that is more a retreat from reality than a penetration of it to a deeper level. How plausible is it, he asks, for the historian to ignore the irregularities and discontinuities in history "as superficial, no more than a shadow play upon the surface, irrelevant to, or their outcome determined by deeper movements beneath the tides of history, to which a scientific or analytic historiography can supply the almanac?" (552).

He is convinced, for example, that it is impossible to provide a reasonable picture of the twentieth century in this way. We cannot account for the division of Europe in that century, he claims, by paying attention only to long-term underlying economic, social, and political trends. Of far greater significance than universal scientific laws, he argues, are unique personalities and events such as, for example, the political opportunism of Lenin in Russia and the actions of Hitler in Germany.[1] He acknowledges that events are not simply

---

1. Dennis Wrong also invokes Hitler's coming to power as an example of the need for an explanatory account of a historical event that goes beyond generalization. It is, he writes, "a typical if momentous

"the result of conscious action or opportunism, whether by individuals or groups" (556), and agrees that the historian cannot ignore the long-term political, social, and economic trends, yet maintains, and I think rightly so, that the real is not only to be found in the rational (rationalizable) aspects of reality, but also in its contingencies and subjectivities (558). For Braudel, on the other hand, those contingencies and subjectivities are mere "surface disturbances" and "crests of foam." For him, to give place to what he calls the *longue durée,* and thereby to get beneath the surface of history, is more than a routine expansion of historical studies; it amounts to a displacement of traditional history. As Braudel puts it:

> For the historian, accepting the *longue durée* entails a readiness to change his style, his attitude, a whole reversal in his thinking, a whole new way of conceiving of social affairs....
> [I]t is in relation to these expanses of slow-moving history that the whole of history is to be rethought, as if on the basis of an infrastructure. All the stages, all the thousands of stages, all the thousand explosions of historical time can be understood on the basis of the depths, the semistillness. Everything gravitates round it. (33)[2]

For Bullock, this amounts to a rejection of history and a failure to see that human life is a mixture in which different elements, the superficial, the profound, the ephemeral, and the lasting, are not separated out but flung together and juxtaposed, often in a confusing and bewildering way; in which the reaction of men to their historical circumstances is extraordinarily varied, and in which an emerging pattern is liable to be disrupted, modified, and often changed out of recognition by the impact of events and the actions of men, and the emergence of new trends which were not, and could not be foreseen (559).

Whereas Bullock's concern was restricted to the assault on traditional history by those who would seek explanations in terms of infrastructure beneath its surface, mine involves more recent "beneath-the-surface" type proposals to account for the full social and cultural richness of human behaviour that I think may amount to the displacement not only of history but of the social sciences as well. I have in mind here the proposal by John Tooby and Leda Cosmides for the creation of an Integrated Causal Model (ICM) for explaining the full range of human behaviour, and that of Jerome Barkow (1989) for creating a framework for a "Vertically Integrated Explanation" (VIE) of human social and cultural behaviour.[3]

---

historical example ... for our interest in knowing how it came to happen in the supposedly advanced and enlightened society of early twentieth-century Germany is hardly satisfied by grouping it with other instances of the ascendancy of authoritarian dictators" (2005, 97).

2.   This is clearly evident in Braudel's *The Mediterranean and the Mediterranean World in the Age of Philip II* (1972 [1949]) where he divides history into three movements of time: geographical time, social time, and individual time. He proceeds there to contrast "the brilliant surface of history" (vol. II, 1243) in individual time with "the strong tides of history" that carry the "surface disturbances [and] crests of foam" that comprise "the history of individuals and events" (vol. I, 21) on their strong backs. For Braudel, the individual is "imprisoned within a destiny in which he himself has little hand" (vol. II, 1244), and the event is described as "flotsam" that is essentially "ephemeral" (vol. II, 1243). As a structuralist, Braudel admits that he is little tempted either by the individual or event, and he writes: "I would conclude with the paradox that the true man of action is he who can measure most nearly the constraints upon him who chooses to remain within them and even to take advantage of the weight of the *inevitable,* exerting his own pressure in the same direction. *All* efforts against the *prevailing tide of history*— which is not always obvious—are *doomed to failure*" (vol. II, 1243–1244; emphasis added).

3.   I focus attention on these works, even though it is nearly two decades since they were first published because of their pervasive and continuing influence on scholars in the humanities, and particularly on scholars in Religious Studies.

Such frameworks, they maintain, will make possible "multiple level, mutually compatible explanations of behaviour" (1989,4) that will displace what they call the Standard Social Science Model (SSSM) of explanation.[4] Before setting out the reasons for my concern, however, I want to acknowledge some hesitation in criticizing these proposals. First, I find all proposals for explaining human behaviour that seek to work within the boundaries of knowledge established by the other sciences wholly acceptable; second, Barkow plainly asserts in his writing (and Tooby and Cosmides come close to that at a variety of points in their major essay on the topic) that his aim is not to replace the social sciences, but only to have them submit to what we might call the boundary conditions that knowledge in the natural sciences sets for knowledge claims in other fields; and finally, I fully agree with the fundamental assumption adopted by all of them that historical, social, or cultural realities are not *sui generis*, and that a proper understanding of them requires that we attempt to causally locate these realities inside the larger network of scientific knowledge; that we recognize that such realities must be presumed to be part of a larger natural system.

### "Encompassing Explanatory Generalizations": Can History Be Reduced to Biology?

Despite the explicit commitments of Tooby, Cosmides, and Barkow to an integration of social scientific and biological knowledge in explaining human behaviour, and my agreements with some of the explicitly stated objectives of the VIE and the ICM proposals, it seems to me that their proposals do more than simply displace the Standard Social Science Model of explanation. In my judgment, that is, their proposals do not only exclude social science explanations as *alternative* routes to understanding the full range of human behaviour, but rather seem also to make impossible even *complementary* explanatory contributions to those provided by biology and evolutionary psychology. Although the Standard Social Science model is criticized and rejected by Barkow, Tooby, and Cosmides, there is not even a sketch of an alternative kind of social science that they might consider an acceptable framework for delivering genuine explanations of human behaviour that complement those provided by evolutionary biology and evolutionary psychology. I cannot here provide a full-blown argument to establish the suspicions I have of the VIE and ICM proposals but will look briefly at some of the implications I think those proposals hold.

In "The Psychological Foundations of Culture" John Tooby and Leda Cosmides essentially put forward an argument that universals underlie the variableness of overt behaviour (45) and that these universals are essentially biological. They write: "From a perspective that describes the whole integrated system of causation, the distinction between the biologically determined and the nonbiologically determined can be seen as a non-distinction" (46). This appears to me to imply that culture is nothing other than just another biological phenomenon; simply another bit of mental behaviour wholly explicable in terms of "evolved psychological mechanisms that cause it to exist" without culture itself having any causal powers (118). They also write: "…nothing the organism interacts with in the world

---

4.  They seem to presume that all social scientists take social and cultural factors (realities?) to be *sui generis*, and they take Émile Durkheim to be the founder and chief exponent of this "doctrine." I will not enter a debate over the correct interpretation of Durkheim on this matter. Suffice it to say that there is no justification for the assumption by Durkheim's (cognitive) critics that treating social levels of reality as having causal force or power is equivalent to assuming such a level to be *sui generis* and therefore beyond, or in need of, explanation. On this matter see R. Keith Sawyer's *Social Emergence: Societies As Complex Systems*; especially chapter 6, "Durkheim's Theory of Social Emergence," (2005, 100–144).

is nonbiological to it, and so for humans cultural forces are biological, social forces are biological, physical forces are biological, and so on. The social and cultural are not alternatives to the biological" (86). Even though on one level of analysis the erasure of the distinction between biological and social/cultural reality makes sense, and, in some sense, justifies the claim that the social and the cultural are not *alternatives* to the biological, it does not, in my estimation, justify the claim that the social and cultural do not constitute emergent levels of reality that can provide complementary explanatory accounts of human behaviour. Invoking social structure, culture, learning, and the like in explanatory accounts of human behaviour (that is, involving "downward causation"[5]) need not constitute alternatives to biological and psychological explanations but may, rather, complement such explanations; nor need such complementary explanations deny, as Tooby and Cosmides seem to imply, "that cultural and social phenomena can never be fully divorced from the structure of the human psychological architecture or understood without reference to its design" (122).[6]

Barkow's essay in *The Adapted Mind* entitled "Beneath New Culture is Old Psychology: Gossip and Social Stratification" raises similar concerns for me as do Tooby and Cosmides, for he seems there to espouse a kind of biological reductionism. He writes: "Fortunately, the concepts of vertical integration and evolutionary psychology ... suggest that there is little human that is really 'evolutionarily unanticipated'" (627). In pointing out that old adaptive behaviours in our evolutionary past "underlie complex and novel sociocultural forms" (627) he seems, like Tooby and Cosmides, to imply that social structure and culture are not themselves causal factors in accounting for human behaviour, so much as they are the causal result of underlying psychological and evolutionary forces (635). I am aware of his explicit claim here that we are still in need of the social sciences, as I am of the explicit

---

5.    I have in mind here Douglas Hofstadter's claim that because of what he calls "the upside-down perceptions of evolved creatures," humans are built, as he puts it, "to perceive 'big stuff' rather than 'small stuff'" (173). He is quite aware that it is at the basic level of physics "where the actual motors driving reality reside" (173), but he also notes that thinking creatures know next to nothing about that level of reality even though it makes their living and thinking possible. Thus he maintains that we are "fated" to explain our world "not in terms of the underlying particle physics ... but in terms of such abstract and ill-defined high-level patterns as mothers and fathers, friends and lovers, grocery stores and checkout stands, soap operas and beer commercials, crackpots and geniuses, religions and stereotypes, comedies and tragedies, obsessions and phobias, and of course, beliefs and desires, hopes and fears, dreads and dreams, ambitions and jealousies, devotions and hatreds, and so many other abstract patterns that are a million metaphorical miles from the microworld of physical causality" (172–173). See also R. Keith Sawyer's treatment of sociological theories of emergence in his *Social Emergence: Societies as Complex Systems* (2005). He argues there that emergent social properties cannot be wholly analyzed in terms of the individuals who constitute society and that as at least in some sense autonomous, they exert causal force on individuals. In *The Fabric of Reality: The Science of Parallel Universes—and Its Implications* (1997) David Deutsch also argues against both reductionism and holism and for a philosophy of emergentism that escapes what he calls the "initial state plus laws of motion" framework of explanation. He writes: "There is no reason to regard high-level theories as in any way 'second-class citizens.' Our theories of subatomic physics, and even of quantum theory or relativity, are in no way privileged relative to theories about emergent properties" (27). (See also note 7 below).

6.    There is no good reason to believe, as Tooby and Cosmides apparently do, that cultural and social phenomena must be wholly divorced from notions of design or untouched by human psychological architecture for them to have causal force or power. Emergent realities—that is, the products of microforces underlying and giving rise to those patterns at the human level of perception—may nevertheless function as a "collective entity" whose causal force can be "mapped" without recourse to the micro-level of explanation.

170

claim in his earlier work, *Darwin, Sex, and Status: Biological Approaches to Mind and Culture*, that he is not a reductionist and that "the social sciences are not to be replaced by biology but to be made compatible with it" (213). Although the fault may be mine, I do not see in what sense Barkow thinks the social sciences can provide complementary accounts of human behaviour, since in his framework, neither social structures nor culture have causal power to influence human behaviour. He announces his opposition in this work to the view that humans are cultural animals, and he criticizes social scientists for assuming "that our cultures, not our heredity determine our behaviour" (40) as if it can only be heredity or culture (but not both) that has causal influence. *Therefore, in my judgment, his criticism of social scientists for relegating the influence of biological evolution to the distant past despite recognizing that culture is a product of such evolution, can be appropriately matched with criticism of evolutionary psychologists who assert the importance of the social sciences, yet seem to insist that social structures and culture have no causal effect on human behaviour.*

I have no doubt that "in the final analysis," as we say, everything—every aspect of everything in the world—can be explained in terms of our most basic science; physics. Whereas Barkow, Tooby, and Cosmides, (and those who follow them) seem ready to account for all of human behaviour in terms of evolutionary psychology and evolutionary biology, we might with equal justification ask for an explanation of all biological phenomena in terms of biochemistry and chemistry, and all of that, were we looking for the Ultimate Cause(s) of all human behaviour, in terms of the four basic causes discovered by physicists, namely, gravity, electromagnetism and the strong and weak nuclear forces. Not to take that reductionist route while excluding all recourse to larger patterns or emergent levels of reality beyond the biological or psychological as bearing causal significance is simply arbitrary. But there is good reason for not taking such a route, as Douglas Hofstadter (2007) has recently pointed out:

> The point is that one gets into very hot water if one goes the fully reductionistic route; not only do all the objects of "the system" become microscopic and uncountably numerous, but also the system itself grows beyond bounds in space and time and becomes, in the end, the entire universe taken over all time. There is no comprehensibility left, since everything is shattered into a trillion trillion trillion invisible pieces that are scattered hither and yon. Reductionism is merciless (48).[7]

---

7.  I point out here, still drawing on the work of Douglas Hofstadter, that within a materialist framework all "realities" at the human level of existence are epiphenomena; that is, realities comprised of a very large number of "deeper" (more simple) levels of reality. As Hofstadter puts it: "An epiphenomenon … is a collective and unitary-seeming outcome of many small, often invisible or unperceived, quite possibly utterly unsuspected events. In other words, an epiphenomenon could be said to be a large-scale *illusion* created by the collusion of many small and indisputably non-illusionary events" (93). To call these "realities" epiphenomena, therefore, is simply a shorthand way for pointing to macroscopic phenomena that have some kind of perceptible "logic" and "structure" to them—"a kind of life of their own" that, at our level of experience of the world, demands a different vocabulary from that of physics. If we do not use a different vocabulary from that of physics, we will be swamped by an overwhelming complexity at the level of myriads of particles, as Hofstadter puts it, where "there are no natural sharp borders in the [human] world" (47). Thus, depending on the level chosen as one's focus, there are different causal forces at play in the various patterns churned out by the sub-atomic particles. Thus, according to Hofstadter, "mental properties … reside not on the level of a single, tiny, constituent but on the level of *vast abstract* patterns involving those constituents" (30). "If this all seems topsy-turvy," he writes, "it certainly is—but it is nonetheless completely consistent with the fundamental causality of the laws of physics" (50).

I suggest here, then, that Barkow, Tooby, and Cosmides may be limiting too severely the range of possible explanations by what appears to be their apparently reductionistic approach to explaining human behaviour essentially within a biological framework, while, paradoxically, refusing to fully embrace reductionism by moving beyond evolutionary psychology and biology to wholly mechanistic causal explanation of that behaviour. They seem ready, that is, to accept downward causation at the biological and psychological levels of reality, but still appear to be blind to patterns of reality at the level of the social and cultural that may well have shaping influence on human behaviour.

## "The Persistence of the Particular": History as Non-Fictional Story

Although I believe social scientific and cultural explanations can complement the work of the evolutionary psychologists, I do not intend to provide an apology here for the social sciences, as necessary as such an apology may be, given the crimes and misdemeanors with which philosophers like Karl Popper have indicted some social scientists.[8] Nevertheless, given the overarching theme of this volume, I do want to focus some attention on the nature of the historical enterprise as providing us with a peculiar kind of knowledge of human behaviour that, although not scientific in any strict sense, (and does not, therefore, run afoul of Popper's critique of historicism), is not unscientific and does complement the scientific knowledge of human behaviour championed by Tooby, Cosmides, and Barkow.

In answer to the question in the title of this paper, then, I *suggest*, following Gustav Johannes Renier's (1950) understanding of the historical enterprise, that in a not unreasonable sense, history is primarily, although not totally, a surface matter; that is, that the fundamental task of the historian is simply to tell a story that accurately preserves the memory of our various pasts by providing accounts of the emergence and development of particular sets of human events and experiences. I find Renier's version of history in his account of its purpose and methods apt, in that he neither ignores the importance of science to the historian, nor the importance of what the sociologist Dennis Wrong calls "the persistence of the particular" in human experience; that is, the desire "to know more about historical and biographical experiences and situations than what they have in common with others that are similar" (2005, 99). "This much is certain," Renier wrote, "the man who has not communicated to his fellow human beings, by publication or by private circulation, a story of past events … is not a historian" (4). The essential task of the historian, that is, is to tell tales "of human collectivities going through active and passive experiences and of individuals who lived in societies, *influenced them, [and] were influenced by them*" (189; emphasis added).

Although distinguishing history from science, Renier insisted that the historian needs to make use of "the results achieved by workers in other fields of human knowledge" (111), including such disciplines as geography, sociology, and psychology. "All these techniques and sciences," he wrote, "are aids in the historian's work, but they are on different levels: some are servants, some allies" (111). He had no doubt that the "philosophy" that guides the scientist should also guide the historian in every aspect of her/his work, for in his mind, history is not seen as an alternative mode of explanation of human behaviour to that provided by the sciences. "We may conclude," he wrote, "that the methods of science are not those of history, but that both science and history approach their method in the same spirit …" (154).

---

8.  See here Sir Karl Popper's two volume *The Open Society and Its Enemies* (1962 [1945]) and his *The Poverty of Historicism* (1966 [1957]).

What is particularly refreshing about Renier's approach is that it remains open to the results of research and new scientific discoveries in a wide range of fields and disciplines. To tell an acceptable story, in fact, requires the historian to make use of the best knowledge available about human nature because that knowledge constitutes the basis for what he calls "the serialization of events into a story" (192). However, serializing the events that concern the historian, he insisted, requires the historian to assume only so much as "will put no strain on anyone's intellectual integrity" (193). Thus he wrote:

> We have agreed that human behaviour is human nature in action. There will be no dif-
> ficulty in our agreeing that character is habitual behaviours .... To acquire an understand-
> ing of human character and of human behaviour means, therefore, to become skilful in
> predicting successfully the actions of one's fellow human beings. This skill can be acquired
> by observation, from literature, and from doctrines of psychologists (193).

Renier, then, is almost ecstatic about the value of science to the historian in accounting for particular events and for linking them together in a way that at first sight might have appeared unconnected and so "unfit for use in a story" (205). And I have no doubt that he would have readily acknowledged the value of evolutionary biology and psychology for the work of the historian. As he concluded the matter:

> To explain an action is to situate it in a causal sequence. This means that more order can
> be introduced into our picture of human behaviour. Mystery and guesswork are receding
> together with their references to chance, free choice, temperament, providential interven-
> tion, or the whim of the gods (198–199).

Nevertheless, he simultaneously acknowledges what Dennis Wrong (2005) refers to as the "resistance of history and biography to encompassing explanatory generalizations" (99). It is clear therefore that in his mind, science and history are not alternative explanations of human behaviour; they are, rather, complementary explanations. The historian is not content simply to invent or imagine connections among events, nor is he/she ready to substitute fiction for a story in which the connections between and among events are real.

Given Renier's view of the nature of the historical enterprise, and the specific nature of its subject matter, it is clear that the historian provides a genuinely complementary knowledge about human behaviour, (that is, about the past experiences of particular human societies), to that provided by the natural and biological sciences, even though history is not a sci-ence. It is able to do so first, because it is "a discipline which approaches its subject-matter in the same spirit as science" (245) and, second, because its specific subject-matter is the particularities of human behaviour rather than the generalizations about our "human na-ture." Historians, therefore, clearly carry out their work within a framework of explanatory pluralism.[9]

## A Brief Excursus on Barkow

Before bringing this to a conclusion, I wish to return to Barkow's recently published com-ments on the value of Darwinism for social scientists (2006), because I think he is right

---

9.  "Explanatory pluralism" for historians (and other social scientists) is preferable to both VIE or ICM
    frameworks of understanding because it does not presume that a clean, tight fit between and among all
    the sciences is likely to be achieved—let alone reductions of history or the social sciences to the simple
    ingredients of physics such as space, time, and subatomic particles—yet recognizes that the natural sci-
    ences, in some sense at least, set boundary conditions for their work.

to decry the fact that so many social scientists and historians are missing the import of the Darwinian revolution for their work. For all my concerns raised above, I find the latest articulation of his position on the social sciences in *Missing the Revolution* (2006) persuasive. I fully agree with his claim there that axiomatic physics is a poor model for the social sciences, and that the "evolutionarily informed, vertically integrated social science" he envisions, need not even resemble the natural sciences (2006, 33), although its accounts ought to be "*comparable* with what we think we know of human evolution ..." (2006, 29). It seems obvious, therefore, that the scientific standards of universal laws have only limited relevance to understanding biographical and historical phenomena given the reality, as Bullock has noted, that unique events and particular personalities also have an important impact on social and cultural life. Consequently, I agree with Barkow that those headed into the social sciences and history ought to receive some training in evolutionary biology and psychology (2006, 33) but that this "does not mean that our students must begin by becoming biologists or psychologists ... anymore than biologists must begin by becoming chemists" (2006, 34).

## Three Historians on "Delving Beneath the Surface of History"

In *Human Nature in Rural Tuscany: An Early Modern History* (2007) Gregory Hanlon attempts to make use of evolutionary psychology in accounting for the peculiar character of the behavior of people in a seventeenth-century Tuscan village. "If the postulates of evolutionary psychology are correct, and I believe they are," he writes in the Introduction, "we could apply them to any given society in history and understand better why people acted the way they did. It connects the physical sciences with the human sciences and explains the largest number of facts with the smallest number of assumptions" (2007, 8). Although Hanlon compares his suggestion here to the approach taken by Fernand Braudel and maintains that "insights derived from evolutionary psychology will transform the way historians understand not only family life, kinship, and sexuality, but also politics, violence, and cooperation" (2007, 8), it is not clearly evident to me how this knowledge has "transformatively influenced" his descriptive historical account of village life in seventeenth-century Montefollonico; without reading the Introduction to the volume, and some of the introductory material of several chapters, I would have been hard pressed to see the peculiar value of evolutionary psychology to his overall account of life in Montefollonico. This is not to say that I think evolutionary psychology and the cognitive sciences are useless in understanding past human behavior. Indeed, I find David Lewis-Williams's invocation of evolutionary thought and the neurosciences in accounting for San spirituality (*San Spirituality: Roots, Expression, and Social Consequences* [2004]) and the religious experience of Upper Paleolithic people (in his earlier *The Shamans of Prehistory: Trance an Magic in the Painted Caves* with Jean Clottes [1998]) to bear true transformative explanatory influence.

It is of interest to compare Hanlon's exercise with that of Charles Radding who, in his *A World Made by Men: Cognition and Society 200–1200* (1985), sets out "to make sense of the culture and society of the Middle Ages by studying the reasoning people then used" (1985, 33). Unlike Hanlon, Radding argues that a proper explanation here requires a rejection of what he calls "the *Annales* or Geertzian conception of *mentalité* as that which is shared among all members of society" (1985, 28). Radding does not object to generalizations about cognition—which he refers to as "mentalities"—but he does not use that term to refer either to society as a whole having a mind which is subject to evolutionary development or, by implication, to some underlying process or processes of thought that are determinative and unchanging. Consequently, he sets out to examine the "changes in reasoning of real men and women over the centuries" (1985, 31). Human beings, he maintains, "must … be seen as living in a dialectical relationship with their traditions, influenced by the values and ideas they are taught but also, and at the same time, bending those traditions to fit their minds. Culture, therefore, should be regarded not as an entity distinct from human intelligence but as the interaction of cognition and tradition" (1985, 28). Contrary to Braudel, therefore, Radding does not view "[t]he dominant mentality of an age … [as] simply mirror[ing] social and economic activities" (1985, 143). Nor, by implication more than argument, does Radding equate "mentality" with "automatic" cognitive processing in the brain; rather he sees "mentalities" as ways of reasoning and the use of ideas that influence and change traditions and social structures. In this regard Radding contrasts the influence of the mentality that resulted from belief in and reliance on supernatural forces to that which emerged from the appeal to reason and reasons. The fundamental point of Radding's argument, therefore, is that human beings are not wholly passive with respect to cultural forces (nor wholly determined by underlying cognitive structures/forces resulting from our evolutionary development).

Daniel Lord Smail's more recent book, *On Deep History and the Brain* (2008) is of particular value in this discussion for although his "deep history" recognizes that the "existence of brain structures and body chemicals means that predispositions and behavioral patterns have a universal biological substrate that simply cannot be ignored …," he nevertheless acknowledges that this does not entail adopting "a crude determinism" (2008, 114). Indeed, Smail is highly critical of a radical biological reductionism in the explanation of human behavior. In concert with David Buller (2005) he criticizes the evolutionary psychology of the Barkow, (and Tooby and Cosmides) type, and insists that the biological inheritance of cognitive modules cannot by itself account for history (2005, 143). He maintains, in fact, that such views make it impossible to fashion a deep history that can produce "a seamless narrative that acknowledges the full chronology of the human past" (2005, 3) because it makes it "impossible to narrate any deep history of change, of migration, of cultural adaptation: one moves straight from the environment of evolutionary adaptation to the present with little need to pause in between" (2005, 149). He concludes by saying that "when evolutionary psychologists stress the ideas of Stone Age brains acting clumsily in modern environments, they produce a narrative little different from that of Genesis, where the expulsion from paradise led to pain, misery, and suffering. We can do better than this" (2005, 149).

## Conclusion: The Need for Explanatory Pluralism

To conclude, I draw on the work of Michael Carrithers who, in my judgment, provides an excellent summary account of the relations between and among history and the social sciences on the one hand, and evolutionary biology and psychology on the other in his account of *Why Humans Have Culture* (1992). The interactional bias in human thinking explained in terms of our evolutionary heritage, he claims, operates as an evolutionary ratchet. He maintains, that is, that each increase in sociality is matched by an increase in the intricacies of collective life which suggests "that organisms may produce changes in the environment, changes which redound on themselves, creating a circle of positive feedback" (1992, 48–49). This, therefore, essentially amounts to "the invention of history" by which Carrithers means that a stage is reached where "human social arrangements and their unintended consequences become a selective force in themselves" (1992, 49). Recognizing this to be the case, therefore, demands a framework of explanatory pluralism for a coherent and persuasive account of human behaviour.[10]

# References

Barkow, Jerome H., Leda Cosmides, and John Tooby, eds. 1992. *The Adapted Mind: Evolutionary Psychology and the Generation of Culture*. New York: Oxford University Press.

Barkow, Jerome. 1989. *Darwin, Sex, and Status: Biological Approaches to Mind and Culture*. Toronto: University of Toronto Press.

————. ed. 2006a. *Missing the Revolution: Darwinism for Social Scientists*. New York: Oxford University Press.

————. 2006b. "Sometimes the Bus Does Wait." Editor's Introduction. In Jerome Barkow ed., *Missing the Revolution: Darwinism for Social Scientists*. New York: Oxford University Press:

Braudel, Fernand. 1972 [1949]. *The Mediterranean and the Mediterranean World in the Age of Philip II*, 2 vols. London: Collins.

————. 1980 [1958]. "History and the Social Sciences." Translated by Sarah Mathews. In Fernand Braudel, *On History*, 25–54. Chicago, IL: University of Chicago Press.

Buller, David J. 2005. *Adapting Minds: Evolutionary Psychology and the Persistent Quest for Human Nature*. Cambridge, MA: MIT Press.

Bullock, Alan. 1978. "Is History Becoming a Social Science? The Case of Contemporary History." *The History Teacher* 11(4): 549–561.

Carrithers, Michael. 1992. *Why Humans Have Cultrues: Explaining Anthropology and Social Diversity*. Oxford: Oxford University Press.

Clottes, Jean and David Lewis-Williams. 1998 [1996]. *The Shamans of Prehistory: Trance and Magic in the Painted Caves*. New York: Harry N. Abrams.

Deutsch, David. 1997. *The Fabric of Reality: The Science of Parallel Universes—and Its Importance*. Harmondsworth: Penguin Press.

Hanlon, Gregory. 2007. *Human Nature in Rural Tuscany: An Early Modern History*. New York: Palgrave/Macmillan.

Hofstadter, Douglas. 2007. *I Am a Strange Loop*. New York: Basic Books.

Lewis-Williams, J. David. 2002. *The Mind in the Cave*. London: Thames and Hudson.

Lewis-Williams, J. David and D.G. Pearce. 2004. *San Spirituality: Roots, Expression, and Social Consequences*. Walnut Creek, CA: Altamira Press.

————. 2005. *Inside the Neolithic Mind*. London: Thames and Hudson.

Murray, Oswyn. 2001. "Introduction" to Fernand Braudel's *Memory and the Mediterranean*, ix–xx. New York: Alfred A. Knopf.

Popper, Karl R. 1962 [1945]. *The Open Society and Its Enemies* (Vol. 1: *The Spell of Plato*; Vol. II: *The High Tide of Prophecy: Hegel, Marx, and the Aftermath*). New York: Harper and Row.

————. 1966 [1957]. *The Poverty of Historicism*. London: Routledge and Kegan Paul.

Radding, Charles M. 1985. *A World Made by Men: Cognition and Society 400–1200*. Chapel Hill:

---

10. In *The Persistence of the Particular* Dennis H. Wrong comes to a similar conclusion from a sociological perspective. He writes: "One might say that the sociologist searches for the *necessary* conditions for the existence of durable social phenomena while the historian seeks the inevitably historically specific *sufficient* conditions. The explanation of *any* social phenomena thus synthesizes the general and the particular rather than subsuming the latter under the former" (107). See also Ian Tattersall's *Becoming Human: Evolution and Human Uniqueness* (1998).

University of North Carolina Press.

Renier, Gustave Johannes. 1950. *History: Its Purpose and Method*. London: George Allen and Unwin.

Sawyer, R. Keith. 2005. *Social Emergence: Societies as Complex Systems*. Cambridge: Cambridge University Press.

Smail, Daniel Lord, 2008. *On Deep History and the Brain*. Berkeley: University of California Press.

Tattersall, Ian. 1998. *Becoming Human: Evolution and Human Uniqueness*. New York: Harcourt Brace and Company.

Tooby, John and Leda Cosmides. 1992. "The Psychological Foundations of Culture." In *The Adapted Mind: Evolutionary Psychology and the Generation of Culture,* edited by Jerome Barkow, Leda Cosmides, and John Tooby, 19–136. New York: Oxford University Press.

Wiebe, Donald. 1991. *The Irony of Theology and the Nature of Religious Thought*. Montreal-Kingston: McGill-Queen's University Press.

Wrong, Dennis H. 2005. *The Persistence of the Particular*. New Brunswick: Transaction Publishers.

# — 13 —

## Past Minds: Present Historiography and Cognitive Science

### Jesper Sørensen

The preceding chapters of this volume are all dedicated to investigating some aspect of the intricate relations between cognitive theorizing and historiography. Motivated by the rising popularity of cognitive science in the scientific study of religion, Luther Martin and I found it pertinent to address the promises, and problems, arising when different research strategies using different methodologies and traditionally addressing quite different questions are combined. Thankfully, the contributors to this volume have addressed these problems from numerous perspectives and I shall include some of these in the discussion below.

The scientific study of religion is illustrative of how historical investigations depend on and interact with other scientific approaches. Broadly conceived, investigations into religion have been informed by two sources: First, the anthropological and sociological methods of in-depth field studies and quantitative analysis have been used to construct synchronic pictures of the role of religious ideas in particular social groups. Second, and most prevalent in the dedicated departments of "Religious Studies," investigations of religions have been solidly embedded in a philological-historical tradition, describing historical and often extinct religious traditions as circumscribed by a particular language and/or textual corpus and building on a hermeneutic approach of textual studies. This distinction between what can roughly be defined as social science and historical approaches has been problematized within the last 60 years or so, as anthropologists and sociologists have become increasingly aware of the importance of history when describing contemporary human groups, and conversely, historians have recognized that historical events take place within human groups with particular social systems and social dynamics.[1]

This rapprochement between historiography and social science has been so successful that Donald Wiebe (Chapter 12) can discuss and criticize evolutionary psychology's understanding of social science, when he in fact (and in line with the aim of the book) more or less solely addresses its relation to *historical* explanations. This illustrates the gen-

---

1.    The conflict between interpretative and social scientific approaches has, of course, persisted in both the academic study of religion and historiography more broadly (see Iggers 2001a and 2001b). However, while aspects of this conflict reflects a basic disagreement on the epistemology and even ontology of historical 'facts', part of the conflict can be understood as a simple reflection of different scholarly endeavors.

eral agreement of sociologists, anthropologists and historians that in order to describe particular events, actions and beliefs we need to address both the agents' past, in so far as this has effect on contemporary motivations, and the social context, in so far as this forms a 'super-structure' that constrains or even determines individual actions and beliefs. That being said, the accent has of course differed as to *what* the focus of explanation is, and the emphasis on the causal role of individual events and social structures respectively. As expressed by historian Keith Thomas in his reply to anthropologist Hildred Geertz's criticism of his book *Religion and the Decline of Magic* concerning the approach to ideas belonging to particular historical settings: "[Historians] differ from some anthropologists ... in thinking that attention has to be paid to the actual content of those ideas no less than to their structure. Historians will continue to be more interested in local and temporal differences of content rather than in structural similarities." (Thomas 1975, 108). According to this view historians aim to excavate clues to 'what really happened' at a particular point in time (whether distant or proximate) and how particular beliefs and events are chained together in narrative strings, whereas social scientists focus on the underlying structural conditions and constraints. The relation, however, is asymmetric. The latter not only legitimize and give credentials to the narrative strings claimed by the historian, but also facilitate the comparison between structures belonging to different periods and territories and thereby to the construction of structural ideal types, such as "chiefdom," "hunter-gatherer," and "late-modern capitalist society."

The above discussion points to the rather trivial fact that the historiographical endeavor of linking particular events into narrative strings is always embedded within an explanatory framework that furnishes the underlying building blocs when *causal* connections are established between otherwise distinct events. In the attempt to transgress historicism, historiography has turned to social science to supply more or less universally applicable models of social systems and social dynamics and, whether originally inspired by Marx, Spencer, Durkheim or Weber, such models have informed explanations of historical findings. Historiography's reliance on social science models for connecting events has, however, a rather ironic aspect. Traditional social science models are namely either more or less ahistorical (e.g. Durkheim) or posit the succession of a fixed set of socio-cultural systems characterized by a state of equilibrium between the relative power and interests of institutions, classes or other types of social agents. Thus change, the very raw material of historiography, is to some extent regarded as epiphenomenal by the social science models used by historians as their underlying explanatory model, *unless* we are concerned with either "phase-transitions" between distinct equilibrium-like socio-cultural systems (e.g. the emergence of "modernity") or changes of particular social agents seen as a necessary and inherent outcome of the emergence of a new social system developing towards its natural equilibrium (e.g. the process of secularization as an 'natural' part of modernity). In the first case, however, particular historical events are of little or no explanatory value and focus is instead directed to the emergence and disappearance of a number of entities constituting the structural lattice of a particular social state. In the second case, explanations of change risk becoming mere tautologies, as when the process of secularization is explained as a result of modernity—a socio-cultural system that, among other things, is defined by being secular. In both case, concrete historical events function as *examples* of predefined macro-sociological changes, rather than singular data in need of an explanation.

At this point, I need to introduce a caveat. The discussion above should not be understood as a rejection of the utility or explanatory value of descriptions of stable socio-cultural systems through ideal typology. Freezing the flux of human social behavior into synchronic descriptions of stable relations between idealized social agents has been of immense importance in unraveling fundamentals of human behavior such as the exchange of gifts (Mauss 1954), or relations of dominance, authority and economic development (e.g. Weber 1976). Nor do I imply that historians and social scientists alike are not aware of these problems and have addressed them in numerous ways. The relation between 'tradition' and 'change' has been widely discussed in the social sciences and historiography and we find numerous attempts to transgress the opposition between system and history (see A. Geertz 1992, 145–181 for an overview). I merely wish to point out the inherent tension pointed out by Thomas, namely that between the structural description of a number of steady, social systems and the unraveling, understanding, and perhaps even explanation, of particular historical events. Further I would like to suggest that cognitive science, evolutionary psychology and dual inheritance theories are helpful when attempting to bridge this explanatory gap. If steady, socio-cultural systems are approximations of a limited range of human organizational structures, we need to explain why *those* and not other patterns are successful. We also need to explain to what extent and how such social structures influence human conceptions, beliefs and motivations. In short we need reliable models of human psychology in order to relate socio-cultural systems to concrete individual actions. This, in turn, brings us to the realm of historiography, as most events of interest to the historian are human actions and as such the result of one or more cognitive system interacting with and within the social and physical environment. Psychology is thus an intrinsic part of both social science and historiography as both operate with human agents to which are ascribed particular mental capabilities, such as memory, symbolic faculties and motivations. Unfortunately, there has been a great reluctance to acknowledge or even downright hostility towards this basic fact and, in an attempt to establish the explanatory adequacy of the social sciences, Durkheim's alleged rejection of psychology as necessary for understanding social facts has been canonized. This is an unfortunate situation since it entails that both social science and historiography work with *implicit* psychological models more informed by folk theories of the mind than by scientific reasoning. In recent years, however, the rejection of psychology from both historiography and social science has been under attack and numerous scholars have called our attention to the fruitfulness of incorporating psychological theories into historiography. But this can be done in numerous ways, and in the remainder of this chapter I shall discuss this problem, first as a relation between stable and contingent factors and, second, as it crystallizes in different investigative endeavors.

## Stable Structural Constraints and Contingent Historical Events

Even if it is recognized that both social science and psychology are needed in order to construct and explain historical events, how these factors are related are by no means obvious. In the following I will made a crude analytical distinction between three modes of construing the tripartite relation between *history* (understood as the attempt to understand relations between particular events), *socio-cultural systems* (understood as the modeling of stable modes of social organization as well as public, symbolic representations)[2] and *psy-*

2. The often-marked distinction or even conflict between approaches emphasizing the role of symbolic systems and calling for an interpretative method and, on the other hand, approaches focusing on social institutions and calling for an explanatory method is disregarded. What is important is that both argue for the importance of collective and social level of meanings, power, structure etc.

181

*chology* (understood as the modeling of individuals' neuro-cognitive systems). The purpose of this modeling is to not to place individual scholars under a particular heading, but rather to supply a framework for discussing the relation between stable and contingent factors in historical investigations.

### Social determinism

Historians' and social scientists' frequent rejection of the relevance of psychology for investigating social facts is generally based on a more or less implicit assumptions that the mind is a blank slate upon which culture inscribes itself during socialization. Whether inspired by Durkeim's claim of the social as *sui generis* or the extreme learning paradigm of behaviorist psychology, psychological dispositions of individuals or even whole societies are understood to be a result of particular social and/ or historical circumstances. As such, psychology is made equal to particular historical events, as both are explicable by reference to an underlying model of the socio-cultural system that supplies the causal framework. Both concrete historical events and the mentality of historical agents are understood as the *product* of particular social configurations. Figure 13.1 describes this relation.

The socio-cultural system, whether conceived as one of a number of relatively stable types or an idiosyncratic symbolic system, is understood as the source of structural stability. Social scientists differ as to how they construct typologies and models of the social system, as well as what aspects of social reality are deemed to be of prime importance (whether conceptual, economic, political, ethnic, kinship, gender, etc.). However construed, the structures depicted by the models are understood as the major causal factor in understanding both particular historical events as well as the psychological dispositions of individuals belonging to a particular social group. For instance, Durkheim's radical distinction between primitive societies defined by mechanic solidarity and modern industrial society defined by organic solidarity led Lucien Lévy-Bruhl (1985) to juxtapose two major forms of mentalities: a pre-logical mentality determined by individuals being constrained by the conceptual structure inherent in primitive societies, and a logical mentality informed by the logical conceptual structure of modern industrial society. By arguing that the social structures determined individual thought process, Lévy-Bruhl became the founding father of what has been dubbed "cognitive relativism" (Littleton 1985). The most famous expression of this position is perhaps the so-called Sapir-Whorf hypothesis that, in its strong formulation, claims that even the most fundamental aspects of cognition, such as perception of space

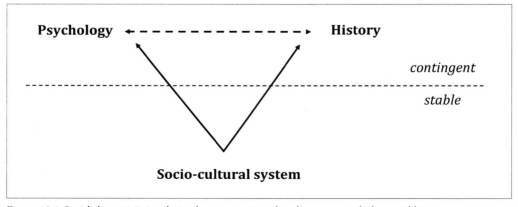

Figure 13.1 Social-deterministic relation between socio-cultural system, psychology and history.

and time, are determined by the conceptual structure that each individual is socialized into. Less radical ideas of the effects of particular social systems on individuals' psychology are more widespread, but it is a common assumption in the humanities and social sciences that a significant part of our psychological makeup is a product of the socio-cultural system we are born into and, in general, claims of stable or innate psychological factors are looked upon with scorn and are alleged to essentialize or, even worse, naturalize certain human features at the expense of others.

The dotted line connecting History and Psychology in Figure 13.1 expresses that both can be understood as mediating factors. Thus, historical events are conceived as the product of individuals' actions (that are determined by socio-cultural systems, e.g. in historical materialism) and, inversely, human individuals are thought of as constrained by immediate historical factors (that are temporary expressions of stable socio-cultural systems). In both cases, the causal structure underlying historical events is constructed by means of an implicit assumption of *absolute socialization*, according to which individual minds reflect social systems. In this framework, change can only be conceived as a product of (a) ecological changes (e.g. the little ice age in the European Middle Ages), (b) "inevitable" macro-historical changes (e.g. the transition from "feudal" to "capitalist" society), or (c) micro-historical changes (e.g. individuals acting against the common mentality due to pathology, "genius" etc.).

## Psychological determinism

Another way of construing the relation between history, socio-cultural systems and psychology claims that only fundamentals of human psychology form a stable structure and that both historical events and socio-cultural systems ultimately are explicable as expressions of laws of psychology. This is illustrated in Figure 13.2.

One of the most refreshing and invigorating, but also controversial, recent approaches based on a version of psychological determinism is evolutionary psychology. Addressing numerous aspect of human behavior, from sperm competition and mate choice, over precautionary behavior and infanticide, to group formation, language and the role of art and literature, evolutionary psychology has proposed a number of hypotheses and explanations based on insights from evolutionary biology and cognitive science (see Buss 2005, for a comprehensive overview). Even though evolutionary psychology cannot be described as a

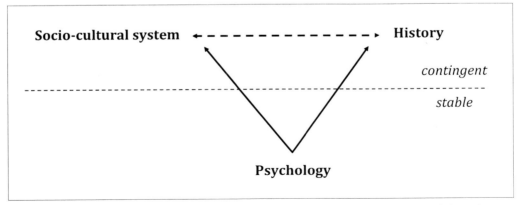

Figure 13.2 Relation between psychology, socio-cultural system and history according to Psychological Determinism.

single and unified research program without internal controversies, a number of proposals form a common core of the approach. First and foremost, evolutionary psychology argue that human psychology should be understood in Darwinian terms. Just as the function of other organs is explained as adaptations to particular selective pressures, human psychological dispositions are understood to be adaptations to conditions prevalent in a hypothesized Environment of Evolutionary Adaptedness (EEA). Since the EEA is conceived as a long stable period in the Pleistocene in which humans lived in relative small groups of hunter-gatherers with no major genetic changes subsequently occurring in the relatively short time since, humans can be popularly described as having a "stone age mind in a modern world." Second, these adaptations are expressed in an extensive network of dedicated cognitive modules. Accordingly, human cognitive processing is domain-specific as different types of information is processed by different cognitive modules that evolved to solve particular adaptive problems in the EEA (Boyer and Barrett 2005). For instance, humans have specialized cognitive modules dedicated to processing information about faces, as these allow for fast, and early developed decoding of emotional states of fellow group members as well as tracking of individuals enabling, thereby, mental representations of complex social relations. The ability to track persons and read emotions helped solve recurrent problems involved in group-living by giving access to difficult-to-fake emotional signals as well as a "tracking-device" enabling individuals to distinguish "co-operators" from "cheaters" based on previous interaction.

However, and this is the third point, the cognitive domains will have different degrees of innate informational specificity. This means that whereas input conditions of some modules might be relatively fixed from birth, others can be modified in response to the type of information available from the environment. Thus, language acquisition seems to follow a universal trajectory where, however, grammatical particulars are acquired from environmental stimuli. This, in turn, "configures" the system to a specific language environment, and impedes subsequent acquisition of alternative structures. In other words, language acquisition is an innate mechanism, triggered by the generally insufficient environmental stimuli of parents' and other caretakers' vocalization, that brings a necessary structure to the acquisition of a particular language. Seen in this light, mental modules are more precisely described as a host of *learning systems* predisposed to activate when presented with some but not other types of information and following particular algorithmic trajectories.

Fourth, as mental modules are construed as learning systems predisposed to a particular domain of information, they can be "fooled" by information that seems to fit the bill. For instance masks and other graphic illustrations of faces are likely to be processed by some of the same mechanisms that process "real" faces, and this enables the development of artisan traditions even if these have had no adaptive function in themselves. Thus, historical and social formations do not have to correspond directly to evolved, human adaptations but can be conceived of as *by-products* of adaptations that evolved to solve other problems. Conversely, this distinction between a proper and an actual domain (Sperber 1996) allows for emergence of a plethora of historical and social processes that "parasitize" on evolved cognitive system and are regarded thereby as both relevant and important by the human cognitive system. In both cases, however, the ultimate explanation of contingent social and historical phenomena rests on the stable psychological system and its mode of activation.

The direct relevance of evolutionary psychology to historical inquiry is disputed (e.g. Smail 2007; Wiebe, Chapter 12). An obvious benefit is a more sophisticated understanding of human psychology in general and in particular the identification of stable motivational factors underlying human behavior. This assists historical analysis by replacing implicit psychological assumptions with explicit theories relating information from the environment, cognitive processes and behavioral patterns—a concern that informs all chapters in this volume. One of the crunch questions, however, is exactly the degree to which, and exactly how, contingent historical factors as well as more stable social organizational patterns influence human behavior. Is it only a matter of particular historical situations giving form to otherwise stable dispositions? Do social structures entail the internalization of particular learning mechanisms thus influencing more fundamental cognitive processing (Heintz, Ch.2)? Or do we find feedback processes according to which historical events and/or socio-cultural systems to a significant extent modify the selective pressure of humanity?

### Dual inheritance theories

The importance of adaptive processes argued by evolutionary psychologists points to two fundamental questions: first, what counts as the selective environment and second, whether genetic inheritance is the only relevant mode of transmitting information. Dual Inheritance and Co-evolution theories argue that humans actively influence the selective pressure of their own species by modifying their environment through particular types of behavior (e.g. "niche-construction" as argued by Odling-Smee 1994, 1995; Laland and Brown 2006; and Levy, Chapter 3). Human adaptation has taken place in a social environment for millennia and therefore aspects of society and culture function as a selective force leading to particular human adaptations. The degree and time-scale of this process is disputed and it depends, to some extent, on findings concerning the speed of human genetic modifications (Laland and Brown 2006). Recent results in population genetics indicate that human cultural evolution has in fact led to an increase rather than a decrease in sustained genetic modifications, so instead of making genetic change superfluous, cultural evolution might have sped up the process (Hawks *et al.* 2007). However, even without allowing for a significant change of humans genetics due to historical factors, the *communicative* aspect of human culture, i.e. the intentional modifications of the environment in order to communicate, enables the transmission of behavior-modifying information between individuals thus creating a second inheritance tract (Plotkin 2001, 2002), or what has been called "Social Cognitive Causal Chains" (Sperber 1996; Heintz, Chapter 2). In Figure 13.3 below, this second inheritance track forms part of the socio-cultural system and together with evolved human psychology it constitutes the relatively stable structure that constrains contingent historical events. Further, as cultural learning takes place through such historical events (i.e. particular learning situations), these feed back into and slowly modify both human organizational patterns and psychology. This is represented with the dotted line feeding back from History to both Social system and Psychology.

The classic example of how human cultural patterns impose a selective pressure is the distribution of human lactose tolerance. Humans belonging to societies organized around husbandry for a consistent period of historical time have developed a high degree of lactose tolerance enabling mature individuals to digest milk (in contrast to other humans and all other mammals) and the pervasiveness of this mutation is directly correlated with the distribution and cultural importance of husbandry. In order to explain this fact, both evolutionary theory (e.g., specifying conditions for spread of genetic mutations through a population) and cultural history (describing the development and spread of a particular cultural practice) are necessary (Durham 1991). Whereas husbandry has obvious consequences for social organization, the direct impact on evolved human psychology from cultural practices

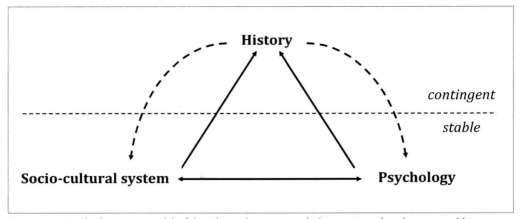

Figure 13.3 Dual inheritance model of the relation between psychology, socio-cultural system and history.

such as tool-making, agriculture and architecture is less described. Thus, a crucial factor in this discussion is the role of *symbolic communication* in the creation of a human evolutionary niche (Deacon 1997). Symbolic communication enables a much wider distribution of information than previously found, but it also notoriously enables deceit and manipulation on a much grander scale. It could be argued that besides changing the physical and social environment, humans in fact inhabit a 'cultural niche' that has effectively selected for particular traits such as the ability to communicate symbolically and the ability to decode collective intentionality inscribed in institutions and artifacts such as money (Searle 1995; Plotkin 2002). This comes down to the relative importance of cultural influence on psychological dispositions *vis-à-vis* evolved constraints, a topic I shall return to below.

## Explanatory Goals, Levels and Timeframes

The distinctions presenting the relative position of history, psychology and socio-cultural systems in three explanatory approaches is, of course, a rather crude attempt to analytically highlight a number of epistemological ground positions. But, while emphasizing certain relevant features, it hides other equally relevant features. One obvious omission is the articulation of explanatory goals in any scientific investigation. At first glance, inquiries into particular historical events are usually guided by the attempt to construct a historical narrative or a coherent structure of evidence by means of all available scientific tools, both psychological and social-scientific. Besides specifying what really took place, most historians use underlying theoretical constructs, not only to distinguish relevant from irrelevant events or phenomena, but also to establish causal or probable relations between these. Such inquiries will, almost necessarily, involve multi-causal explanations if the full complexity of any historical situation should be adequately captured (see chapters by Chalupa and by Lisdorf). Inversely, and more contested, particular historical events can serve as testing cases for predictions made by social and/or cognitive theories (e.g. Whitehouse 2005; Whitehouse and Martin 2004; Czachesz, Chapter 11). This is trickier as it is unclear how historical material can test particular hypotheses rather than the mere adequacy and, ultimately, the relevance of their *application* to a given historical material. In fact, such endeavors generally end up using historical cases as more or less well-founded illustrations of particular theoretical claims. As such, historical cases are more likely to function as an indication of the fruitfulness or prospects of a theoretical construct rather than an actual test. More rigorous testing of particular hypotheses is better performed in a laboratory setting or, perhaps, in "natural experimental condition" during field studies of living societies. Thus in the following I shall restrict my discussion to the use of cognitive theorizing when explaining particular historical events, i.e. to the question of how cognitive science can inform historical inquiries.

## *Micro-history: Transmission and pragmatics*

Based on the premise that psychology is an inherent aspect of all historical inquiries, two arguments for the utility of cognitive science can be offered initially. First, whether explicit or implicit, the concept of *transmission* of knowledge between people is central to most historical explanation (Martin, Chapter 1). Not only is historiography itself about transmission of knowledge about the past (amongst other things); it crucially presumes that individual historical actors themselves, consciously or unconsciously, are able to *represent* and *remember* past events, modes of discourse and ideas about the world transmitted to them from other individuals. Thus, if a historian aims to explain the importance of the 1864 loss of Schleswig-Holstein to Prussia for Danish decision-makers negotiating the relationship to Germany during the First World, he or she will have to assume that knowledge or ideas about the Danish-Prussian war in 1864 is transmitted between people by means of public representations. Further, it is assumed that this leads to the formation of mental representations in individual decision-makers, that they are used either explicitly or implicitly in discourse and that these representations have some impact on motivations underlying concrete decisions and actions. As such, the investigation is really concerned with long chains of transmissions of representations, or what Sperber has called Social Cognitive Causal Chains, and how these might influence and motivate people's behavior at a particular point in time (Sperber 2006; Heintz, Chapter 2). The importance of cognition rests on the fact that representations are not poured from one mind to another in an uncorrupted and neutral manner. Not only are they influenced by the explicit interests of actors—a fact that historians are of course well aware of—but our cognitive system introduces consistent biases as to the relative *relevance* of information (what is remembered), as well as systematic *distortions* in the process of acquisition (how they are remembered). The importance of cognitive constraints of transmission of religious ideas have been lucidly demonstrated by Pascal Boyer (1994, 2001), but there is no reason to believe that these processes should not influence the transmission of other types of knowledge as well (e.g. Sperber 1996, 2006).

Further, representations of other people's social status, interests and past behavior have crucial impact on actors' judgments about the *reliability* of the information achieved and strongly inform the degree and form of responsive behavior (whether hostile or cooperative). The ability of individuals to recall other agents' roles in particular events and to represent their present intentional states are critical when historians investigate a range of historical events and their interconnections. And again, cognitive science supplies a much more sophisticated psychology by pointing to the large number of mechanisms generally subsumed under the heading of Theory of Mind mechanisms. Theory of Mind is a set of universal principles that structure our perception and conception of other people, such as perceptual qualities of agency (e.g. self-movement); that actions are guided by information from the environment; that information leads to the formation of belief-states; that belief-states underlie intentional states; that actors have certain attitudes towards their own actions; and that the unfolding of these mechanisms follows a specific developmental trajectory (Gopnik and Wellman 1994; Leslie 1994, 1995; Frith and Frith 1999). Not only do historians implicitly use Theory of Mind to imbue historical agents with particular intentional states thereby connecting actions and motivation, they also implicitly ascribe Theory of Mind to the historical agents themselves.

Constraints imposed by our cognitive system on transmission and on interpersonal communication add valuable theoretical knowledge to investigations into concrete historical situations. When seen from a temporal perspective, this approach concerns *micro-history* as it focuses on individuals' processing of information in concrete, pragmatically defined situations. An individual cognitive system engages a range of problems in its environment based on a number of cognitive processes addressing particular types of information. Whether attempting to explain particular historical events or the distribution of certain representations within a population, such an "epidemiological approach" (Sperber 1996), which specifies a relation between cognitive constraints and the relevance of environmental information, has much to offer historiography (Heintz, Chapter 2). Cognitive science and evolutionary psychology can help inform such inquiries by pointing to stable constraints on the cognitive processing of information received as well as species-specific motivational factors. As we shall see, however, it is disputed whether the underlying methodological individualism of this approach is sufficient when engaging in historiography.

### Macro-history: Adaptations, co-evolution and "deep history"

Addressing historical events with the aid of cognitive theorizing does not necessitate evolutionary explanations. Cognitive science has been working for decades to specify both local and universal cognitive operations through empirical testing, and there is still some resistance to the 'biological turn' and its more or less explicit questioning of "multiple realizability" models of cognitive processing (Bickle 2003). However, if one attempts to explain why humans have some and not other cognitive abilities, the functioning of the brain and body, and by extension evolutionary theorizing, becomes highly relevant to historians and, perhaps, even indispensable. Further, a natural history of the human species must include the evolution of our cognitive capacities, even if our evidence is indirect and sometimes even conjectural. When models of evolved cognitive capacities are used to explain historical events it actually therefore amounts to a situation in which a long-term or macro-history, i.e. evolution, is used to make sense of micro-history.

But how do we understand human macro-history itself? Historians have a long tradition of disregarding the long-term history of humans and leaving it to paleontologist and archeologists. The very concept of "pre-history" points to its role as a unknown dark territory of human development preceding the emergence of "proper" history, most notable with the advent of written records (Smail 2007). More recently, however, this position has been questioned and scholars have embarked on a journey into this uncharted territory where the distinction between "natural" and "cultural" history is blurred, if not dissolved. I have already pointed to the role of the human evolutionary past in the discussion of evolutionary psychology where an Environment of Evolutionary Adaptedness is constructed in order to explain the emergence of a range of psychological dispositions. Building upon this framework, archeologist Steven Mithen (1996) has explained the emergence of the modern mind as an expanding degree of "cognitive fluidity" according to which an increase in the ability of distinct cognitive modules to interact enabled an emergence of symbolic thinking during the middle and higher Pleistocene. Typical of this approach, however, Mithen's history ends with the advent of agriculture and in this sense it reinforces a distinction between the stable psychological makeup of human "natural history" and a subsequent expression of these natural endowments in "cultural history."

However, there are dissenting voices as to how to understand the early history of the human species as well as its development into the present. Psychologist Merlin W. Donald has argued that human natural and cultural history forms a continuum that can be described in terms of four stages of cognitive and cultural evolution (Donald 1991; 2001). Emerging from an "episodic culture" shared with higher primates containing episodic event perception and self-awareness, early hominids transitioned into a "mimetic stage" characterized by the expansion of material culture and transmission of knowledge by means of imitation. The emergence of modern *Homo sapiens* was accompanied by a second transition into a "mythic stage" characterized by transmission mediated by language and other types of symbolic communication as well as the construction of mythical narratives underlying systems of governance. Finally, with the emergence of the "theoretic stage," humans found themselves immersed in a full-scale symbolic environment containing complex formalisms and massive externalized storage of information. Donald argues that brain development of the homo line cannot be understood separately from this cumulative cultural development and he places a particular emphasis on how cultural artifacts function as externalized information storages effectively transcending individual storage capacity as well as imposing both a selective and developmental pressure on individual phenotypes. He agrees with evolutionary psychologists that our past is with us into the present (all stages are still found in present culture), but rather than a dichotomy between a stone-age brain and a modern world, Donald argues for a co-evolutionary process of brain and culture through a succession of stages with distinct cognitive and cultural characteristics (Donald 2001).

Historian Daniel Lord Smail (2007) also rejects the radical dichotomy between Pleistocene adaptations and present day environment. He argues that historical developments should understood as a continuous narrative that links our pre-homo and homo ancestors to modern *Homo sapiens* in a culturally diversified modern world. Whereas Donald points to the importance of externalized storage, Smail emphasize how historical development entails a change in sustenance, broadly conceived, that influences human brain chemistry and that, in turn, influences both cognition and emotions. Thus, the transition from hunter-gatherer into agriculture might have had serious impact on cognition due to chemical changes in the brain caused by the change in diet. Smail lists three point that he argues reinstates history and culture as an active player in human evolution. First, even though a number of emotions and cognitive processes have deep evolutionary roots, they should be regarded as dispositions that are molded by cultural traditions. For instance, disgust is a universal emotion with a particular range of bodily expressions, but what is deemed disgusting is highly flexible, both on an individual and a cultural level. Second, universal cognitive dispositions often depend on both the correct learning environment as well as the availability or amount of specific neurotransmitters. Both of these, however, are dependent on factors such as cultural practices, individual life-history and genetic differences between individuals. In fact, genetic polymorphism has potentially played a significant role for emergence and development of historical phenomena, as different cultural environments have either protected or aimed to eradicate a particular behavioral trait (e.g. atheism, see Saler and Ziegler 2006; or Jewish intelligence, see Levy, Chapter 3). Third, we, more or less deliberately, change our brain-chemistry by ingesting food, drink and other substances. In addition, all cultures in known history have developed a wide range of techniques, such as rituals, sport, reading, singing, playing music and telling stories, which all have the explicit goal of changing our brain chemistry and thereby our cognitive and emotional functioning (Smail 2007).

One cannot help thinking of the old "culture and personality school" in American anthropology with its notion that different cultural 'patterns' molds individual psychology in a particular direction by rewarding and punishing particular behaviors (e.g. Benedict 1934). However, in contrast to this version of socio-cultural determinism, Smail, Donald and other co-evolutionists argue that cultural practices construct environments that impose selective pressures on the evolution of human cognitive capacities and have been doing so increasingly for millions of years. Humans have adapted to a cultural niche of their own making. It is also argued that particular cultural practices change how our predispositions unfold during development of the individual organism. Accordingly, deep history matters, not because of its contrast with a modern environment, but because it can be used to map a continuous narrative of gene-culture co-evolution.

### Meso-history: material culture, cognitive models and the immunology of cultural systems

The reinstatement of cultural history into the explanatory framework points to another relevant timeframe: the longer periods of apparent stability and prevalent trends within a particular territory and/or political dominion—the *longue durée* of the *Annale* school of historiography (see chapters by Lisdorf and Martin). The rejection of the claim by some historians and social scientists that such entities as "cultures," "discourses" or "symbolic systems" determine and therefore explain individual behavior should not lead to the opposite extreme that the socio-cultural environment has no or only superfluous influence. Even if the latter can be considered only a *proximate cause* dependent on ultimate evolutionary processes, it will not render it epiphenomenal when attempting to describe particular human behavior rather than universal tendencies. Thus seeking status is, most likely, a universal human trait that motivates particular types of behavior. However, even if status markers expose a number of universal features, *how* status is acquired differs tremendously as its attainment will be dependent on motivations for achieving particular sub-goals whose existence can only be explained by recourse to history and local contextual knowledge.

This example points to a level of analysis distinct from both the concrete pragmatic situations of everyday interaction between individuals as well as the macro-historical narrative of cognitive evolution. It addresses the role of more stable discourses of legitimization; of symbolic systems such as particular languages; of widespread cultural models; and the mechanisms that ensure some degree of stability in these. In fact, it can be argued that it addresses the level of science itself (whether historiography, cognitive science or physics) as a practice of knowledge expansion and transmission that has stabilized over time due to a number of constraining features. When scholars modestly explain that scientific progress is a result of "standing on the shoulders of giants" it points to this feature of knowledge accumulation that enables the development of new theories and explanations based on available models and modes of inference. Heintz (Chapter 2) is therefore right when he points to the role of enculturation in individual cognitive processing. Building on the epidemiology of representation presented by Sperber (1996), Heintz argues that individuals not only acquire cultural forms that merely mold already existing cognitive processes. Cultures also contain a large number of learning systems that enable individual cognitive systems to process information in a novel way—learning how to learn is a central element in the development of individuals in any cultural environment. Without reifying the concept of culture, we might talk about "cultural learning styles" as relatively stable, culturally transmitted modes of reasoning about particular types of information.

An obvious way these manifest themselves is through the cognitive constraints imposed by material culture. We are stuck with the QWERTY keyboard, despite its apparent short-comings (it was designed to *slow down* typing), and many young people today have developed an extreme agility in one of their thumbs (with corresponding changes in the brain) due to new means of communication (texting on mobile phones). Technology thus imposes simple action routines that are internalized into procedural memory, but often these have wider ramifications, as when towns are planned for transportation by car, or mobile phones makes it possible for the communication industry and subsequently the national intelligence services to track people's movement. On a basic cognitive level, interacting with tools entails an automatic recognition of an inherent intentional structure—a tool is *made* by someone *for* something—and it thereby facilitates the emergence of shared intentions (Liénard and Sørensen, forthcoming). More profound cognitive changes due to the invention of particular types of technology have been argued for the case of literacy. Thus anthropologist Jack Goody has argued that the invention of literacy is a necessary condition for the subsequent emergence of historical consciousness, critical thinking and ultimately a (proto-) scientific tradition as it fixes the thoughts of individual authors in written texts in contrast to the imperceptible change and transformation of irrelevant aspect of a tradition found in societies confined to oral means of communication (Goody and Watt 1968; Goody 1977, 2000). Further, material culture not only changes the way we think in particular areas. It also allows thinking to become externalized in technological processes and aspects of computational processes to be distributed among several individuals. The invention of the abacus allowed new and faster arithmetic methods and was critical in substituting the Arab numerals for the Roman, and many processes, such as steering an aircraft-carrier demands the concerted cognitive effort of several individuals (see Hutchins 1995).

However, not only material culture and technology influence human cognitive processing. American cognitive anthropology has a long tradition investigating the role of so-called "cultural models" (Holland and Quinn 1987; Strauss and Quinn 1997) or "cultural schemas" (D'Andrade 1995). Informed by connectionist models of human learning, it is argued that individuals acquire a large number of models or schemas during ontogeny and that these inform cognitive processing. The, always imperfect, internalization of publicly available cultural models, transforms these into cognitive models used in both interpretation and expression (Shore 1996). An obvious example is linguistic codification of spatial and temporal relations. While rejecting a strong Whorfian hypothesis according to which language categories determine human cognition, it has nevertheless been shown that spatial relations, for instance, are differently processed by individuals having different languages as their mother tongue. Thus Tzetal speakers generally understand relative changes in spatial relations in absolute terms ("north") corresponding to the Tzetal codification of space based on an absolute "uphill"/"downhill" model. In contrast, Dutch and English speakers understood the same changes in relative terms ("left") corresponding to the prevalent use of relative terms in both English and Dutch (Boroditsky 2003). This "weak" Whorfian hypothesis thus claims that cultural models influence particular types of cognitive processing, but it does not claim that culture *determines* such processing, nor that this is not build upon a universal competences available to all.

Other types of cultural models are conceptually entrenched metaphors (Lakoff and Johnson 1980, Lakoff 1987). Some of these are found more or less universally. Thus, a cultural model specifying "knowing" in terms of "seeing" (e.g. "I see what you mean") is widespread, most likely because it builds upon a basic experience of acquiring knowledge by means of sight. Other cultural models are more culture-specific and point to conceptual structures and ideological features of a particular group and point in time. Hence, Trobriand Islanders consistently conceptualized the domain of "gardening" in terms of 'seafaring' including the "anchoring" and "mooring" of the harvested yams in the "canoe" (log house), and clearing the garden of pests and diseases by sending them on a sea journey (Malinowski 1935). Such models are not merely means of expression. Even though Trobrianders were perfectly well aware of the difference between gardening and seafaring, blending these domains (Turner and Fauconnier 2003) enables the import of novel inferential structures and bolsters the authority of individuals in one domain by its activation in another domain (Sørensen 2007).

This points to the more ideological aspects of cultural models. While these highlight some aspects of a domain, they hide other aspects. The modern capitalist model "time is money" is now a widespread and widely accepted notion of time in most industrialized countries. As this model is obviously tightly related to the emergence of capitalist economy and its ethos of accumulation of resources within an exchange system (Weber 1930), it is equally obvious that time was not always conceptualized this way and that it might not be so in the future. This is a perfect example of how historically contingent cognitive models can influence how aspects of reality are conceived in particular situations as well as how ideologies and discourses are constructed and internalized.

This brings me to the last point in this section. Cultural models seem to have a self-preserving effect by effectively constraining the introduction of new ideas and concepts. Cultural models are really small networks that connect a number of independent concepts into a relational structure. Each concept will potentially be connected to a number of (mutually inconsistent cultural) models—"time" can be construed as many other things than "money"—but each of these models will relate the concept to a particular domain and connect it to an inferential structure. This model-dependency of individual concepts is a constraining factor on the spread of ideas and concepts through transmission. Whereas local pragmatic situations as well as evolved human cognitive dispositions together form the basic mechanism of an "epidemiology of representations" (Sperber 1996), the constraining effect of cultural models on the transmission of representations points to a corresponding "immunology of cultural systems" (Sørensen 2004) that explains why equally cognitive optimal representations have a differential spread. Two short examples can illustrate the function. Despite heavy proselytizing for about 40 years, the attempt to convert westerners to the version of Hinduism exposed by ISKCON (better known as the Hare Krishna movement) has utterly failed. Even though their teaching involves minimally counter-intuitive representations and therefore should spread easily according to an epidemiological approach to religious ideas (Boyer 1994, 2001), very few people have converted or even shown remote interest. This might be explained by lack of trust in the missionaries, but this hardly distinguishes ISKCON from more successful missionary movements. Another, and more compatible explanation would be that the lack of success is, at least partly, the result of the incompatibility of ISKCON's ideas and practices to widespread cultural models in the western world. Their concepts have nothing to "cling on to" and their acceptance therefore involves a more radical replacement of cultural models than most people are willing to endure.

In contrast, an originally Indian concept of reincarnation has been hugely successful in spreading in the western world during the last 150 years, but even in this case we see the activity of the cultural immunological system. Reincarnation was introduced into the western world on numerous occasions during the last two thousand years, but without any success until esoteric groups, such as the Theosophical Society, introduced it from India in the latter half of the nineteenth century (Sørensen 2000). However, during its introduction the concept transformed from a negative concept of eternal rebirth in a cruel world into a positive concept of eternal progress of the individual soul. The concept had success as soon as it could connect to a successful cultural model of evolution and progress (Sørensen 2004). In short, the immunological argument is that large number of cultural models creates cultural systems that are somewhat recalcitrant to radical change, but are still flexible and amenable enough to allow for gradual change and modification.

Analyzing the cognitive foundations of culture-specific cognitive models should not be understood as an argument for either a cognitive or a cultural relativism. Just as universally specified and evolved cognitive capacities give rise to thousands of different languages constrained by common structural principles, cultural models are constrained by universal principles of categorization, domain-specific reasoning and memory. For the historian, however, it reinstates history as an investigation of change and of a competition among available cultural models that, together with pragmatic and evolved cognitive constraints inform individual historical agents.

## Conclusion

Does paying attention to cognitive and evolutionary theorizing ease the tension described by Thomas between a historiography focused on excavating facts and finding out "how it really was" and the structural system underlying any historical event? No simple answer can be given to this question. As I have tried to show, the answer first depends on how the meta-theoretical relation between History, Psychology and Socio-cultural systems is construed. Different models entail different ways of understanding historical events and, in particular, to what extend such events have real causal consequences. Second, the answer depends on the nature of the investigation—whether it primarily concern *micro- meso-* or *macro*-historical problems. Theories that fruitfully engage one level might not have much to say on another level, and the historian could take the luxury position of eclectically choosing the theories best suited for his or her particular investigation and leaving the finer intricacies and details of cognitive and evolutionary theorizing to experts in these fields. One might also argue that the relation between event and system depends upon a distinction between a descriptive historiography and the explanatory ambitions of evolutionary and cognitive science. Whereas the former describes historical events, the latter explains causal regularities.

As always, however, things are not simple and clear-cut. Theoretical assumptions about human cognitive functioning influence the judgment of the relative relevance of particular pieces of evidence for a historical description. No description is devoid of theoretical assumptions and, whether implicit or explicit, criteria are critical when sorting relevant from irrelevant information. Further, in regard to recent history, historiography works on the, I believe, correct assumption that temporal distance enhances the ability to re-construct "what really happened," whereas historical actors themselves are constrained by a limited and often distorted viewpoint. The discrepancy between the historian's perspective and the historical actors' limited knowledge highlights the necessity of adequately understanding the actors' access to knowledge and how that knowledge informed the actions that constitute historical events. Sorting out relevant from irrelevant information and "reconstructing" historical actors' access to knowledge both involve psychological models—first as relevance is usually found in relation to the conception of what might have influenced actors' actions, and second as the reconstruction of the actors' point of view necessitates models of communication and differential spread of information.

The dependency on psychological models does not diminish when we turn to more distant history or to meso-historical understandings of stable historical trends as the individual historical actor recedes into obscurity. Rather, understanding the relation between internalization of stable cultural models, learning systems as well as institutional and material culture, on the one hand, and universal cognitive dispositions, on the other, enhances the need of proper cognitive modeling. Stability of new cultural forms depends on both a "fit" with cognitive systems, as well as its compatibility with already established models. Finally, when investigating the deep history of humanity, its macro-history, the distinction between natural and cultural history seems to dissolve into a co-evolutionary description of continuous interdependence and cultural niche-construction as human beings increasingly alter their selective environment. Again cognitive science becomes highly relevant as such inquiries need to wrestle the profound as well as highly controversial question of human cognitive evolution.

As cognitive processes are a result of evolutionary processes, both natural and cultural, historiography's engagement with cognitive models relate historical actors to the larger evolutionary unfolding. And what could be a more proper celebration of Darwin's bi-centenary than a renewed investigation of the how natural and cultural history intertwine to produce the plethora of observed human behavior.

## References

Benedict, Ruth. 1934. *Patterns of Culture*. Boston, MA: Houghton Mifflin.

Bickle, John. 2003. "Multiple Realizability." In *Encyclopedia of Cognitive Science,* edited by L. Nadel, 143–150. London: MacMillan Press.

Boroditsky, Lea. 2003. " Linguistic Relativity." In *Encyclopedia of Cognitive Science,* edited by L. Nadel, 917–921. London: MacMillan Press.

Boyer, Pascal. 1994. *The Naturalness of Religious Ideas: A Cognitive Theory of Religion*. Berkeley: University of California Press.

———. 2001. *Religions Explained: The Human Instincts that Fashion Gods, Spirits and Ancestors.* London: Vintage.

Boyer, Pascal and H. Clark Barrett. 2005. "Domain Specificity and Intuitive Ontology". In *The Handbook of Evolutionary Psychology, edited by* David M. Buss, 96–118. Hoboken: John Wiley and Sons.

Buss, David M., ed. 2005. *The Handbook of Evolutionary Psychology*. Hoboken: John Wiley and Sons.

D'Andrade, Roy. 1995. *The Development of Cognitive Anthropology*. Cambridge: Cambridge University Press.

Deacon, Terrence. 1997. *The Symbolic Species: The Co-evolution of Language and the Human Brain*. London: Penguin Books.

Donald, Merlin. 1991. *Origins of the Modern Mind: Three Stages in the Evolution of Culture and Cognition*. Cambridge, MA: Harvard University Press.

———. 2001. *A Mind So Rare: The Evolution of Human Consciousness*. New York: W. W. Norton.

Durham, William H. 1991. *Coevolution: Genes, Culture and Human Diversity*. Stanford, CA: Stanford University Press.

Frith, Chris D. and Uta Frith. 1999. "Interacting Minds—A Biological Basis." *Science* 286: 1692–1695.

Geertz, Armin. 1992. *The Invention of Prophecy; Continuity and Meaning in Hopi Religion.* Knebel: Brunbakke Publications.

Gopnik, A. and Wellman, H. M. 1994. "The Theory Theory." In *Mapping the Mind: Domain Specificity in Cognition and Culture,* edited by Lawrence A. Hirschfeld and Susan A. Gelman, 257–293. Cambridge: Cambridge University Press.

Goody, Jack. 1977. *The Domestication of the Savage Mind.* Cambridge: Cambridge University Press.

———. 2000. *The Power of the Written Tradition.* Washington, DC: Smithsonian Institution Press.

Goody, Jack and Ian Watt 1968. "The Consequences of Literacy." In *Literacy in Traditional Societies,* edited by Jack Goody, 27–68. Cambridge: Cambridge University Press.

Hawks, John, Eric T. Wang, Gregory M. Cochran, Henry C. Harpending and Robert K. Moyzis. 2007. "Recent acceleration of human adaptive evolution." *Proceedings of the National Academy of Science (PNAS)* 104(52): 20753–20758.

Holland, Dorothy and Naomi Quinn. 1987. *Cultural Models in Language and Thought.* Cambridge: Cambridge University Press.

Hutchins, Edwin. 1995. *Cognition in the Wild.* Cambridge, MA: MIT Press

Iggers, George G. 2001a. "Historiography and Historical Thought: Modern History (Since Eighteenth Century)." In *International Encyclopedia of the Social and Behavioral Sciences,* edited by Neil J. Smelser and Paul B. Baltes, 6798–6804. Amsterdam: Elsevier

———. 2001b. "Historiography and Historical Thought: Current Trends." In *International Encyclopedia of the Social and Behavioral Sciences,* edited by Neil J. Smelser and Paul B. Baltes, 6771–6776. Amsterdam: Elsevier.

Lakoff, George. 1987. *Women, Fire, and Dangerous Things: What Categories Reveal about the Mind.* Chicago, IL: University of Chicago Press.

Lakoff, George and Mark Johnson. 1980. *Metaphors We Live By.* Chicago, IL: University of Chicago Press.

Laland, Kevin N. and Gillian R. Brown. 2006. Niche Construction, Human Behavior, and the Adaptive-Lag Hypothesis. *Evolutionary Anthropology* 15: 95–104.

Leslie, Alan M. 1994. "ToMM, ToBy, and Agency: Core architecture and domain specificity." In *Mapping the Mind: Domain Specificity in Cognition and Culture,* edited by Lawrence A. Hirschfeld and Susan A. Gelman, 119–148. Cambridge: Cambridge University Press.

———. 1995. "A theory of agency." In *Causal Cognition: A multidisciplinary debate,* edited by Dan Sperber, David Premack and Ann J. Premack, 121–149. Oxford: Clarendon Press.

Lévy-Bruhl, Lucien. 1985. *How Natives Think.* Princeton, NJ: Princeton University Press.

Liénard, Pierre and Jesper Sørensen. (in press). "Tools for Thought." In *Origins of Religion, Cognition and Culture,* edited by Armin Geertz. London: Equinox Books.

Littleton, Scott C. 1985. "Lucien Lévy-Bruhl and the Concept of Cognitive Relativity." In Lucien Lévy-Bruhl, *How Natives Think.* Princeton, NJ: Princeton University Press.

Malinowski, Bronislaw. 1935. *Coral Gardens and Their Magic.* 2 vol. London: George Allen and Unwin Ltd.

Mauss, Marcel. 1954. *The Gift: Forms and Functions of Exchange in Archaic Societies.* London: Cohen and West.

Mithen, Steven. 1996. *The Prehistory of the Mind: A Search for the Origins of Art, Religion and Science.*

London: Thames and Hudson.

Odling-Smee, J. 1994. "Niche construction, evolution and culture." In *Companion Encyclopedia of Anthropology,* edited by Tim Ingold, 162–196. London: Routledge.

———. 1995. "Biological Evolution and Cultural Change." In *Survival and Religion: Biological Evolution and Cultural Change,* edited by E. Jones and V. Reynolds, 1–43. Chichester: John Wiley and Sons.

Plotkin, Henry. 2001. "Some Elements of a Science of Culture." In *The Debated Mind: Evolutionary Psychology Versus Ethnography,* edited by Harvey Whitehouse, 91–109. Oxford: Berg.

———. 2002. *The Imagined World Made Real: Towards a Natural Science of Culture.* London: Penguin Books Ltd.

Saler, Benson and Charles A. Ziegler. 2006. "Atheism and the Apotheosis of Agency." *Temenos* 42(2): 7–41

Searle, John. 1995. *The Construction of Social Reality.* London: Allen Lane.

Shore, Bradd. 1996. *Culture in Mind: Cognition, Culture, and the Problem of Meaning.* Oxford: Oxford University Press.

Smail, Daniel L. 2007. *On Deep History and the Brain.* Berkeley: University of California Press.

Sørensen, Jesper. 2000. Theosophy: Metaphors of the subject. *Temenos 35–36:* 225–248.

———. 2004. Religion, Evolution, and an Immunology of Cultural Systems. *Evolution and Cognition* 10: 61-73.

———. 2007. *A Cognitive Theory of Magic.* Lanham, CA: AltaMira Press.

Sperber, Dan 1996. *Explaining Culture: A Naturalistic Approach.* Oxford: Blackwell Publishers.

———. 2006. "Why a deep understanding of cultural evolution is incompatible with shallow psychology." In *Roots of human sociality: Culture, cognition and interaction,* edited by N. Enfield and S. Levinson, 431–449. Oxford: Berg.

Strauss, Claudia and Naomi Quinn. 1997. *A Cognitive Theory of Cultural Meaning.* Cambridge: Cambridge University Press.

Thomas, Keith. 1975. "An Anthropology of Religion and Magic, II." *Journal of Interdisciplinary History* 6(1): 91–109.

Turner, Mark and Gilles Fauconnier. 2003. *The Way We Think: Conceptual Blending and the Mind's Hidden Complexities.* New York: Basic Books

Weber, Max. 1930. *The Protestant Ethic and the Spirit of Capitalism.* London: Allen and Unwin.

———. 1976. *Wirtschaft und Gesellschaft.* Tübingen: J.C.B. Mohr.

Whitehouse, Harvey (2005): *Modes of Religiosity: A Cognitive Theory of Religious Transmission.* Walnut Creek, CA: AltaMira Press.

Whitehouse, Harvey and Luther Martin, eds. 2004. *Theorizing Religions Past: Archeology, History, and Cognition.* Walnut Creek, CA: AltaMira Press.

# Index

CPSIA information can be obtained at www.ICGtesting.com
Printed in the USA
BVOW061251260812

298777BV00005B/1/P